ACTS
The Birth of the Church

BY E. M. Blaiklock
   Commentary on the New Testament
   Acts: The Birth of the Church

ACTS
The Birth of the Church

A Commentary by
E.M. Blaiklock

Fleming H. Revell Company
Old Tappan, New Jersey

Library of Congress Cataloging in Publication Data

Blaiklock, E M
    Acts, the birth of the Church.

    1. Bible. N. T. Acts—Commentaries. I. Bible. N. T. Acts. English. Blaiklock. 1980. II. Title.
BS2625.3.B56   226'.607   80-11891

ISBN 0–8007–1106–8

FOREWORD

Luke wrote two books: his story of Christ and the story of the first beginnings of the Christian Church. The second was a piece of history rapidly channeled into the work of two great men—the apostles Peter and Paul—and was the natural sequel to the first book. If God's intrusion into human history is the mightiest event since creation, it follows that the founding of the Church upon the Living Christ is the most significant project entrusted to human hands. Luke's narrative of Christ flowed naturally on to what his apostles did.

Notable characters for good and ill moved through the history of the first century. Great movements took form and shape. The vast political system called the Roman Empire assumed character, coherence, and direction. The order it brought out of the chaos into which the pre-Christian centuries were falling determined the shape of modern Europe. It is not by accident that the crease across the map, which divides what we call East and West Europe today, is not remote from the old frontiers of Rome. Rome gave the world much and, in the immensely important decades in which the New Testament was written, alarmingly revealed the maladies of which she was ultimately to die.

Interwoven with that of the empire is the story of the founding of the Christian Church. Certainly no one writer's experience could compass that whole story, but the economy of Scripture has given us, though not all we should like to know, at least all we need. Culminating in the account of the most important events in the life of one of the greatest men of all time—Paul of Tarsus—the Acts of the apostles tells how the Church reached many of the great cities of the empire, how it laid its foundations, built its structure, confronted society, and clashed with Caesar and Caesar's system.

But let the story tell itself. It is a tract of that ancient history whose languages and literature it has been my task to teach, over almost a lifetime. I have learned to view it as a whole, as well as pursue its details in their contexts of time and place. It has been a joy to spend time with Luke again, to watch his mind at work, to observe the friend behind whom he stood, and to follow the unfolding of his narrative.

The translation contains nothing novel or strange. For completeness and to facilitate the use of the book as a manual of study, it seemed a useful idea to include one. The comments may contain some of those insights which sometimes come with the passing of the years. I have had in mind to reach those who, in this overbusy life, have no time for searching in more detailed and exhaustive tomes. With deference and hoping thus to serve, I offer it to those who wish to read.

ACTS
The Birth of the Church

1

Dear Theophilus
(Acts 1:1–3)

In my first book, Theophilus, I described what Jesus began to do and to teach up to the day when—after giving instructions, through the Holy Spirit, to the envoys he had chosen—he was taken up. And it was to them that he showed himself alive, after his sufferings, by many proofs, being seen by them over forty days and speaking of what concerns God's kingdom.

Thus did Luke, the loved physician-friend of Paul (Colossians 4:14), the only Greek among the writers of the New Testament, begin one of the most important books of all time. It is beyond valid dispute that the "first book" was the Gospel which goes by Luke's name. The second book was certainly written to carry the Christian story forward to a vital point in the ministry of Paul; to link that great man's work with the evangelism of the Twelve; and to demonstrate to the wide Roman world, which Paul understood and coveted, that the faith was no movement of underground sedition, but, in fact, the empire's hope. That, after Paul had written his last word and before John wrote Revelation, Rome chose Caesarism, is one of the vaster tragedies of history. Had Luke written a third book, his fairly obvious intention, he might have intruded into those disastrous years which began after the Great Fire of Rome in the summer of A.D. 64.

As it is, in his second book he has left us a document of

first-century history, which is accurate in detail, as archaeology and epigraphy most satisfyingly demonstrate; vivid in its narrative; and instructive in matters of Roman law, society, administration, and provincial life. Classical historians—from William Mitchell Ramsay, in the early years of the century, to A. M. Sherwin-White, and others of more recent years—have been eager to recognize these facts. Luke was not only a participant in much of what he describes (16:10–17; 20:5–15; 21:1–18; 27:1–28:16) but a competent historian in his own right, a man of trained mind and polished style.

While Paul was in Roman protective custody, Luke had time and leisure to work on both his books. The dating criteria waver a little at this point; but if one places it at that traumatic time at the end of the sixth decade of the first century and imagines Luke's friend free to travel the land for facts, much falls into place. Luke found the eyewitnesses who made the opening chapters of his Gospel possible (Luke 1:1–5), and uncovered the details of "the acts of Peter," the first half of Acts. The province clearly had not yet exploded into the catastrophe of the First Rebellion. Jerusalem stood. The Jews, not the Romans, were the persecutors. The signs of growing tension were visible, with international Jewry restive; but there was still hope that the empire might be the shield of the church, and not its scourge. The date of composition can hardly have been later than A.D. 62.

Theophilus is unknown, so that it cannot be said that the absence of title (Luke 1:3) is of any significance. Luke was anxious to win him for Christ and so assures him that the Gospel—closing with the beautiful Emmaus story, in Luke's best style—is only the beginning (1) of a longer tract of history. He begins again, with the "convincing proofs" of the Resurrection, the commissioning of the apostles, and the assault upon the world.

The Commission
(Acts 1:4–8)

And, during this time of fellowship, he charged them not to leave Jerusalem, but to wait for, "The promise of the Father, which," he said, "you have heard about from me. John, indeed, baptized with water, but you, in a few days, will be baptized with the Holy Spirit." So, there, together with him, they began to ask questions, "Lord, is it now that you are establishing the kingdom for Israel again?" He said, "It is not for you to know times and occasions, which the Father has placed under his own control, but you shall receive power when the Holy Spirit has come upon you, and you will be my witnesses in Jerusalem and in all Judaea and in Samaria and to the end of the earth."

It was during these weeks of living closely with his men that the Lord left their faith in his Resurrection unassailable. The word of verse 4 is not a common one ("As he ate bread with them . . ." [LAMSA], "as he shared a meal with them . . ." [KNOX], "And while staying with them . . ." [RSV]). The fact of the Resurrection did not spring up in a distant province, like the myth of Nero's reappearance. It did not emerge with the lapse of legend-making years. It was the core of the apostles' first preaching, as the next chapters will show. It was revealed in Jerusalem, a short walk from the empty tomb, in the presence of those who, with horror or with awe, knew the tomb was empty: Joseph, Caiaphas, Nicodemus. The King James Version is justified in adding "infallible" in verse 3 ("sure tokens" [ROTHERHAM BIBLE], "convincing proofs" [NAS]).

The company was still bewildered, but bidden await "the promise," which John was not to put into writing for another sixty years. It is an interesting exercise to observe how much of the fourth Gospel was known by the Church and written into the New Testament before John supplied words and background. They had Joel's oracle (Joel 2:28–32), which Peter was to quote (2:17–21), and only with that endowment came clarity of mind and certainty of message (John 14:16, 26; 15:26).

He would seem to have taken them to Bethany, on the Mount of Olives, and to have paused while the magnificent view of Jerusalem, across the steep Kidron Ravine, was still in view. It was there that they had heard the apocalyptic words of his prophecy, so it was a place and moment of deep solemnity (Luke 24:49–52). Perhaps it was in the early morning, the roads empty, and the sun, climbing over the Moab ridges, just gilding the city. His last words embraced Luke's book and all history (8) and established a principle of outward movement for all time. They were a guideline for evangelism, with many implications.

The Ascension
(Acts 1:9)

And these words said, as they looked, he was taken up and a cloud took him from their sight.

This said, he disappeared. The modern mind finds difficulties in the story, and medieval art does not help. The sudden severance of fellowship is part of Luke's story (Luke 24:50–52; Acts 1:9–11; 2:32–35). He merits respect as a first-class historian. He examined his witnesses (Luke 1:1–4). He was not present on the occasion, though he could possibly have been the unnamed one of the two who actually saw a similar disappearance at Emmaus (Luke 24:31).

Art inevitably pictures the levitation of a robed figure into a Constable sky. What happened was that Christ passed, almost instantaneously, into another dimension. They could only describe it as a shimmer, perhaps an upward dazzle, a swift blur-ring of outline, and he was gone, as they had seen him go before (Luke 24:31; John 20:19, 26). Any Classical scholar (and the art and exercise of translating into Greek still survives), if asked to translate the above description into intelligible first-century Greek, could hardly find words other than those Luke chose. (This is from one who, after a lifetime's teaching of ancient Greek, can write it with ease.)

It was necessary that there should be some moment which indicated final separation, before the coming of "the Comfort-er" (John 16:7). The Creed, therefore, must include the Ascension, and the word *up* does not express a "three-tiered universe." The Greeks had long known the world was round, and we, who know the same, still go "up" and "down," in meteoro-logical phraseology.

The Coming Again
(Acts 1:10, 11)

> And while they were gazing skyward at his departing, sudden-ly two men in white garments were standing by them, who said, "Galilaeans, why stand looking heavenwards? This Jesus, who has been taken up from you into heaven, will come in the same way as you have seen him go into heaven."

There was nowhere else to direct their startled gaze but up-wards. He must have seemed to rise and obviously was no long-er with them, and the whole adjacent slope was empty. Futile it was, then, to gaze, as the two sudden visitants said, and, in saying, placed the Second Coming of Christ into place and time. Avoid misinterpretation, again. The angels merely say that, at a moment and at a place, the same being whose depar-ture they had witnessed, would resume the fellowship which that moment had severed (11). He himself had promised his returning (John 14:3), a climax to God's dealings with man (Romans 8:19–23; 1 Corinthians 15:23–28; Ephesians 1:14).

Pause for a moment and consider. This extraordinary story of a risen and ascended Christ shows nothing to any well-trained classicist of the forms and fashions of myth. It is idle to deny that the writer did not derive his information from prime sources. Nor is it possible to doubt his ability, as a historian, to sift evidence and scrutinize his facts. There is no reason why he should write so well and convincingly of a riot scene in Ephesus and report gullibly of a Pharisee's astonishing experience on the Golan Heights, why he should so accurately write the best story of a shipwreck in all ancient literature and then talk nonsense of what eleven men saw near Bethany. Sir William Ramsay, brought unexpectedly to a profound conviction that Luke was a fine historian, rapidly faced this dilemma, as he says in *Was Christ Born at Bethlehem?*:

> It became more and more clear that it was impossible to divide Luke's history into parts, attributing to one portion the highest authority, as the first-hand narrative of a competent and original authority while regarding the rest as of quite inferior mould . . . . The history must stand as a whole, and be judged as a whole . . . .

The Upper Room
(Acts 1:12–14)

Then they returned to Jerusalem from the hill called the Olive Grove, just over half a mile from Jerusalem, and went straight to the upper room, their place of meeting—Peter, James, John, Andrew, Philip, Thomas, Bartholomew, Matthew, James (Alphaeus' son), Simon (the one-time Zealot), and Judas (James' brother).

These all continued, with one accord in prayer, along with the women, Jesus' mother Mary, and his brothers.

In short, they obeyed orders. Their regular meeting place was the scene of the Supper (Luke 22:12), the likeliest place, as they rightly divined, for the promised visitation. Luke lists the names, omitting Judas to demonstrate that the chosen band, so varied in temperament, was in place unanimously. Luke uses the adverb rendered "with one accord" (better translated "with one mind") ten times. It occurs once elsewhere in the New Testament (Romans 15:6).

Luke, perhaps in a Macedonian tradition, always makes much of the place of women in the Church, but also stresses the presence of Christ's brothers, strong-minded men like James and Jude, of later reference, who had once been their elder brother's stern critics (John 7:3–5). To be rejected by his own kin was part of the Lord's "temptations" ("in all points . . . like as we are," as Hebrews 4:15 [KJV] says). That such men, at risk of all, were now with the band is strong proof of the Resurrection—not merely of the empty tomb, a physical fact beyond dispute.

Observe the priority given to Peter. James was to become head of the doomed Jerusalem church, but Peter assumed, by common consent, the task of leadership, as the next eight verses demonstrate.

Peter Takes Action
(Acts 1:15–22)

And it was at this time that Peter rose in a gathering of the brethren and spoke (the total number present was about 120). He said, "The Scripture, brethren, in which the Holy Spirit made a prophecy, through the mouth of his servant David, about Judas,

who was a guide to those who arrested Jesus and had his allotted
part in this ministry, had to be fulfilled." (This man bought a
piece of ground with the price of his wickedness, fell headlong,
and so ruptured midmost, that all his bowels burst out, as everybody in Jerusalem knew—so that piece of ground was called
in their language, *Aceldama,* or "the field of blood.") "For," (Peter went on) "it stands written in the book of Psalms: 'Let his
dwelling be deserted and no one live in it,' also, 'let another take
his office.' So, then, one of those men who have been in our
company during all the time that the Lord Jesus went about
among us, right from John's baptism to the day he was taken up
from us, must become, along with us, a witness of his resurrection."

Any attentive reader of the New Testament narratives is
bound to note, in word and event, a striking consistency of
characterization; Philip and Thomas provide examples, but Peter is preeminent. He was irked by inactivity. He was prone to
release emotion in speech, sometimes wisely, sometimes not
(Matthew 16:16, 22, 23). For the same reason, he was quick to
promote action (Luke 9:33; John 20:3; 21:3). He was also
ready, as his sermons and his first epistle show, with an apt
word from the Old Testament. His qualities of leadership made
him persuasive. They had been told to wait in Jerusalem, not to
begin organizing the Church, but Peter's reaction to such pas-
sivity was typical.

Note Luke's parenthesis on Judas. It does not contradict the
story Matthew probably had not yet written down (Matthew
27:3–10). The priests were legalists of the first order. With the
polluted silver flung at their feet, they bought a burial plot for
waifs and called it, appropriately, perhaps in grim irony, the
field of blood. It was necessarily a remote and abandoned corner in some local ravine. What more likely place would the

remorseful traitor choose to hang himself and remain unnoticed till the rope broke and shattered his remains down some rock face? "A field of blood, indeed," horrified observers would say.

The Election
(Acts 1:23–26)

And they put forward two: Joseph Barsabas, also called Justus; and Matthias. And they prayed, "Lord, you who know the hearts of all, show the one you have chosen of these two, so that he may take his place in this apostolic ministry, from which Judas turned aside to go to his proper place." They drew lots, and the lot fell on Matthias, and he was given a place among the eleven apostles.

Perhaps Peter's fertile mind had already grasped the notion of a "royal priesthood" (1 Peter 2:9); and the priestly prerogatives of the Old Testament (*see* Ezra 2:63), within whose thought his mind habitually ran, would suggest the form of procedure. He had not waited for the new enablement, and some words of Christ were no doubt loud in his mind (Matthew 19:28). Later vacancies seem not to have been filled, unless James, the Lord's brother, in such fashion took the place of John's brother James (Acts 12:2, 17).

A little naively, perhaps, the assembly assumed that God would choose one of their two candidates (24). Whether God's choice was specifically Paul is nowhere directly stated, save that Paul claimed apostleship (a term wider than the Twelve: Luke 11:49; 2 Corinthians 8:23; Philippians 2:25). We hear no more of the good Matthias, save for a tale of martyrdom in Ethiopia.

Summary

Thus, in the city which had done its Lord to death, the Church was born, convinced that he had walked in risen life among them. They were ready for their assault upon the world. Perhaps their meeting place was an upper room in the house of Mary, mother of Mark (12:12), but, wherever it was, there the hinge of all history was turning. The world was never to be the same again.

When was it? An informed guess might place the birth of Christ in the autumn of the year we call 5 B.C. If he began his ministry when he was "about thirty years of age" (Luke 3:23), the events in the first chapter of Acts could have been in A.D. 29. There can be no absolute certainty when history was taken out of the hands of the rulers of the world.

The Emperor Tiberius, an embittered man of fifty-six years, had taken over the empire when Augustus died in A.D. 14. Dour and hard, he had done his best to make the perilous frontiers secure. Like the great Augustus, who was baffled by domestic tragedy, Tiberius had been unable, pathologically suspicious as he was, to secure a firm succession—which was to prove a fatal problem of the principate. In A.D. 26, at the suggestion of Sejanus, his powerful minister, he had retired to Capri, whence he was able, in A.D. 31, cleverly to strike down the same Sejanus, who had plotted against him. The portents, the succession, the scourge of the army coup, were high and dark. Sejanus had appointed Pilate, for his own ends, to the Judaean procuratorship. Tiberius had a little over five years left to live.

But another force was moving. The Twelve were able men, by no means the dozen "ragamuffins" of Prussian Frederick's letter to Voltaire. Some of them were trained in the most prosperous industry in Galilee; these men had given up more than nets to follow. But it took more than shrewd and nimble wits to launch the Church on its career of conquest. The next chapter shows how this was true.

2

Pentecost
(Acts 2:1–13)

When Pentecost came, they were all together in the same place, when suddenly came a noise from heaven, like that of a mighty rushing wind, and filled the whole house where they were sitting. They saw what appeared to be tongues of fire, which parted and came to rest on each of them. They were all filled with the Holy Spirit and began to speak in different tongues, as the Spirit gave them utterance.

There were Jews living in Jerusalem—men of God from every people under heaven. When this sound was heard, a crowd gathered in astonishment, because each of them heard them speaking in his own language, and they were bewildered and astounded, saying, "Look, are not all these who are speaking Galilaeans? How then are we each one hearing them speaking in our own native tongue?—Parthians, Medes and Elamites, residents of Mesopotamia, Judaea and Cappodocia, Pontus and Asia, Egypt and Libyan Cyrene, Roman visitors, Jews and proselytes—we hear them proclaiming the great works of God in our own language." Amazed and puzzled, they asked one another, "What does this mean?" Others jeered and said, "They are drunk with new wine."

Pentecost was the harvest festival, falling fifty days after the offering of the "wave sheaf" of the Passover (Leviticus 23:15–21). There was an appropriate symbolism in the "firstfruits" of the Church falling thus timely after Christ's fulfilling sacrifice (1 Corinthians 5:7; James 1:18).

Wind and fire (2, 3) were symbols of God's presence, but God was neither wind nor fire (1 Kings 19:11, 12). In both connections, Luke, as in the story of the Ascension, wrestles with language to express an unearthly occurrence. It was "like" a wind, "like" fire. We, "heirs to centuries of logical analysis," of C. S. Lewis's phrase, must beware of too vigorous an attempt to visualize. This is certain: It was an act of God, designed to demonstrate that, though they had seen their Lord depart, as he had promised, God was with them in utterly transforming power.

The language phenomenon is equally mysterious. Before dogmatism can be indulged, a number of difficult facts must be fitted convincingly into a coherent pattern, a feat which so far remains unaccomplished. It will help to tabulate them thus:

1.   Those who heard were all godly Jews, both of Jerusalem and the Dispersion, the latter group on pilgrimage (6). Foreign-nationality converts to Judaism would be among them, though Italian members of the Roman synagogue were the only ones specifically mentioned (10).

2.   The nations listed were those among whom the expatriate Jews lived, with synagogues extending from the Persian Gulf to Rome. Both Greek and Aramaic each served as a lingua franca in the whole area. Some would know Latin, certainly the Romans, and Pilate recognized a trilingual capacity in Judaea (John 19:20). The well-educated would know Classical Hebrew, and Peter, whose knowledge of the Old Testament was phenomenal, would be numbered among these. Paul was certainly quadrilingual.

3.   The urban Jew of the Dispersion would be quite as unlikely to know the language of the native countryside where he

dwelt, as a multilingual South African (who might understand and speak Dutch, in addition to English and Afrikaans) would be to understand a Bantu dialect. The foreign names given to the expatriate Jews reflected the insolence of the metropolitan religious leaders.

4.   The phenomenon could not have been the ecstatic psychological phenomenon manifested even among pagan devotees of emotional cults. Whether that type of utterance was the practice Paul sought to damp in Corinth, or whether that disordered church, in a polyglot community, was actually given to multilingual worship, is not clear.

5.   Tongues was not a miraculous and permanent endowment of foreign languages—a fact which is demonstrated by Paul's perilous adventure at Lystra, where no sudden understanding of the local Gallic dialect came to his aid.

6.   Undoubtedly, expatriate Jews would speak their Aramaic or Greek with strong dialectical variations. Even in a world of tight communications, anyone can distinguish between American, Australian, South African, and New Zealand English (or even Oxford and London, and Boston and Dallas). The word in verse 6 is actually *dialektos,* though, admittedly, this word can be used for "language." A point to note in this connection is the remark of verse 7: "Are not these all Galilaeans?" The dialect of Galilee is said to have differed, especially in gutturals, from pure Judaean, much in the way that Highland Scotch differs from standard English.

7.   Is there significance in the fact that the skeptics heard nothing but incoherence (13)? The word *mock* (KJV) is an indication of closed and scornful minds.

8.   The phenomenon of Pentecost seems to have been almost unique. It recurs at the "Gentile Pentecosts" of Acts 10:46 and 19:6. Apart from the equally complex and difficult situation in Corinth, which finds a small place in the first epistle and

demanded a ministry of interpreters, "glossolalia," as it is
called, had small place in the early Church. It has no mention
in the Gospels, save in Mark 16:17, in a brief passage which
conservative scholars, zealous for the authority and integrity of
Scripture, generally believe was added to Mark. It finds no
mention in Paul's letters, other than the one already quoted, no
mention in Peter's, James', Jude's and John's writings. Such a
situation forbids overemphasis for any position.

9. Paul spoke of the phenomenon as a passing phase (1
Corinthians 8).

The same conservative scholars, without dogmatism (which,
for all points of view, is here impossible), incline to the belief
that the Pentecostal phenomenon involved exalted speech: lifted in purity and clarity above all dialectical barriers to compre-
hension; language of compelling precision beyond the native
ability of the speaker; a communication so penetrating and persuasive that each hearer, in very truth, heard the Christians
speak "his own language," giving words and utterance to inex-
pressible needs and aspirations. Can that be the meaning of the
miracle? That there was a miracle, at the first meeting of the
Church and the world, is beyond all doubt.

Peter Explains
(Acts 2:14–40)

Standing with the Eleven, Peter raised his voice and spoke to
them, "Jews and all dwellers in Jerusalem, let this be known to
you, and attend to my words, for these men are not drunk, as
you suppose—it is only the third hour of the day—but this is
what was predicted by the prophet Joel: 'And it shall be in the
last days,' says God, 'that I will pour out of my Spirit upon all
flesh, and your sons and daughters shall prophesy, and your

young men shall see visions, and your old men shall dream dreams, and even upon my servants and maidservants in those days, I will pour of my Spirit, and they will prophesy. And I will show wonders in heaven above, and signs upon the earth beneath, blood and fire and fog of smoke; the sun shall be turned into darkness and the moon into blood before the coming of the great and manifest day of the Lord. And it shall be that everyone who shall call on the Name of the Lord shall be saved.'

"Men of Israel, hear these words: Jesus of Nazareth, a man attested by God to you by the deeds of power, the wonders, and signs which God did through him among you, as you yourselves know—this man, given up by the set purpose and intention of God to you, by the hands of wicked men, you crucified and killed. And God raised him up, loosing him from the agonies of death, for it was not possible for death to master him. David said about him, 'I have kept the Lord before me always, for he is on my right hand that I be not shaken. That is why my heart is glad and my tongue rejoices, and my body, too, shall rest in hope: because you will not abandon me to the place of death, nor will you suffer your holy one to see corruption. You have shown me the paths of life; you will fill me with joy in your presence.' Brethren, it may be frankly said to you, about the patriarch David, that he died and was buried, and his tomb is among you to this day. But, being a prophet and knowing that God had solemnly promised him that 'of the fruit of his loins he would set one upon his throne,' in foresight he spoke of the resurrection of the Messiah, because neither was his body 'left in the place of death' nor did his flesh 'see corruption.' This Jesus God raised up, and you are all witnesses of the fact. Raised to the right hand of God, he has received from the Father the promise of the Holy Spirit and has poured out that which you both see and hear. For David did not go up to heaven, but he said, 'The Lord said to my Lord, Sit at my right hand until I make your enemies a footstool

for your feet.' Let all the house of Israel then know for certain
that God has made this Jesus, whom you crucified, both Lord
and Messiah."

When they heard these words, they were stung to the depths
and said to Peter and the other apostles, "Brethren, what shall
we do?" Peter said to them, "Repent and be baptized each one of
you in the name of Jesus the Messiah, for the forgiveness of your
sins, and you will receive the gift of the Holy Spirit, for the
promise is yours and your children's and for all who are afar off,
as many as the Lord shall call." And with many other words he
witnessed to them and exhorted them, saying, "Be saved from
this bent generation."

Peter's sermon is a most important document of Church history. Interpolations and various tamperings with the text have
been imagined, largely by commentators untrained in the disci-
plines of Classical literary criticism. It should not be forgotten
that the first century was not an illiterate age and that the first
sermon of the leader of the Church would be recorded and
stored. Anyone who carefully reads Peter's first letter—written,
though it was, thirty years later—will be aware of a similarity of
manner. A word translated "intention," above (KJV's "fore-
knowledge"), appears, for example, in 1 Peter 1:2 and nowhere
else in the New Testament. Nor is "all who are afar off" (39) an
added touch by the globally minded Luke. It is part of the
passage from Joel (Joel 2:32) in the Septuagint version and also
from Isaiah (Isaiah 66:19). The command to be baptized derived from basic Christian practice as old as the early ministry
of Christ (38).

Peter's method was to anchor the new faith in the Old Testament. He was speaking to Jews (22) and was quick to use his
massive knowledge of the Old Testament (*see* 1 Peter 1:10–12).
He turned first to Joel, who was possibly the earliest of Israel's

literary prophets (perhaps an older contemporary of Amos and Hosea, from the ninth century before Christ) (Joel 2:28–32). It was a remarkably apt quotation, covering not only Pentecost, but the wide and varied human pool from which the Lord had drawn, and was drawing, his witnesses (18). The apocalyptic passage was not immediately relevant to his purpose (19, 20), but it led to the evangelistic verse of the close (21). Nor, indeed, would any who were alive in the land forty years later and saw the trampling of Israel and the siege of Jerusalem, find verses 19 and 20 without grim significance.

Picking up a phrase of the Lord's (Matthew 22:41–46), Peter then turns to Psalms 110:1. Christ's empty tomb was as real as the occupied sepulcher of David, probably visible on Zion's hill. He repeats the accusation of corporate crime (23, 36). The issues are stabbingly clear (38) and strike home (37–40). Peter, of course, after the manner of Old Testament prophecy, spoke words of wider meaning than his immediate intention. He probably saw a reformed Judaism embracing its Messiah, and indeed, that course was open. The Jews, like Rome later, faced a crisis and took the wrong road.

It was part of Luke's purpose to make the process of this rejection clear. It was also his aim to show that Christianity was not a "mystery religion," imposed on the simplicities of Jesus' teaching by the Greek-minded Paul. In so many ways, Peter's sermons are Pauline. He will show how Paul's whole Gentile ministry was founded in the words and doings of the first leader of the Church.

The Church Emerges
(Acts 2:41–47)

So those who received his word were baptized, and there were added to them on that day about three thousand souls. And they continued loyally in the apostles' teaching and company, in breaking bread, and in prayer. A sense of awe was everywhere, and many wonders and miracles were done by the apostles. The believers shared everything they had, and they would sell possessions and property, distributing to all, according as anyone had need. They would meet together regularly, every day, in the temple, and breaking bread in their homes, took their food with gladness and sincerity of heart, praising God and winning respect from the whole community. The Lord added daily to their company those who were being saved.

The idyllic state was not to continue, but it cannot be doubted that the undeniable fact of the empty tomb and the shattering emotional tempest which had marked the harvest festival had shaken Jerusalem. A harvest of three thousand is well within the bounds of possibility.

Clearly the Church had no thought of separation from temple Judaism. The expulsion was to come from the hierarchy, who had closed the synagogues to Christ and were similarly to reject Paul. The first Christians were devout and instructed Jews with minds opened to prophetic exposition; and, in numberless cases, they were still under the influence of the giant movement led by John the Baptist, three years earlier.

Their "breaking of bread" was simply partaking of a common meal. It was such abuses as those which arose in later years in Corinth, which led to the separation of the *agape* or love feast and the more formal celebration of the Lord's Supper. In the East, eating together was and is a common symbol of unity and fellowship. The experiment in community living obviously did not include the sale of houses (46) and was a practice too fragile to last. It may have been a factor in the later poverty in the Jerusalem church, which Paul sought to relieve.

Summary

Difficulties, theological or exegetical, concerning the Pentecostal phenomenon of tongues, should not cause the inner lessons of Pentecost to be lost on the Church. The Church needs, above all else, a baptism of conviction, a revival of personal commitment, a new note of certainty, and a drive to convert. Social activity, as this chapter shows, emerges from active fellowship cemented by a dominant conviction. The Church is a community of saints, not an organization for charity, though James—who lived through these days of fervor—was quick to stress that the two go in necessary conjunction. And those preoccupied with tongues do better so to train the tongue they have, that it can speak of Christ with persuasion, potency, and charm. All who can speak have the gift of one tongue.

Historically, the emergence of a world figure should be noted. A fisherman from Galilee, so demoralized, a few weeks before, that he denied his Master with the crudest language of unregenerate days, had become a power in a hate-ridden city. He was to be a force in the civilized world. A vast church named after him dominates Rome, where the Caesars' triumphal arches crumble and their palaces and fora are broken walls and truncated column shafts.

3

At the Gate Beautiful
(Acts 3:1–11)

Peter and John were going up to the temple at the hour of prayer—the ninth—just when a man, lame from birth, was being carried along. They used to put him daily by the gate of the temple which is called Beautiful, to beg from people going in. Seeing Peter and John about to go into the temple, he began to ask them for money. Peter, looking straight at him, along with John, said, "Look at us." He gave attention to them, expecting to receive something from them. But Peter said, "I have no silver and gold, but I give you what I have. In the name of Jesus Christ of Nazareth, walk." And, taking him by the right hand, he pulled him up. And immediately his feet and ankles were strengthened. With a leap, he stood up and began to walk and went into the temple with them, walking, jumping, and praising God. And all the people saw him walking and praising God, and they knew that this was the man who used to sit begging by the temple's Gate Beautiful, and they were filled with wonder and astonishment at what had happened to him. As he held fast to Peter and John, everybody gathered, running, round them in amazement, at the portico called Solomon's.

Luke orders his material with supreme care. In 2:43 he has said that the apostles performed many miracles. He chose one of them for two reasons. He is still preoccupied with "the acts of Peter," a theme prominent in the first half of his book. And this incident led to the first, or Sadducean, persecution.

31

He had the story from Peter. A sensitive reader of the Greek New Testament will recognize the terse, factual, and slightly rugged style of Mark's Gospel. Mark had his narrative from Peter, and it is possible, at times, to catch the words and emphases of Peter's style of narrative. A strong mark of authenticity lies on the story: Peter's straight look (4) and vigorous aid (7) (as the Lord had once aided him [Matthew 14:41]), and the fact that the man "held fast" to Peter and John (11), as though hardly believing that the miracle was real. He had held on to people all his life. The psychological truth is striking. The faith which healed him was in his returning Peter's look and getting to his feet. His "jumping" (8) was also a joyous attempt to reassure himself. These people were human beings, not puppets.

Peter's Second Sermon
(Acts 3:12–26)

When Peter saw the people, he replied to them, "Men of Israel, why are you amazed at this or stare at us as if by our own power or goodness we had made this man walk? The God of Abraham, Isaac, and Jacob, the God of our fathers, has glorified his Servant, Jesus, whom you surrendered and repudiated before Pilate, when he had decided to set him free. But you repudiated the Holy and Righteous One and asked for a murderer to be set free for you, and you killed the Master of Life. But God raised him from the dead, a fact of which you are all witnesses. And by faith in his name, this man, whom you see and know, his name has made strong. Yes, faith that comes through him has given him this perfect health, as you all can see. Now, brethren, I know that you acted in ignorance, as did your rulers, too. And God has thus fulfilled what he foretold through the words of all the prophets, that his Messiah would suffer. Repent, then, and turn back for your sins to be wiped away, so that times of refreshing may come from the presence of the Lord and that he may send the Messiah, Jesus, who has been appointed for you—he whom heaven must receive, until the times of universal restoration, which God promised long ago through the voice of his holy prophets. Moses said, 'The Lord God will raise up a prophet for you, as he raised me, from your brethren. You will listen to everything he tells you. And it shall be that every soul that does not listen to that prophet shall be cut off from the people.' And all the prophets, from Samuel onward, who have spoken, have also proclaimed these days. You are heirs of the prophets and the covenant which God made with your fathers, when he said to Abraham, 'In your descendants shall all nations of the earth be blessed.' To you first God sent his Servant, when he raised him up, to bless you by turning each one of you from your evil ways."

Luke had the scholar's gift of summarizing an address, as his book demonstrates on a dozen occasions. His mind is working now in the Servant Songs, which close the writings of Isaiah. With a new enlightenment of mind, Scripture was falling into place, as the Holy Spirit performed his promised function (John 16:13). They were days of intense intellectual and spiritual excitement. Peter had grasped what Joel and David meant. Now it was Isaiah and Moses. The word describing Jesus should be translated, therefore, "servant" not "son" (13, 26).

The attack is fearless and frontal. God had set his glory on his Servant; but loudly, treacherously, the Jews repudiated him. Pilate, in fact, would have set him free, had he not been cowed by the Jews' clamor. He could not afford another complaint to the emperor, especially when his patron, Sejanus, was playing for high stakes in Rome: nothing less than the principate itself. Horror was compounded when they chose a terrorist hero over the Sinless One, freed Barabbas, and murdered Christ.

In precisely the manner of the earlier address, Peter turned to appeal. Nothing had happened which was outside what God had permitted (16–18). They had, in fact, witnessed a vast consummation of history, already plain to see in the prophets (19–26). The royal Messiah of their ancient expectations was still to come. He had already come in Jesus, rejected, crucified, risen, in order that one forgotten facet of the covenanted word could be fulfilled: the blessing of all nations, in Christ. Peter's mind is still moving in those closing chapters of the great Isaiah—he who had a clear glimpse of a world at peace under God.

Summary

A repeated note in all three chapters so far is the relevance of the Old Testament. "Salvation," said the Lord, "was of the Jews" (John 4:22), and this is what he meant. Tear the Old Testament out of the New, and very little is left. Christ, to be sure, broke suddenly into history; but that saving intrusion, had the Scriptures been read aright, had been from the beginning foretold. The Holy Spirit now made it crystal clear, and Peter is reaping the harvest of a lifetime's pondering, reading, and memorizing the ancient oracles. He demonstrates, in fact, the duty which lies upon a Christian to store the mind with God's word. It is thus that guidance, inspiration, insight, and understanding can come. When God's will and message stand revealed, the slothful and inattentive can hardly expect a special communication. Peter is a bright example of biblical preaching. Any other kind of preaching is useless.

4

Enter the Sadducees
(Acts 4:1–7)

They were still speaking to the people, when the priests, the commandant of the temple, and the Sadducees descended on them, disturbed greatly because they were teaching the people and proclaiming, in Jesus, the resurrection of the dead. They laid hands on them and, seeing that it was already evening, put them in custody until the next day. But many of those who had heard what they said believed, and the number of men proved to be about five thousand. On the morrow their rulers, the elders, and the scribes assembled in Jerusalem, along with Annas, the high priest, Caiaphas, John, and Alexander, and all the high priest's family. They stood them in the midst and began to question them, "By what power or in whose name did you do this?"

History was repeating itself. The Christians were using the temple court for proclamation. The Sadducees, who, by long tradition, monopolized the high-priestly office, saw such places as their own preserve. The Lord had similarly clashed with them when he cleaned away the scandal of their cattle market. Hierarchies have always sought to prevent free Christian teaching. Tyrant and cabal find it dangerous.

Urban and organized Judaism had crystallized, in the first century, into the sects of the Sadducees and the Pharisees. Of the latter group, more later. The Sadducees may derive their name from Solomon's high priest Zadok, but this is only one of

several explanations. What is relevant to Luke's story is the
position of the Sadducean priesthood at this time. There were
Pharisees on the Sanhedrin and among the priests, but it does
appear that the Sadducees, mainly men from rich and aristocratic families, dominated the hierarchy.

In policy the two groups sometimes found collaboration expedient. Christ offended both, and they closed ranks against
him, as they were to unite against the Church. It was natural
enough that the Pharisees should be the first to clash with
Christ. He moved among the masses, from which they stood
removed. Sadducees appeared by the Jordan, when John was
under official investigation, and with the Pharisees, earned de-
nunciation (Matthew 3; John 1). Jesus coupled the leaven of
both sects, in the sense that he regarded both as equally pernicious in doctrine.

The Sadducees appear among the inquisitors of Passion
Week, when they appropriately met defeat on Mosaic grounds
(Matthew 22:23–33; Mark 12:18–27; Exodus 3:6). As a sect,
they were not prepared to admit that the oral law of the Pharisees went back to Moses, and they did not believe in the resurrection. Hence a deep root of their materialism, their cynical
collaboration with the occupying authorities, and preoccupation with the good things of life. Hence their opposition to
Christ, who attacked their temple commerce, and also, in their
suspicious eyes, had all the marks of a potential "messianic"
disturber of their peace. The opposition to the apostles logically
followed. The messianic peril was enhanced, they would conclude, by Peter's reported utterances; and it was alarming to
them that their repudiated doctrine of resurrection should
emerge in the same context, to heighten the peril of popular
demonstrations in the electric atmosphere of the most difficult
city in the Roman world. They had fallen in with Caiaphas'
cynical remedy for the situation (John 11:49, 50); and, now, in

the very courts of the temple, the dead Messiah seemed menacingly alive again.

Peter's Third Address
(Acts 4:8–12)

Then, Peter, full of the Holy Spirit, said to them, "Rulers of the people and elders, if we are defending ourselves today for a good deed done to a cripple, about how this man is cured, let it be known to all of you and to all the people of Israel that, in the name of Jesus Christ of Nazareth, whom you crucified and whom God raised from the dead, in him this man stands before you whole. This is 'the stone, rejected by the builders'—you— which has been made 'the chief stone of the corner.' And there is no salvation in any other. Nor is there another name given under heaven by which we must be saved."

How much Luke used his undoubted gift of condensation cannot be determined; but here, as elsewhere, the gist of the speaker's theme is conspicuously clear and his personality and habitual approach manifest—laced with relevant Scripture, fearless, challengingly direct, and uncompromisingly evangelical. There is clear and significant recollection of recent words (Matthew 21:42) and a familiar quotation that Peter, equally significantly, was to use again (Psalms 118:22; Isaiah 28:16; 1 Peter 2:7). A bare ninety words of Greek set forth Peter's unanswerable defense and the universal Christ. Peter liked the quotation about the stone. *Petros* was the name that Christ had given him (John 1:42).

Authority Baffled
(Acts 4:13–31)

Observing the courageous speech of Peter—and of John—and understanding that they were laymen of no formal training, they were amazed and took note of the fact that they had been with Jesus. Observing, too, the man who had been healed standing with them, they had no answer to give. Ordering them to withdraw outside the Sanhedrin, they conferred together, saying, "What shall we do with these men? That a notable miracle has been performed by them is obvious to everybody living in Jerusalem, and we cannot deny it, but to stop the matter spreading further among the people, let us warn these men to speak to no one else anymore in this name." And, summoning them, they ordered them not to speak or teach at all in the name of Jesus.

Peter and John replied, "Do you judge whether is it right, in God's sight, to listen to you rather than to him, for we cannot do other than speak of what we have seen and heard." With further threats, they let them go, not finding any means of punishing them, because of the people—because everyone was praising God for what had happened, for the man to whom this miracle of healing had happened was over forty years old.

When they were set free, they came to their own folk and told them what the chief priests and elders had said. At which, in unanimity, they raised their voice to God, "Lord, Maker of heaven and earth and all which they contain, you spoke by the Holy Spirit, through the mouth of our father David, saying, 'Why do the nations rage and the peoples devise empty plots? The kings of the earth stand together and the rulers assemble against the Lord and his Messiah.' For, in truth, there gathered together in this city—against your holy Servant, Jesus, whom you anointed—Herod and Pontius Pilate, with the Gentiles and the tribes of Israel, to do what your hand and counsel had before decided would happen. And now, Lord, look upon their threats and grant to your servants with all boldness of speech to speak your word, stretching forth your hand for healing and signs and wonders to be done through the name of your holy Servant, Jesus." And when they had prayed, the place where they had met together was shaken, and they were all filled with the Holy Spirit and spoke the word of God with boldness.

The first half-dozen verses show Luke at his brief, muscular best. Like Pilate, the Sanhedrists had all the evidence they required for a just decision. They admitted the brave and open speech of the two accused. They grasped the plain fact that such confident eloquence flowed from their association with Jesus. They saw that they were *unlettered* men, which does not mean that they were illiterate. The synagogue schools gave a sound basic training. Theirs was the ridiculous attitude of some of the lesser academic products of some prestigious universities today: What the disciples manifestly knew had not been learned in the proper schools—in a word, theirs! There was also the patent evidence of the healed man bravely standing with his helpers. They were unwilling to take the step of justice and dismiss them. Their decision was dominated, as was Pilate's, by their fear and their political involvements. It was the scene of John 7:45–53 over again. It is a fine piece of reporting, no doubt direct from Peter to Luke. Or was Paul in the assembly? It is well to watch Luke's every word. The healed man was "standing" with them. The words *straitly threaten* (17 KJV) reflect a Hebraic construction of emphasis. The actual statement is almost audible.

Luke goes on to show the awareness of the apostles that they were setting forth a principle for the Church (19, 20). The Athenian dramatist Sophocles wrote his greatest tragedy, *Antigone*, on this theme: To whom is ultimate allegiance owed—to humanly constituted authority or to God, the final arbiter of good? Antigone died. So have myriads of Christians. On this occasion, a baffled Sanhedrin grudgingly set its prisoners free.

"They came to their own folk": always a good plan when the world has been harsh. Peter led the group in prayer, and his prayer was stored in the archives of the Church. Peter's voice and manner are by now familiar to the reader of Acts. The assembly followed, wholeheartedly (24). Peter, as always, was ready with Scripture (25, 26; Psalms 2:1, 2). He spoke again of the Suffering Servant (27). John the Baptist had brought Isaiah to life through the land. Peter carried on the tradition. He handed it all over to God.

Barnabas Appears
(Acts 4:32–37)

The host of the believers were one in body and soul, and no one called anything he had his own. They held all things in common. With great power, the apostles were testifying to the Resurrection of the Lord Jesus, and great grace was on them all. There was no needy person among them, for those who held land or houses would sell them and bring the proceeds of the sale and lay it at the apostles' feet, and it would be distributed to each according to his need. And Joseph, a Cypriot Levite, called Barnabas (the word means "Son of Encouragement") by the apostles, sold a farm he had, brought the money, and laid it at the apostles' feet.

The story, it has been alleged, is a "doublet" of the earlier account of the abortive experiment in community of possessions. Luke, no doubt, heard many such accounts. He was not a fool, but demonstrably a sound and perceptive historian. He had two good reasons for speaking again of the incident already described (2:44, 45). One was that, in the next episode of his narrative, he is to tell the somberly significant story of Ananias and Sapphira; and he wishes to introduce an important figure. It is his way (*see also* 6:5, 7:58) to mention people of more than ordinary importance a little ahead of their major appearance in the story.

In passing, observe that the practice was not to strip off all possessions. It was a poverty-stricken land, and the Christians were all determined not to follow the Lord's rich fool (Luke 12:16–21). They sold, evidently, surplus property. Barnabas, the first Hellenistic Jew to appear in the narrative, forerunner of Stephen, Philip, and Paul, must have held some property in Cyprus; and, having moved, like many a modern Israeli, to the homeland, felt it surplus to his legitimate needs. Mary retained her house. It became a Christian meeting place. Note, too, that both of the next chapters demonstrate emerging difficulties in the distribution of capital, the first sign that it was unlikely to continue. These were the days of first, fine rapture.

Summary

Luke has already made his first point. The Church had laid firm hold on the first of its prescribed objectives: Jerusalem (1:8). It had done so by the proclamation of the Resurrection of Christ, in the place where any flaw in that story could have been most easily detected. It had led to confrontation with those guilty of the murder of Christ. The "power of his resurrection" (Philippians 3:10) was obvious: the dynamism—that is, the fearless confidence, the spiritual invincibiilty—which arose from an unshakeable conviction that he who had died, lived. It is difficult to kill a conviction by maltreating or eliminating those who hold it. Luke is showing this to his friend Theophilus and also skillfully showing the battle lines shaping, the core of the Christian message, and Peter's powerful leadership.

5

The Two Deceivers
(Acts 5:1–11)

A man named Ananias, along with his wife, Sapphira, sold a piece of land and sequestered some of the price, with his wife's full knowledge. He brought a part of it and laid it at the apostles' feet. Peter said, "Ananias, how is it that Satan has so possessed you that you should lie to the Holy Spirit and sequester part of the price of the land? While it was unsold, it belonged to you. When it was sold, you had it entirely in your own hands. Why did you conceive such an action? You have not lied to men, but to God." When Ananias heard these words, he fell down dead. Everyone who heard the news was terrified. The younger men took over, shrouded the body, and buried it.

About three hours after, his wife, not aware of what had happened, came in. Peter asked immediately, "Did you sell the land for such and such a sum?" "Yes," she said, "that was the amount." And Peter said, "Why have you both conspired to try the Spirit of the Lord? Look, those who have buried your husband are just coming in, and they shall carry you out, too." Instantly, she fell dead at his feet. The young men came in, found her dead, carried her out, and buried her by her husband. Terror struck all the Church and all who heard about it.

The story has a touch of Hebrew narrative style—brief, stripped of all extraneous detail. There must, for example, have been some compelling reason for the rapid burial without even the wife's knowledge. And surely there must have been, in any ordered society, some official check on sudden death. Perhaps the tragic events took place on temple territory (12), and priests, anxious about pollution, commanded all haste. Peter, again, may have been Luke's informant; and, ready of speech though Peter was, he was not a waster of words.

It is a sad tale, and those who have accused Luke of idealizing the picture, in the early days, have their answer in the ruthless manner in which he tells of this first intrusion of lying and hypocrisy into the community. Peter is clear that the couple had no obligation to sell or to give, wholly or in part. His severity sprang from the recollection of such stern words as those of Matthew 23, only a few weeks old. And here was the old leaven fermenting in the new bread. The serpent had slipped into Eden. The two deceivers were not robbing God, but lying to him; and, having seen Barnabas honored for his deed, they coveted similar standing. Peter saw the destructive potentiality of any form of deceit or hypocrisy; and both required a certain hardihood of sin to conceive, organize, and introduce them into the atmosphere of faith and jubilant devotion which was evidently characteristic of those first days of ardent Christian living. The first recorded burials of the Church thus became the burials of two hypocrites.

Persecution Again
(Acts 5:12–26)

And at the hands of the apostles many signs and miracles took place among the people. By common consent they would all meet in the Portico of Solomon. None of the rest ventured to associate with them, but they held them in high regard; and hosts of men and women, becoming believers in the Lord, were being added to their number. They would even bring the sick into the streets and place them on their stretchers and mats, just so that, as Peter went by, his mere shadow might light on this one or that of them. There came a host, too, from communities all round Jerusalem, bringing the sick and those burdened with unclean spirits, who indeed were all being restored to health.

Then there arose the high priest and his party, the sect of the Sadducees, filled with jealousy. They laid hands on the apostles and put them in the public prison. But, in the night, the angel of the Lord opened the prison, brought them out and said, "Be off, and, standing in the temple, speak to the people all the words of this life." Thus bidden, they went early in the morning into the temple and began to preach.

The high priest and his people summoned the Sanhedrin—the whole eldership, that is, of the people of Israel—and sent word to the prison for them to be brought. But the officers arrived, only to find that they were not in the prison. Coming back, they reported, "The prison we found closed in all security, with the guards in place at the gates, but when we opened it we found no one inside." When the commandant of the temple and the high priests heard these words, they were at a loss to know what had happened about them. Then someone came and told them, "Look, the men whom you put in prison are standing in the temple and teaching the people." Then the commandant and his men went and brought them, but without force, because they were afraid of being stoned by the people.

It was a common enough practice to gather for instruction or discussion in the many porticoes or cloisters. Ancient architecture, in all its public buildings, provided these facilities. The Stoics, in fact, derived their name from that of the *Stoa Poikilê,* or "Painted Portico," where the group met in Athens (12). The discussion was such that no one lightly joined in (13), common though it was for bystanders to overhear all proceedings. At the trial of Christ (John 18), the deliberations of the Sanhedrin and the verbal interchanges in the courtyard were mutually audible, and when Paul spoke at Athens, a "woman named Damaris," an outside listener, was converted (17:34). Elihu, in the story of Job, listened to the whole discussion and finally joined in.

All religious revival has its fringe of excitement that begets a measure of superstitious practice, and there is no doubt that a "revival" of great significance was in train on the very ground where Christ had been done to death and where the empty tomb could be inspected. The priesthood found that their measureless crime had left their problem completely unsolved (15, 16).

The story of the second imprisonment rests on Luke's authority, and he no doubt had the story direct from Peter. This is not the place to discuss the basic problem of the Western mind when confronted with a miracle. It is relevant, however, to point out that Luke, whenever his narrative can be tested against established fact, proves to be a historian of meticulous accuracy. An event of the most extraordinary significance was taking place—no less than the founding of the Christian Church on the evidence of a resurrected Lord; and, for all the modern mind's respect for the rule of law and order, a belief in the Author of law and order entails an acceptance of actions and events which fall outside the orbit of the commonly and generally observed.

The Sadducees were naturally anxious for the peace of Jerusalem and were sensitive to a growing hostility among the people at large (26). It was a tense and concerned group which found themselves back in the situation they had sought to meet by crime. They held a position of delicate responsibility. The Romans were sensible imperialists; and, whenever an existing structure of authority functioned efficiently, they saw no reason to change it. Hence Augustus' toleration of Herod, whom, as a man, he disliked. And now the hierarchy served their purpose and lightened the load of the procurator. While the Sadducees controlled the crowd, they were free to pursue their interests. Hence their sensitivity to any popular movement.

Peter's Defense
(Acts 5:27–42)

And the high priest examined them, saying, "We strictly commanded you not to teach in this name, and, look, you have filled Jerusalem with your teaching and plan to bring this man's blood on us."

Peter, along with the apostles, said, "We must obey God rather than men. The God of our fathers raised Jesus, whom you murdered, hanging him upon a tree. Him has God exalted to his right hand, to be our Leader and Savior, to give repentance to Israel and forgiveness of sins. And we are all witnesses of these things, along with the Holy Spirit, which God has given to those who obey him."

When they heard this, they were cut to the quick and were minded to do away with them. But there arose in the Sanhedrin a Pharisee named Gamaliel, a teacher of the Law honored by all the people, and he ordered the men to be moved outside for a little and said to them, "Men of Israel, take care how you propose to deal with these men, for some time ago appeared Theudas, professing to be somebody, to whom about four hundred men rallied, and all who trusted in him were scattered and came to nothing. After him rose Judas of Galilee, at the time of the census, and raised a great following. And he was destroyed, and all who obeyed him were scattered. And I say to you now, 'Keep away from these men and let them go, for if this plan or movement is of men, it will collapse. If it is of God, you will not be able to break them up. Be careful lest you turn out to be fighting

God.' " They were persuaded by him, and, summoning the apostles, they flogged them, commanded them not to speak in the name of Jesus, and let them go.

They went off from the interview with the Sanhedrin, rejoicing that they had been found worthy to suffer dishonor for the name. And all day in the temple and from house to house they went on teaching and preaching the message of Jesus the Messiah.

The authenticity of the speech is striking. In an Aramaic text, it was probably kept in the archives of the Church. Note three pointers to this. First, the grammatical structure of the high priest's opening phrase suggests an Aramaic construction: "Did we not threaten you with a threat . . ." is a translation of a Semitic idiom in which an infinitive construction contributes emphasis. Hebrew is poor in adjectives and adverbs and uses such devices. Second, in verse 32, Peter uses *words* for *things*. It reflects the Aramaic or Hebrew word which serves for both purposes. *Word* implies, in Hebrew, the content of the word, the "things" it represents. Third, in verse 30, Peter uses *tree* for the cross, a phrase he repeats at 10:39 and in his first epistle (1 Peter 2:24). The common word for the instrument of crucifixion was *stauros,* "a stake," and to crucify, was, in common parlance, *to stake.* The *stauros* was a fixture at the place of death; and the crossbeam, carried by the victim, was placed, by some fixing device, across it, forming a capital *T.* It may have been convenient to use sawn-off tree trunks for the stake, and hence the use of *tree* for the cross.

But bipartisan opposition was now organizing (34). The Pharisees were there, in the Sanhedrin, and Gamaliel's wise advice saved the apostles. Note that, wise and applicable though Gamaliel's words were to the existing situation, they have not the status of a divine injunction for all occasions of dissent.

Luke reports them, but they cannot be made a formula for restraint where open error stands in need of correction. The Pharisees, because of their disastrous alliance with the Sadducees and Herodians, against Christ, have a bad name in Scripture. They thought he attacked the Law, wherein lay salvation. Hence the rage of Saul against him. But Gamaliel joins Nicodemus and others (*see* Luke 13:31) as a noble man, one of a great party, born in the days of the Exile, who preserved the Old Testament from damage through vital years. Then, like so many of the institutions of man, the Law became introspective and decayed.

Christ himself had warned against the false messiahs of the sort Gamaliel mentions. Some dating discrepancies over Theudas, as between Luke and Josephus, are simply resolved by supposing there were two of the name. There were a limited number of Hellenized forms of Jewish names. There were also many identical characters, and the land was alive with rebellion. Imagine a future historian confronted with a few scraps of surviving evidence about World War II and asked to believe that Admiral Cunningham, General Cunningham, and Air Vice-Marshal Conyngham simultaneously commanded in the Eastern Mediterranean in the early forties of this century. It is idle to build high speculations on tattered evidence. Luke knew history; so did Gamaliel. If Josephus contradicts, writing sixty years after Gamaliel spoke and thirty after Luke wrote, it is likely to be Josephus who was in error.

6

The Hellenistic Jews
(Acts 6:1–6)

About that time, as the numbers of the disciples increased,
there arose some complaining, among the Greek Jews, against
the Jews of the homeland, that their widows were being overlooked in the distribution of relief. The Twelve called the body
of the disciples together and said, "It is not desirable that we
should leave the teaching of God's word to look after the administration of relief. Brethren, pick out of your number seven men
of good repute, full of the Holy Spirit, whom we shall put in
charge of this need, and we will give all our time to prayer and
the service of the word."

The proposal was unanimously welcomed. And they chose
Stephen, a man full of faith and the Holy Spirit; and Philip;
Prochorus; Nicanor; Timon; Parmenas; and Nicolas, a Greek
convert from Antioch. They presented these men to the apostles,
who, after prayer, laid their hands upon them.

Since the Exile, the Jews had spread through the world. The
Roman poet Horace has a scornful word about them in 30 B.C.
Juvenal, a satirist of more than a century later, speaks of the
Jewish shantytown outside Rome's Capena Gate. Jews made up
more than half the population of Alexandria, which, along with
Rome, was one of the two most populous cities in the whole
Mediterranean. Tarsus had housed a colony of Jews since An-
tiochus Epiphanes had refounded the city in 171 B.C., and Paul

belonged to a section of this minority, which had held the Roman citizenship since the organization of the East by Pompey, in 72 B.C.

The Jewish communities were held ethnically coherent and distinct by their common possession of the Old Testament Scriptures, a reverence for which dated from the ordeal of the Exile. Later, the institution of the synagogue, one of the most significant events in Jewish history, helped unify the scattered Jewish communities that stretched from India and Parthia to Rome and perhaps Spain. Paul found them everywhere and sought always to make the synagogue the bridgehead for his teaching. Often he found the synagogue a hostile power in the community. The Jews of Alexandria gave the world the incalculable advantage of a Greek translation of the Jewish Scriptures, from which the Greek New Testament commonly quotes.

In the synagogues were proselytes, like Nicolas of Antioch (5); these were Gentiles who found the austere Jewish faith and its lofty monotheism attractive amid the decadence and theological chaos of the pagan world. But, inevitably, the Jewish communities absorbed the enquiring spirit of Hellenism; the wider view of life and the world; the philosophical approach; the habits of logical analysis, which somehow are inherent in the Greek language, which the Dispersion naturally adopted, and which, spreading in the wake of Alexander's conquests, made the whole world kin mentally.

Metropolitan Jewry tended to look down on their kinsfolk from abroad. Witness the scornful remark of John 7:35. The "foreign" Jews were mere "Greeks." But, in fact, metropolitan Judaism was dead. It was little more than a monument and memorial which the Hellenistic Jews found when they came to Jerusalem. These were men like Simon of Cyrene, the Jewish visitors of Pentecost, and the rest; and many of them were resident in Jerusalem, as the story of threatened division shows.

Luke has several reasons for relating it. An important step was taken at this time in the organization of the Church. Here was the beginning of the diaconate. Observe, too, the magnanimity by which all seven men chosen for the office were Hellenistic Jews. But we have also noted Luke's habit of a lead-in for characters destined for prominence in the chapters following. Here are two men marked for a large place: Stephen, so soon to die—but not without having the deepest influence on Paul—and Philip, whose story reveals the beginning of an unrecorded inroad of the Gospel into Africa.

Stephen Appears
(Acts 6:7–15)

And the word of God spread, and the number of disciples in Jerusalem increased rapidly, and a large body of the priests were obedient to the faith. Stephen, full of grace and power, was doing wonders and great miracles among the people. Some members of what was called the Freedmen's Synagogue, from Cyrene, Alexandria, Cilicia, and Asia, began a controversy with Stephen, but could not equal the wisdom and the spirit with which he spoke. Then they put up men who said, "We have heard this man speaking blasphemous words against Moses and God." They stirred up the people, the elders, and the scribes, came upon him, seized him, and brought him to the Sanhedrin. And they brought false witnesses, who said, "This man keeps on speaking against this holy place and the Law. We have heard him saying that this Jesus of Nazareth will pull this place down and change the customs which Moses handed down to us." And all those who sat in the Sanhedrin looked hard at him and saw his face like the face of an angel.

Stephen is illustration of how the briefest ministry can count for God. It was his teaching which first showed how Christianity could not be absorbed by Judaism, as the Lord, indeed, had warned (Luke 5:36–39). Christianity superseded Judaism; and Paul's ministry, Luke's major theme, was to make that plain. Stephen's speech was to be a turning point in the life of one who heard it; and Stephen was to die for Paul, as Christ had died for Stephen. Stephen had no doubt been saying in his temple teaching what he had expounded in his address, a theme which Paul was to spread through the world.

The freedmen, who seem to have been from four overseas ghetto communities, were men who had once been slaves and appear to have been the victims of some social disapproval. Perhaps it was a pitiable attempt to gain approval from the proud Jerusalem Jews that prompted their ill-advised attempt to refute a man of Stephen's intelligence and eloquence. They revealed what Paul was also destined to discover painfully: Opposition to the new faith was not confined to Jerusalem, but was to rise, with equal bitterness, among the synagogues of the Dispersion. The scene was to become a familiar one, to Paul.

7

Stephen's Speech
(Acts 7:1–53)

The high priest said, "Are these things so?"

Stephen replied, "Brethren and fathers, listen. The God of glory appeared to our forefather Abraham, in Mesopotamia, before his migration to Haran, and said, 'Leave your land and kindred and get you to a land which I shall show to you.' Then he left the land of the Chaldaeans and migrated to Haran, and thence, after his father's death, God moved him on to this land in which you now dwell; but he did not give him even a standing place to be his own, yet promised to give it to him as a possession and to his posterity, though he had no son. And God told him that his descendants would be strangers in a foreign land who would enslave and ill-treat them for four hundred years. 'And the nation they shall serve,' said God, 'I will destroy, and afterwards they shall come out and serve me in this place.' He gave to him the covenant of circumcision, and so Abraham begat Isaac and circumcised him on the eighth day, and Isaac, Jacob, and Jacob, the twelve patriarchs. And the patriarchs, jealous of Joseph, sold him into Egypt. But God was with him and rescued him from all his troubles and gave him grace and wisdom in the eyes of Pharaoh, the king of Egypt, who made him governor over all of Egypt and his civil service. There came a famine over all Egypt and Canaan and great distress. Our fathers could not find food. Jacob, hearing that there was corn in Egypt, sent our fathers first. On the second visit, Joseph was recognized by his brothers, and Joseph's lineage was made known to Pharaoh. Joseph sent and summoned Jacob, his father, and all his kinsfolk, seventy-five people. Jacob went down into Egypt, and he died, as our fathers did, too. They were moved to Shechem and placed in the tomb, which Abraham bought, for a sum of silver, from the sons of Hamor in Shechem. But as the time of the promise which God had covenanted with Abraham drew near, the people grew and increased in Egypt, until there arose another king over Egypt, who had no knowledge of Joseph. He it was who took clever advantage of our race and persecuted them, making them cast their children out to die.

"Just at that time, Moses was born, and he was divinely beautiful. He was reared three months in his father's house. When he was cast out, Pharaoh's daughter rescued him and brought him up as her own son. And Moses was educated in all the culture of the Egyptians. He became a powerful man in speech and action. When he was about forty years of age, it occurred to him to visit his brethren, the people of Israel. Seeing one of them suffering wrong, he defended him, avenged the sufferer, and struck down the Egyptian. He thought that his brethren would understand that God, by his hand, would liberate them, but they did not understand. The next day he came on two of them fighting and tried to make peace between them. 'Men,' he said, 'you are brothers. Why are you harming one another?' The guilty party pushed him aside, saying: 'Who set you up as ruler and judge over us? Do you want to make away with me in the same fashion as you did with the Egyptian, yesterday?' When he heard this, Moses fled and became an exile in Midian, where two sons were born to him. After a lapse of forty years, in the wilderness of Mount Sinai, an angel appeared to him in the flame of a burning bush. Moses was amazed at the spectacle he saw, and, as he went nearer to look at it, there came the voice of the Lord, 'I am the God of your fathers, the God of Abraham and Isaac and Jacob.'

Moses trembled and did not dare to look. The Lord said to him, 'Take the shoes from your feet, for the place where you stand is holy ground. Truly, I have seen the oppression of my people in Egypt, and I have heard their groaning, and I am come down to deliver them. Come, I will now send you into Egypt'—this Moses whom they rejected, saying, 'Who made you a ruler and judge over us?' him God sent, a ruler and deliverer, by the hand of the angel which appeared to him in the bush. And he led them out after doing wonders and miracles in the land of Egypt, the Red Sea, and the wilderness, for forty years. This is the Moses who said to the children of Israel, 'God will raise you up a prophet from among your brethren, as he raised up me.' This was the man who, among the congregation in the wilderness, was mediator between the angel who spoke to him in Mount Sinai and our fathers: he who received living words to give to you, and to whom our fathers refused obedience, but pushed him aside and turned in their hearts to Egypt, saying to Aaron, 'Make us gods to go before us, for as for this Moses who brought us out of Egypt, we do not know what has happened to him.' That was the time they made a calf, brought sacrifice to the idol, and made celebration over what their hands had made. And God abandoned them to the worship of the host of heaven, as it stands recorded in the book of the prophets, 'House of Israel, victims and sacrifices you offered me forty years in the wilderness, and you set up the tent of Moloch and the star of your god Rompha, the images you made to worship; and I will banish you beyond Babylon.' Our fathers had the Tent of Witness in the wilderness, as the one who spoke to Moses directed him to make it after the pattern he had seen. And this our forefathers received and brought in with Joshua when they took possession of the nations, whom God drove out before our fathers' face, on to the days of David. David found favor in God's sight and desired to find a habitation for the God of Jacob, but it was Solomon who built

him a house. But the Most High does not dwell in that which
hands have made—just as the prophet says, ' "Heaven is my
throne, and earth the footstool of my feet. What house will you
build me?" says the Lord, "Or what is the place of my dwelling?
Has not my hand made all these things?" '

"Obstinate people, heathen in heart and ears. You always resist the Holy Spirit. As your fathers did, so do you. Which of the
prophets did your fathers not persecute? You killed those who
foretold the coming of the Righteous One—whose betrayers and
murderers you have now turned out to be, you who received the
Law by angels' mediation and have not kept it."

Here is the Hellenistic mind at work. The Jews had, first of
all peoples, a theology of history. They knew that it was by
universal and inbuilt moral law that nations rose and fell. The
Greeks added philosophy. Herodotus asked why Greece, with
her small manpower, flung back the enormous might of Persia.
Aeschylus pondered the problems of law and righteousness in
his plays. So did Sophocles. The Jews, who had been in contact
with Greek thinking thus added a dimension to the study of
their own history. Observe the Sanhedrin listening, rapt, to a
story they well knew. It is part of a people's decadence to lose
contact with their past, and today's decay of historical teaching,
in so many quarters of the western world, is part of the peril
which besets our way of life. Sociological and political studies
are no substitute for history. Both are inherent in history well-
taught and understood.

Stephen began with Abraham (2–8), of whose ancestry the
Jews were so proud (John 8:39). He moved onto his accusers'
ground. The charge was that he had spoken words of blasphemy against Moses and the temple. He proposes to show that
their faith went far beyond Moses in antiquity, just as Moses'
tabernacle antedated Herod's and Solomon's temple. Joseph

(9–16) and Moses, on whose career he dwells (20–43), were almost types of habitual Jewish rejection of their own great men. Joseph's brothers, "their fathers," had cruelly treated the beloved son. Moses, who came to offer salvation, turning from a brilliant and aristocratic career to identify himself with a nation of slaves, is a particularly striking example of what the hierarchy had just done to one "who came to his own, and his own received him not" (John 1:11). It was Moses, too, who had told of Christ's coming (37).

Stephen's was a subtle argument, with oratory as subtle. "This Jesus . . ." the Jews had sneered. Stephen echoes the words: "This Moses . . ." (35, 37, 38, 40), attaching it to the very moment of rejection (Exodus 32:1). Israel had scorned her deliverer (40) and worshiped the calf they had made. It is subtly suggested, later, that the temple, too, was "made with hands." They had chosen the blindness which had fallen on them. With Peter's skill, Stephen thrusts home with irresistible quotation.

Stephen reverses the order of the pernicious charges (6:13, 14) and deals logically and chronologically with Moses before the temple. He has, throughout, with a keen sense of history, been undermining the notion that God dwelt in any one place, let alone a place constructed by man. The first revelations of God's plan and purpose took place in Ur and then in Midian (2–4, 29–34, 44–50). The patriarchs themselves were buried, he gently reminds them, in Samaria. The earth and the heaven were God's dwelling place (49; Isaiah 66:1, 2). Nor, in fact, was the temple, even of Solomon, a divinely ordained project, like the tent in the wilderness days. That lovely symbol had been prescribed, after the heathen excesses of the golden calf, to impress great theological truths on an ignorant and debased multitude: That God was among them, but unseen; that sin and death were linked; that man was remote from perfect holiness, but accepted on certain terms. The temple, Stephen implies, was a royal notion which God permitted, but by no means commanded.

His defense is complete; and, in giving it, he has revealed the hierarchy for what their forebears had always been: obstinate to believe, striking down all who challenged their comfortable religion. They were following old beaten tracks (51–53), and it was the clear understanding of a Hellenistic Jew that turned all history against them. Of what use the Law, when they had killed the Just One (52)? Paul was never to forget the speech. He quoted it in Antioch and Athens (13:14–41; 17:22–28), not directly, but in a manner which showed how deeply Stephen's approach was interwoven with his thought and evangelism.

[*Note on text:* In verse 4 and the parallels in Genesis there are minor discrepancies which may result from Stephen's acquaintance with traditions and texts older than those from which our present texts derive. A version of Exodus, for example, from the Qumran caves gives Stephen's Septuagint reading of 75 for Jacob's kinsmen (14), as against the commonly accepted 70 of Exodus 1:5. The translators of the Septuagint clearly had an older text. Verse 6 agrees with Genesis 15:13, but Exodus 12:40 says 430. Like Josephus, Stephen was giving a round number. Such trivial differences in no way diminish the Bible's authority.]

First Martyr
(Acts 7:54–60)

When they heard this, they were cut to the heart and ground their teeth at him. Full of the Holy Spirit, he looked intently heavenward and saw the glory of God and Jesus standing at God's right hand. "Look," he said, "I see the heavens opened and the Son of Man standing at the right hand of God." Shrieking loudly, they covered their ears and rushed on him, one and all. They hustled him from the city and set about stoning him, and the witnesses put their clothes at the feet of a young man named Saul. So they stoned Stephen as he called upon God, saying, "Lord Jesus, receive my spirit." Falling to his knees, he cried with a loud voice, "Lord, do not set this sin to their account." And with these words he fell asleep.

The wild storm of emotion, which swept the assembly, showed Stephen that he was doomed. Perhaps he was accustomed to the hard-hitting but ordered debate of Greek assemblies. Compare the reaction of the Athenian court to Paul's address. Such mass bestiality perhaps took a polished Hellenist by surprise. But, in a flash of insight, he was aware of God, that death was on him, and that it was a scene like Calvary. He had lived for Christ. He determined to die like him. What Roman authority was like at this time is difficult to determine. The stony banks of the Kidron, outside what is now called Saint Stephen's Gate, were near at hand, and the whole scene was over in ten minutes. The Romans kept a low profile in Jerusalem, and the whole garrison, commonly barracked at Caesarea, numbered only 3000 men. Perhaps, if there was at this time any sizable garrison in the Antonia Fort, the commandant chose to overlook a crime in which leading Sanhedrists were obviously involved; or perhaps there was some such temporary diminution of a strong presence as might occur between two procuratorships. It could have been about the time of Pilate's recall, when the departing procurator had apprehensions of his own to occupy his mind.

Dramatically, Saul, who was to be Paul, appears, a silent figure who had acquiesced in the crime (22:20), but was clearly not one of the beserk executioners. A process had begun in his heart.

8

Saul
(Acts 8:1–3)

And Saul was in complete agreement with his murder. And a great persecution arose, at that time, against the Church in Jerusalem, and all its members were scattered through the countryside of Judaea and Samaria, apart from the apostles. Good men buried Stephen and made great lamentation over him. And Saul began ravaging the Church, invading homes and dragging both men and women off to prison.

Luke's purpose is clear in this brief interlude. He has shown us the future Paul standing by, while more brutal hands hurled the deadly stones at the first martyr. He now assures us that the savage sentence had his full approval and that he, Saul, was the prime mover in the fierce persecution which fell upon the Christians in the city. Paul, or Saul, as he should still be called, seemed to shake off a passive acquiescence and became ferocious in his participation. It is common enough for a man under some deep conviction to try, by action and fierce energy, to resist a conclusion pressing upon him with unrelenting force. In fact, Stephen had won a convert; but conversion, for the brilliant Pharisee, meant so agonizing a reappraisement of life that he shrank from it in horror and sought to quell the clamant pull of conviction by throwing all his strength into continued persecution.

Before the end, on the Damascus road, Luke had something

more to say. He told of the ministry of Philip, the first dispersion of the Church, and showed that Paul was not the only
Hellenist with an enlightened view of the new faith.

Philip and Simon
(Acts 8:4–25)

And those who were scattered went round preaching the word.
Philip went down to a city of Samaria and preached Christ to the
people. And the whole population gave attention to what Philip
was saying, as they heard and saw the miracles he did. Many of
those possessed by unclean spirits were delivered from them,
with loud crying; many paralyzed and lame folk were healed,
and there was great joy in that city. A man named Simon, who
had been practicing magic there, held the attention of small and
great in Samaria. He professed to be someone important, and
they were saying, "This man is the mighty power of God." He
had been practicing for some time, and it was for this reason that
they gave heed to him, astounded by his magic. But when they
believed Philip, who was preaching the Gospel of God's kingdom and the name of Jesus Christ, they were baptized, men and
women. Simon believed also, was baptized, attached himself to
Philip, and was amazed at the signs and demonstrations of power which took place.

Now when the apostles at Jerusalem heard that Samaria had
received the word, they sent to them Peter and John, who came
down and prayed with them that they might receive the Holy
Spirit—as yet it had fallen on none of them; they had simply
been baptized into the name of Jesus Christ. Then the apostles
laid hands on them, and they received the Holy Spirit. When
Simon saw that by the laying on of the apostles' hands the Holy
Spirit was given, he offered them money, saying, "Give me this
power that on whomsoever I place my hands he may receive the

Holy Spirit." Peter said to him, "Destruction to you and your money, because you have thought to buy the free gift of God. You have no part nor share in this ministry, for your heart is not straight before God. Repent, therefore, of this evil of yours, and pray to the Lord, if perchance this purpose of your heart may be forgiven. For I see you fallen into the bitterness of envy and the bondage of unrighteousness." Simon answered, "Do you pray to the Lord for me, that none of the things you have said may come upon me." When the apostles had borne witness and preached the word, they returned to Jerusalem, preaching also in many villages of the Samaritans.

Following the example of Christ (John 4) and working outward in the manner prescribed (1:8), Philip moved to Samaria, where his ministry received the approval of Peter and John. This was Luke's purpose. He is about to show Philip moving into Gentile evangelism, and then Peter, alone, before introducing the ministry of Paul. With remarkable art, he is interweaving the ministry of the Hellenistic Jews with that of the apostles.

The sinister figure of Simon is introduced to show that Christianity was not a system of wonder-working. It is true that the apostles and the first inner circle of their colleagues did many extraordinary deeds, especially of healing. The whole drift of the story, however, suggests that this was a passing phenomenon, directly connected with the first movement of the Christian Church into the world. It was not permanent and could hardly have continued along with the preaching of faith. A Christ who step-by-step and universally proves his presence could hardly be a Christ of faith. Observe that no miracle saved Stephen from a horrible death.

Simon was typical of the charlatans of all time: the purveyors of miracle mongering who practice, sometimes on whole communities, the arts of the deceiver. The world is full of people

"who make themselves out to be someone" (*see* 9), who (such is
the gullibility of man) seduce crowds and actually win extraordinary titles ranging from the ridiculous to the blasphemous.

How genuine Simon's conversion was cannot be said, but he
speedily turned out to be one of those whose Christianity con-
sisted of continual experience of the extraordinary (13, 19, 20).
Also, his own desire to make personal advantage out of religion
rapidly became evident, a reversion to his old way of life. Unfortunately, the Church can provide opportunity for such
abuse. Hence the use of the word *simony;* hence, too, the stern
severity with which Peter dealt with the case, as he had done
with the first hypocrites, Ananias and Sapphira. And so Simon
became a name for religious perfidy, along with Balaam (2 Peter 2:15). Gehazi might have joined them. Whether Simon was
shocked into repentance and forgiveness is not finally clear
(24). Legend speaks of a continued career in wizardry and a
sect in Rome in Claudius' time. Luke was well aware of the
dangers which beset the Church. He is to recount more of them.
They still exist in new disguises, but in nature and in origin are
the same.

Philip and the Ethiopian
(Acts 8:26–40)

An angel of the Lord spoke to Philip, saying, "Be on your way
toward the south, the road that goes down from Jerusalem to
Gaza—the desert road." He obeyed and went. And, look, an
Ethiopian royal official of Queen Candace of Ethiopia—her
chief treasurer, in fact, who had come to worship at Jerusalem—
was on his way back and, sitting in his chariot, was reading the
prophet Isaiah. And the Spirit said to Philip, "Go forward, close
to his chariot." Hurrying forward, Philip heard him reading Isaiah the prophet and said, "Do you understand what you are read-

ing?" "No," he said, "how can I, unless someone guides me?" He invited Philip to get up and sit with him. The passage of Scripture which he was reading was this: "He was led like a lamb to the slaughter, and, as a sheep before its shearer is dumb, so he opened not his mouth. In his humiliation justice was denied him. Who shall speak of his posterity? For his life was taken from the earth." The officer asked Philip, "I ask you, about whom does the prophet say this? About himself or someone else?" Philip answered, and, beginning from the same Scripture, preached the Gospel of Jesus to him.

As they were going along the road, they came to some water, and the officer said, "Look, water—what is to stop me from being baptized?" He commanded the chariot to stop, and they both went down to the water, both the officer and Philip, and he baptized him. When they came up from the water, the Spirit hurried Philip away, and the officer saw him no more, for he went joyfully on his way.

Philip was next heard of at Azotus, and he went preaching through all the towns right up to Caesarea. [With some reluctance, verse 37 is omitted. The omission began with the Revised Version, on the strength of the fact that the verse is not found in the most ancient manuscripts. It may have been that Luke wrote it and, in a final draft of his work, erased it for brevity, and that some copyists included the excised words. It may be that a common formula of baptism was inserted into the text, which runs, " 'If you believe with all your heart you may.' And he replied, 'I believe that Jesus Christ is the Son of God.' "]

The story is told in Luke's best manner. It was the custom for a lonely traveler to attach himself to a larger group. The Ethiopian was, of course, reading aloud, a fashion dictated by the ancient manuscript with no divisions between the words—a device of convenience which, strangely enough, was not used in ancient manuscripts. To pray silently, it might be added, was also uncommon, and, indeed, suspect (1 Samuel 1:13).

Gaza was the old city of that name on the ancient caravan route to Egypt. It resisted Alexander and suffered destruction and massacre (Zephaniah 2:4; Zechariah 9:5), recovered somewhat as a market center, and was depopulated again by the Maccabees in 96 B.C. New Gaza was a port, and the Ethiopian naturally took the more direct, shorter, and less traffic-ridden route home. Azotus, a port between Gaza and Joppa, was only a few miles from the place of this remarkable encounter.

The two references to a message from an angel may have been Philip's characteristic way of expressing his sense of overwhelming compulsion from God, perhaps through some context of events or some word spoken. The word *angel* means "messenger" and can be so translated.

Philip told this story to Luke. His itinerant evangelism seems to have ended in the Roman garrison town of Caesarea, where he settled (21:8), the first example of a settled ministry.

How the Ethiopian came to be a Jewish convert may be part of a story a millennium old. Israel's faith had obviously followed the trade routes—up which, a thousand years apart, came the Queen of Sheba and the Magi. The corpus of legend which collected round the queen and Solomon extended over the straits to Ethiopia, with which Southern Arabia (Arabia Felix) had close political and commercial ties. There may easily have been a spark of messianic expectation still alive, for some to bring the typical products of Arabia Felix to Bethlehem and for a senior Ethiopian chamberlain to make a pilgrimage to Jerusalem and to pick his way through a Hebrew (or possibly Greek) roll of Isaiah. The text as recorded is that of the Greek Bible, which is no clearer than the Hebrew in verse 33 and which could be translated: "And who shall describe the wickedness of his generation?" or "Who will calculate the number of his followers?"

Finally, observe how the swift understanding of the Hellenistic Jews had penetrated the message of the Old Testament. Luke had already at length reported the speech of Stephen. Here now is Philip, anticipating the approach of Paul. This was also relevant to Luke's total purpose, which is to make irrefutably clear that Paul had not distorted Judaism, but shown how Christ fulfilled what was already implicit in it. To grasp that fact demanded the emancipated minds of the Jews of the Dispersion.

9

Damascus Road
(Acts 9:1–9)

Saul, breathing murderous threats against the disciples of the Lord, approaching the high priest, asked of him letters to the Damascus synagogues so that, if he should find any of the Way, men and women, too, he might bring them under arrest to Jerusalem. Journeying on, he drew near to Damascus, when suddenly a light from heaven shone all round him; and, falling to the ground, he heard a voice saying to him, "Saul, Saul, why are you persecuting me?" And he said, "Who are you, Lord?" And he said, "I am Jesus, whom you are persecuting. But up, and go into the city, and it shall be told you what you must do." And the men traveling with him stood speechless, hearing, indeed, a voice, but seeing no one. Saul rose from the ground; and, when he opened his eyes, he could see nothing. Leading him by the hand, they went into Damascus. He was sightless for three days and neither ate nor drank. [*Note:* The last clause of 5 and the first half of 6 are from 22:10 and 26:14. They are not here in the best manuscripts.]

After Luke's habit, Saul was introduced as a silent onlooker, while the more brutally minded of his fellow Sanhedrists stoned Stephen the martyr. Saul was a "young man" (7:58), a description that could be used until the age of forty. Saul may have been between thirty-five and forty. He was born in the ancient city of Tarsus; "no mean city," he calls it, quoting Euripides

(*Ion* 8.29.38). Tarsus was in Cilicia, an ancient seat of administration as early as Persian times, a center of learning, the home
of a philosophical school, and the hub of a linen industry.
Paul's trade, tent making, was probably the weaving of this
rough cloth, perhaps mingled with goat hair, and known as
cilicium from the name of the province (18:3).

Tarsus was a confluence of East and West. That is why Paul
could think like a Greek. He alluded to Greek philosophy. He
wrote Greek with skill. Educated also in Jerusalem, under the
famous scholar Gamaliel, he was at home with Jewish thought.
As a member of a privileged group in Tarsus, he held the coveted Roman citizenship. He spoke Latin. In his own right, Paul,
as he was called in Gentile contexts, was an intellectual of the
first order, probably the finest mind of his century, and ranked
with Plato by the eminent classicist T. R. Glover, of Cam-
bridge. It was "no mean man" who fell on the Damascus road.

Saul was an ardent Pharisee; and it was his sectarian zeal
that drove him to persecution of the Christians—an ardor ac-
centuated by the conviction, born of Stephen's speech and
death, if Luke be read aright, that the Christians held the truth.
Fierce action can be assuagement for a tormented mind. The
passive figure of 7:58 has suddenly become the fanatic of the
Sanhedrists' persecution, the Pharisees now in their old, base
alliance with the Sadducees. In spite of his training under the
liberally minded Gamaliel, something drove Saul into the camp
of the right-wing Pharisees; and the only reasonable psychological explanation must be a fierce repression, a passionate desire
to stamp out a conviction that the Christians were right. He
sought and won the office of chief inquisitor for Damascus, for
he had seen that the metropolitan persecution had scattered the
Church. It needed pursuit. The high priest had no authority in
Damascus. His envoy had no right of arrest or transfer. Perhaps
this is further illustration of some relaxation of firm Roman

rule, following Stephen's martyrdom. The Sanhedrin was playing a high-handed and dangerous game, and if the exact date were known, it might be possible to explain it in a Roman imperial context.

There were obviously Christian cells in the Damascus synagogues—folk known as "the people of the Way," probably after John 14:6, a saying known long before the last apostle quoted it. The Sanhedrin had every confidence in the ability of their envoy to awaken the rabbis to the peril of a Christian infiltration and, if there was hesitancy over the legality of the whole proceeding, to undertake punishment. The Jerusalem hierarchy, lashed by Peter and Stephen, exasperated with their inability to destroy the preaching of the Resurrection and, for the moment sensing an opportunity, were eager for swift action, perhaps before a new procurator arrived.

That is why the persecutor probably took the faster road of the two which led to Damascus. It ran through Nablus, crossed the Jordan south of the Galilee lake, ran north over the Golan Heights, and swung northeast to Damascus. Somewhere on this road, possibly near Damascus, and at some time during the week the journey would take, the bitter Pharisee was halted by God's challenge (3). The words were snatched out of Paul's own mind; he knew that he was acting like a recalcitrant ox (5). This was no hallucination, no trick of a disordered mind. Paul was not an epileptic. The intellectual achievements visible in his career and writings show a consistently active, superbly sound, and magnificently creative mind undiminished by hardship and powerful till death. A mist of evil was torn aside. He saw the truth and saw that he could no longer shun, escape, or quench it. Moments of conversion may be sudden, but they are the climax of a process. Judaism had brought no peace, as he was to tell the Romans (Romans 7:14–25), and Stephen's death and vision had shattered him.

It was a strangely different man who stumbled into Damascus and faced three days of extraordinary bewilderment to which he may possibly refer in 2 Corinthians 12:1–4. The earliest acceptable date for the event which was to produce the first European, the Christian heir to three cultures, who was to change the history of the world, is A.D. 33.

Sequel
(Acts 9:10–30)

In Damascus was a disciple named Ananias, and in a dream God said to him, "Ananias." He replied, "Here I am, Lord." The Lord said to him, "Up and go to Straight Street and look in the house of Judas for one named Saul, a Tarsus man; for, look, he is praying, and has seen a man named Ananias coming in and laying hands on him so that he should regain his sight." Ananias replied, "Lord, I have heard from many about this man and what evil he has done to your followers in Jerusalem, and he has authority here from the high priests to put under arrest all who call upon your name." The Lord said, "Be on your way, for this man is a chosen instrument for me to bear my name before Gentiles and kings, as well as the people of Israel, for I shall show to him what things he must endure for my name." Ananias went, entered the house, and, putting his hands on him, said, "Saul, brother, the Lord has sent me—Jesus, who was seen by you on the way by which you came—so that you should regain your sight and be filled with the Holy Spirit." And immediately it was as if scales had fallen from his eyes. He got up, was baptized, took food, and recovered his strength.

He remained some days with the disciples in Damascus and immediately began to proclaim in the synagogues that Jesus was the Son of God. Those who heard were amazed and said, "Is not this the man who ravaged those who called on this name in Jerusalem and came here for the sole reason of taking them under arrest to the high priests?" But Saul became stronger and stronger and overwhelmed the Jews in Damascus, proving that this was the Messiah. After some time, the Jews plotted to make away with him. The plot was made known to Saul; and they kept a watch, day and night, at the city gates, to murder him. The disciples took and let him down through the wall, in a basket. Arriving at Jerusalem, he tried to link up with the disciples, but they were all afraid of him, not believing that he was a disciple. Barnabas, however, took him to the apostles and related to them how he had seen the Lord on the way and that he had spoken to him, and how in Damascus he had spoken openly in the name of Jesus. And Saul associated freely with them in Jerusalem, speaking openly in the Lord's name, talking and debating with the Jews of the Dispersion, who, however, kept plotting to do away with him. When the Christians found out, they took him down to Caesarea and sent him off to Tarsus.

Ananias was called to a considerable act of faith. It was natural enough for anyone in Damascus or Jerusalem to ask whether the conversion of the chief persecutor was genuine or simply a deadly plan for infiltration. Like the brave and gentle Barnabas, Ananias obeyed and perhaps gave the broken convert material for a sentence he was one day to write: "Love believes all things. . . ."

The word "scales" is used in the same context by the man of medicine Hippocrates. No material substance fell from the eyes. It was simply like having semiopaque obstructions removed. Saul saw his benefactor and resumed the normalities of life. Ananias is one of those noble characters who appear briefly in the story, do their one deed of beneficence, and disappear. After Stephen, he was the next great influence in the life of this man who had come so astonishingly to conversion. "Saul, brother . . ." must have been sweet music to the broken man.

"Certain days" (19 KJV) is commonly Luke's formula for a

brief period (*see also* 10:48; 15:36; 16:12; 24:24; 25:13). In the alternative account of the escape through some high opening in the wall (2 Corinthians 11:32, 33), the ethnarch of King Aretas of the Nabataeans is mentioned as the one who sought the arrest of the disturber of the synagogues. How Aretas held authority in Damascus is not known, for the city would appear to have been part of the Roman Province of Syria. Aretas was a problem for the empire. It was his daughter whom Herod Antipas had wronged by his evil liaison with Herodias, and Aretas actually attacked Herod's frontiers in A.D. 28. It was a piece of effrontery which Rome could hardly overlook, but they were quite desperately anxious to keep peace along their unstable eastern frontier. It was not until the middle thirties that Vitellius, the governor of Syria, moved against the insubordinate border prince—no very great show of eagerness. The expedition, at any rate, had not moved beyond Jerusalem when Tiberius died in March A.D. 37. Uncertainty over the eastern policy of his successor—the mad Gaius, or Caligula—might have made Vitellius pause; and the young Gaius had his likes and dislikes among the petty rulers, whose unwritten contract with the empire was simply to keep the peace. Very little is known of undulations and variations in the border areas of the region, and it would seem that Damascus was in an equivocal position. It is odd that there is no record of coinage issued in Damascus between Augustus' death and Nero's accession. The statement in the letter to Corinth about Aretas' assumption of authority in the city is evidence that Rome was not, at the time, judicially active in the area, and that the Nabataean ruler presumptuously, by Gaius' gift or by exercise of undisputed tenure all through Tiberius' principate, governed Damascus. It is unfortunate that such uncertainties forbid the use of this incident to pinpoint the time of Saul's conversion.

Fourteen years, over which Luke passes (Galatians 1:15–2:1), follow. They were years of manifold adventure (2 Corinthians 11:24–32), but to detail them is not part of Luke's purpose. He is busy, at this point, welding together the careers of Peter and Paul, to show beyond dispute that the development of global Christianity was part of the commission (1:8) and not the perverse innovation of the brilliant rabbi from Tarsus. He is to turn us again to the "acts of Peter," before the "acts of Paul" hold the stage of his historical purpose.

Paul's three years' ministry in Damascus (Galatians 1:17, 18) is passed over in silence with the rest. We are simply left to imagine him in his native Cilicia, exercising his great gifts in the most difficult of all spheres: the prophet's own country.

Philistine Coast
(Acts 9:31–43)

So the Church through all Judaea, Galilee, and Samaria, being built up and doing its work in the fear of the Lord and by the Holy Spirit's help, was increasing in numbers.

And Peter, in the course of a general visitation, came down to the Christians who lived at Lydda. He found there a man named Aeneas, bedridden with paralysis for eight years past. Peter said to him, "Aeneas, Jesus Christ heals you. Get up and make your bed." And everybody in Lydda and the Sharon plain saw him and turned to the Lord.

In Joppa was a disciple called Tabitha (Dorcas, in Greek). She was continually busy doing good and ministering to need. It was at that time that she fell ill and died. They washed her and laid her in an upstairs room. Since Lydda was not far from Joppa, the disciples, hearing that Peter was there, sent two men to him with the appeal "come down to us without delay." Peter went along with them. When he arrived, they took him to the upper room, and all the widows stood round him in tears, showing him the

dresses and cloaks which Dorcas had made when she was with
them. Peter put them all out, fell on his knees, and prayed. Turning to the body, he said, "Tabitha, get up." She opened her eyes,
saw Peter, and sat up. He gave her his hand and helped her to
her feet. Calling the Christians and the widows, he set her before
them, alive. All Joppa knew about it, and many believed in the
Lord. And he stayed for a time in Joppa, with one Simon, a
tanner.

It would appear that, with the conversion of the most fanatical of its organizers, the heart went out of the Jerusalem persecution. The Church grew, and Peter began to exercise the sort
of episcopal function, along the Philistine coast, that he had
already assumed in Samaria. The key story is to be told in the
next chapter, but this brief interlude, with its two stories of
healing, is designed to show that, in the course of his visit to the
Philistine coast and the congregations which Philip had no
doubt founded (8:40), Peter was in the full stream of his apostolic ministry. It is curious to observe with what consistency he
organized his authenticating miracles after the exact procedure
of his Master (Luke 8:49–56; John 5:6–9). Luke is not, of
course, claiming that the whole population of Lydda was converted. As Calvin sensibly remarked on the passage: ". . .
Scripture puts 'all' for the most part, for many, or the common
sort of men." The East is accustomed to hyperbolical language
(2:5).

Lydda, Lod today, and the site of Israel's international air-
port, was separate from Joppa in the first century. Both now
merge in the great city of Tel Aviv, which spreads its buildings
and smog over a coast which was sand dunes not much more
than half a century ago. Useful harbors are not found along the
eastern coast of the Mediterranean, and any formation of land
that offers a modicum of shelter is eagerly taken up by ship-

ping. Today, Carmel's bold mass gives shelter, from one direction, for Haifa. At Joppa, the now almost completely eroded remains of an offshore reef once gave a sort of haven. It can provide little today.

It is ancient ground. Joppa is mentioned in the tribute lists of Thothmes III, the dynamic pharaoh who conducted the first recorded military campaign in history—a drive north to battle with the Hittites on the Orontes River. That was in 1472 B.C. and was the beginning of two centuries' dominance along all that coast. It became Philistine territory. From the days of Abraham, these Cretan tribes had held a foothold on the coast and indeed gave Palestine its name. But the Hebrews were never able to do more than confine the European intrusion, until the area was occupied by the Maccabees, in the great Jewish liberation movement between the Testaments.

In these tempestuous days, at Joppa, dire things were done to Greeks and Gentiles; and it must have been difficult for Christians who had found refuge from Jerusalem's persecution there, if they dared to think of Christianity as a movement apart from Judaism. The whole tradition of Joppa, since the Jews at long last mastered it, was one of Jewish pride and intransigence. But here, too, was instruction for a man moving, as Peter was, toward a strange new liberalism. The streets would be crowded with sailors from Greece, Italy, and Phoenicia, a cosmopolitan crowd, almost a foretaste of the enormous Tel Aviv which today runs north from the weary port.

Summary

Peter is about to meet his great adventure, and the theme of Acts is assuming final unity. Managing his material as skillfully as Charles Dickens ordered his interwoven plots, Luke has led us to a vital point in his history of one outward surge of the

Church. He has shown the strife and tribulation of those early days, the varied and manifold nature of persecution, and the adjustments of conduct and organization which events and personalities thrust upon the Church. He has shown the rise and prominence of Peter and intermingled his doings with those of the remarkable band of Greek-speaking Jews. There is little left to do in the setting of the stage for the apostle to the Gentiles, whose dramatic conversion has set him in full view, before he was withdrawn for a span of years.

10

Cornelius
(Acts 10:1–8)

There was a man, in Caesarea, called Cornelius, a centurion of the so-called Italian Cohort, a religious man who feared God, as did his whole household. He gave generously to the people and always prayed to God. About the middle of the afternoon, he saw clearly, in a vision, an angel of God coming to him and saying, "Cornelius." He looked hard at him and was alarmed, but said, "What is it, Lord?" The angel replied, "Your prayers and your deeds of benevolence are known and remembered by God. And now, send men to Joppa and fetch one Simon, called Peter. He is a guest of one Simon, a tanner, whose house is by the sea." When the angel who had spoken to him was gone, Cornelius called two of his household servants and a devout soldier, one of his regular bodyguard, told them everything, and sent them off to Joppa.

The story moves to Caesarea, some thirty miles north of Joppa, up the long, open coast. That surf-beaten and harborless littoral has already been noticed. The coast is strewn with ancient harbor works, where engineers have striven to provide a haven for ships. The sea has won in every case, and the endless assault of the waves has broken down and swallowed mole and breakwater, all the way up the old Philistine coast to the jutting promontory of Carmel.

At Caesarea the Mediterranean had its hardest task. Herod I

spent twelve years, from 25 to 13 B.C., building his great port
there. It was a matter of life and death for him to give the
Romans a safe bridgehead. His subtle diplomacy aimed at serving Augustus—whose eastern legions, after all, kept him in
power—and at conciliating the Jews, his restless and resentful
subjects. Hence the apparent contradiction of a temple to Augustus, whose perron can still be seen, at Samaria, and a temple
to Jehovah, in Jerusalem. It is a testimony to Herod's ruthless
ability that he carried through this dual policy and, in the end,
died in his bed.

Caesarea gave the Romans an entry and a base. The seawall
was a notable triumph of engineering. How the blocks of lime-
stone, some of them fifty feet long, were put in place to form
the mole—itself some two hundred feet wide and standing in
twenty fathoms of water—is not known. It would tax all the
resources of a highly mechanized society. The seawall curved
round to form a haven. Behind it, on the low, sandy shore, a
semicircle of wall protected the town, its houses, racecourse,
theatre, and temples.

Today, nothing of Herod's harbor is visible from the boulder-
strewn shore. The dry dock for the galleys may still be traced.
The theater, with its high curve of seats, is prominent and finely
restored. It is there that Pilate, for some reason, set up an inscription, discovered in 1961 and bearing fragments of Pilate's
name, with the letters *D D D (dedit, donavit, dedicavit)*, presumably, a formal phrase meaning "gave, donated, dedicated."
There are sundry Roman foundations. Somewhere among those
stones, Philip had his house, Cornelius his barrack room, and
Paul his cell. Crusader ruins dominate the scene, for the Frank-
ish invaders saw the advantage of Caesarea as a beachhead, as
clearly as did Herod and his Roman masters. North of the town
is a fragment of a vast aqueduct that brought in water from
some distant spring and that must have been the fortress's most

vulnerable link. Surely somewhere the archaeologists must find vast storage tanks. Water would be a problem for the garrison, even with uninterrupted command of the sea-lanes.

Cornelius was a senior centurion, a commander, like Julius (27:1), of a special-duties regiment. Whether Philip had established himself in Caesarea at this time cannot be said; but the character of the five centurions briefly mentioned in the New Testament encourages the conjecture that they were men of special excellence, perhaps with a sympathetic leaning toward Judaism, and wisely seconded for service in that most difficult of all the provinces. There is evidence in one or two first- and early second-century Latin writers that Judaism had important converts among the Romans. A centurion of Capernaum was the first to receive the benediction of the Lord (Luke 7:9). Cornelius was a man like him—attracted, perhaps, by the Old Testament and following, in almsgiving and prayer, the help and inspiration it afforded.

Peter
(Acts 10:9–23)

On the morrow, while they were on the way and drawing near to Joppa, about midday, Peter went up to the housetop to pray. He was hungry and wanted something to eat; and, while they were preparing, he fell half-asleep and saw heaven opened and a container let down to earth by the four corners, in which there were all manner of quadrupeds, reptiles, and birds. And a voice said to him, "Up, Peter, kill and eat." And Peter replied, "By no means, Lord. I have never eaten anything common or unclean." And the voice came a second time to him, "What God has made clean, you must not make common." This happened three times, and the container was taken back to heaven.

And while Peter was puzzling over the meaning of what he

had seen, there were the men sent by Cornelius. They had just asked the way to Simon's house and were at the door, calling and asking whether Simon, called Peter, was staying there. And while Peter was pondering over his vision, the Spirit said, "Look, two men are asking for you. Get up, go down, and accompany them without misgiving, because I have sent them." Peter went down and said to them, "See, I am the person you are looking for. What is the reason for your visit?" They replied, "Cornelius the centurion, a good, God-fearing man who stands high in the estimation of the whole Jewish people, has been commanded by a holy angel to send and invite you to his home and to hear what you have to say." He invited them in and lodged them. The next day he set out with them, accompanied by some of the Joppa Christians.

Peter had much to think about as the tanner's guest. Simon must have spread a leather tarpaulin of stitched skins on his flat roof, suspended on poles at the four corners. It was a cool place, and as Peter stretched out on his couch to pray, the sea breeze lifted and dropped the canopy above him.

He had much to fill his thoughts as he looked up at the covering over the open housetop, with the waves a monotone beneath. The last five years had done much to a Galilaean fisherman. First there was the transforming wilderness ministry of John, then the blessed years with Christ, the horror of the trial and the crucifixion, Pentecost, persecution in Jerusalem, and now what seemed to be developing into a nationwide ministry.

And now, here he was, a guest of this Christian of unclean trade. We have Paul's own testimony (Galatians 2:11, 12) that Peter found it difficult to divest himself of Jewish prejudices, and whimsically or uneasily he watched the billowing cover above him. It is a homely touch typical of Peter. He went upstairs to pray, felt hungry, and then his thoughts drifted into somnolence. It was an "ecstasy" says the Greek: that half-waking, half-sleeping state in which reality is withdrawn and objects around assume a significance apart from themselves. Christ built much that he said on what was at hand: the lilies of the field, the plowlands above the lake, the vine over the temple gate. The same Lord now spoke to Peter in terms of what he saw.

Peter's own protest and the reply are quite typical of other interchanges between the Lord and his impulsive disciple (Matthew 16:22, 23; John 13:8) and ended typically with the warmhearted man's complete surrender. The threefold repetition might also be a signal from God, reminding Peter of a beach in Galilee (John 21:15–17). Then reality, the visitors, and Cornelius' message took over.

Caesarea
(Acts 10:24–48)

The following day they reached Caesarea. Cornelius was expecting them and gathered his family and close friends together. When Peter was at the door, Cornelius bowed low before him and offered him reverence. Peter raised him up, saying, "Arise. I am a man, too." Talking together, they went in, and Peter found many assembled and said to them, "You know that it is unlawful for a Jew to associate with or visit those of another race, but God has shown me not to call any other human being common or unclean. Therefore, when I was summoned, I came without hesitation. So I want to know for what reason you sent for me." Cornelius replied, "Three days ago, at this hour, I was at home for midafternoon prayer and suddenly a man stood before me, in shining clothes, and said to me, 'Cornelius, your prayers are heard and your acts of mercy remembered before God. So send to Joppa and summon Simon who is called Peter. He is a guest in the house of Simon the tanner on the seashore.' So I sent immediately to you, and it was good of you to come. That is why all of us are now here in God's presence to hear everything the Lord has bidden you say."

So Peter began and said, "Truly, I am beginning to understand that God is no regarder of people, but in every nation the man who holds him in reverence and does what is right is acceptable to him. The word which he sent to the people of Israel, announcing the good news of peace through Jesus Christ, who is Lord of all: that word you know which went through all Judaea, beginning from Galilee, after the baptism which John proclaimed, how God anointed Jesus of Nazareth with the Holy Spirit and power—Jesus, who went about doing good and healing all those who were in the devil's power, because God was with him. And we are witnesses of all he did in Judaea and Jerusalem. They killed him, hanging him on a tree. God raised him up on the third day and granted him to be seen—not to all the people, but to witnesses whom he had chosen beforehand: to us, who ate and drank with him after his resurrection from the dead. And he commissioned us to preach to the people and to declare solemnly that this is he ordained by God as Judge of the living and the dead. To him all the prophets bear witness that forgiveness of sins is received through his name by all who believe in him."

While Peter was speaking, the Holy Spirit fell on all those who heard his words. And the Christian Jews who had come with Peter were astonished that the gift of the Holy Spirit was poured out on the Gentiles, too. For they heard them speaking in ecstasy and giving glory to God. Then said Peter, "Can anyone refuse the water that these may be baptized, who have received the Holy Spirit, as we also did?" And he told them to be baptized in the name of Jesus Christ. Then they asked him to stay for a few days.

Perhaps it was the establishment of a Christian cell in the Roman garrison town which led to Philip's long ministry there. There is no doubt that a senior officer would gather believers round him. Rome, later to be Paul's major objective, was already invaded. Luke regarded the encounter as one of paramount importance, as is shown by the leisurely narrative with its repetitions. Peter's Joppa experience is fully related again in the next chapter. Luke knew what he was about. He can be ruthlessly brief when it suits the plan of his work. Vital events he details at length.

Here he has four objects. First, he stresses that the door to Rome and the Gentiles was opened by Peter. He was using the keys (Matthew 16:19). To be sure, Philip had opened up the whole Philistine coast, had penetrated Samaria, and sent a converted Ethiopian royal official back to Africa and his queen; but this was a major inroad by the Jewish leader of the Church of Jerusalem. Second, he was showing the Christology of Peter as identical with that of Paul: Jesus the Man, Christ the risen Lord, and Jesus Christ the Judge of this world and the next (16:31). Third, he was showing Peter, who had known and walked with Christ, as the witness to the risen reality and future cosmic role of the Man from Nazareth. Fourth, and of less importance, he was showing an apostle assuming his special role. The apostle, like the prophet, was one whose work was to end with the rounding of the New Testament canon. That is why Peter does not himself baptize (48; *compare* 1 Corinthians 1:13–16).

11

Peter Reports
(Acts 11:1–18)

The apostles and brethren in Judaea heard that the Gentiles had accepted the word of God; and, when Peter went up to Jerusalem, the strict Jewish element took strong exception to him, saying, "You visited people who were not true Jews and took food with them!"

But Peter began and explained the whole matter to them in detail. "I was in the city of Joppa," he said, "at prayer, and I saw a vision when I was only half-awake—a sort of container, like a big sheet, let down out of heaven to me, held by the four corners. I looked closely at it and saw the four-footed creatures of earth, wild animals and creeping things and birds of the air. I heard a voice saying to me, 'Get up, Peter, kill and eat.' 'In no way, Lord,' I answered, 'because nothing common or unclean has ever passed my lips.' Speaking again from heaven, the voice replied, 'What God has made clean, do you not make common.'

"This was done three times, and then everything was drawn back up into heaven. And, observe, at that very moment three men stood before the house where I was, sent to me from Caesarea. And the Spirit told me to go with them, raising no objections. And there went with me these six brethren, and we entered the man's house. He told us how he saw the angel standing in his house and saying, 'Send men to Joppa, and fetch Simon, called Peter, who shall have a message for you by which you and all your house shall be saved.' And I had hardly begun to speak, when the Holy Spirit fell on them, as it did on us at the beginning. And I remembered the word of the Lord, how he said, 'John indeed baptized with water, but you shall be baptized with the Holy Spirit.' Since God then granted them the same gift as he did to us when we believed on the Lord Jesus Christ, who was I to be able to stand in God's way?" When they heard this story, they had nothing to say and praised God, saying, "Then to the Gentiles, too, God has granted the repentance which brings life!"

Division in the Jerusalem church has already appeared in the narrative. As early as chapter six a "murmuring" was reported about discrimination between the Jews from abroad and the metropolitan Jews. The division evident in this episode is of a much more fundamental nature and destined to form a major problem in the coming ministry of Paul.

It is clear that the converted priests and Pharisees, who formed a strong proportion of the Jerusalem congregation, accepted the facts of the Gospel: that Jesus was the Messiah, that he rose from the dead, and that there was salvation by no other name. They saw the faith as a reforming force in Judaism, destined to wipe away the abuses of the Sadducees, legalistic Pharisaism, and all else which Christ had castigated. Some perhaps less, some more, accepted the sacrificial rituals, kept the historic festivals, and most certainly retained the Jewish sign in the flesh. To become a Christian meant to become a "fulfilled Jew," to use a modern term, but most certainly involved no break with the faith of their fathers and no diminution of Jewish separatism or any open fellowship with Gentiles.

How deep into the conscience and consciousness this ancient prejudice had bitten is shown by Peter himself, the recipient of this most striking divine revelation. Many years later, in distant Antioch, daunted by the continuing prejudices of the stubborn

Jerusalem congregation, he withdrew from a happy fellowship with Gentiles and severed association (Galatians 2).

Judaism had always magnanimously offered hospitality to all who sought acceptance and who fulfilled the Jewish obligations. The synagogues of the Dispersion were a refuge to many Gentiles who, wearied of paganism, sought a pure and upright form of worship such as Judaism had to offer. It was quite another matter to accept the devastating doctrine that Judaism was dead; that the "chosen people," as Paul and Peter in their letters were to teach, had merged and blended in a wider Israel, a royal priesthood; that a new age had dawned and another dispensation.

Proudly conscious of his national privilege, the Jew required a reappraisal and an adjustment almost beyond our imagining to accept the fact that his race had been no more than the temporary custodians of a preparatory religion that was not only fulfilled, but superseded, in Christ. True, in the ancient prophecies there had been hints enough about a global faith, but the Jew had always thought of the nations, convinced at last, pouring to worship in Jerusalem.

Hence Luke's insistence on this story. There were limits to one roll of papyrus, and the twenty-eight-foot roll seems to have been regarded as the limit of the practicable length for an ancient book. Luke knew how large a story he had to tell, but so important does he regard this report to the Jerusalem congregation that he uses his precious space to repeat, in detail, the story of Peter at Joppa and Caesarea.

When they had heard the story, they had nothing to say, though some, with praise to God, remarked upon the quite amazing fact that God seemed to have offered his salvation to the Gentiles also. There is a certain grudging acceptance of the situation. The Roman officer had been accepted, but few could have imagined that the wide world—the Gentile world, not only the Jews in the Gentile world—was opening to a vast outward surge of Christian evangelism that would sweep Judaism from its historic stage. It is probable that many Jewish Christians expected the humiliation of the Messiah to be speedily avenged in a Second Advent more in accordance with ancient expectations of the coming King. No doubt, Cornelius was, by God's grace, an exception, not a portent.

What should stir wonder and thankfulness in the whole situation is the fact that there were minds sturdy enough and hearts devoted to see that the old apartheid was over, that there was a new dawn in the sky and another age—our own.

Antioch
(Acts 11:19–26)

The refugees from the persecution which had broken out over Stephen scattered as far as Phoenicia, Cyprus, and Antioch, speaking the word only to the Jews. There were Cypriots and Cyrenians among them, who, coming to Antioch, preached the message also to the Greeks, that Jesus was Lord. And the Lord's hand was with them. A large number believed and turned to the Lord.

News of these matters came to the ears of the church in Jerusalem, and they sent Barnabas on a mission to Antioch. He came, saw the grace of God, was glad, and encouraged them all, with steadfastness of heart, to be loyal to the Lord, because he was a good man, full of the Holy Spirit and faith; and a considerable number were added to the Lord.

Barnabas went to Tarsus to look for Saul. He found him and brought him to Antioch. They spent a whole year with the church and taught large numbers, and in Antioch the disciples were first called Christians.

It is interesting to watch Luke's mind at work. At leisurely and convincing length he has shown the invasion of the garrison town of Caesarea. One of the senior officers of the 3,000 troops stationed there had opened the door to the task force of Christ. But Luke is now urgent to show that the mission to Cornelius was no more than part of a worldwide movement of the Spirit.

In Jerusalem the fanatical Sanhedrin had tried to stamp out the fire which Pentecost had started. They had simply scattered the sparks, which took fire in Africa, Cyprus, and the north. It may be fairly assumed that the bulk of such refugees were those with some base or connection abroad and that their departure further weakened the liberal and Hellenistic wing of the Jerusalem church, leaving it more than ever in control of the exclusive element.

Ironically, then, the persecution of the Church spread its witness. The Church sprang up in Antioch of Syria, or Antioch on the Orontes—a great and beautiful city that was a confluence, like Tarsus, of East and West, a melting pot of Greek and Eastern cultures. Antioch had been the old capital of the Syrian kingdom: that central successor of Alexander's partitioned empire, from which the Maccabaean rebellion had freed Israel. The city was now five centuries old and the headquarters of the Roman eastern legions. The Church, in finding a second capital, established a second cell in a Roman garrison town.

This act took the Church into a metropolis of vice. Antioch, a cosmopolitan port and a soldiers' town, was notorious for its evil living. It was the third city in the empire, after Rome and Alexandria, and some claimed it was the second. Juvenal, the Roman satirist, writing half a century after this event, alleged that Antioch had corrupted Rome. A rabble of subtle Greek immigrants, quackeries, whoredoms, and debaucheries had found Rome a place of profit. "The Orontes," Juvenal claimed, "has become a tributary of the Tiber."

Here was the new wave of evangelism, fed by the Hellenistic

Jews in Stephen's and Philip's succession, who began openly to preach to the Greeks (19, 20). This must be the meaning of "Grecians" (KJV), for the evangelists themselves were Hellenists, that is, Greek Jews. Jerusalem, already conditioned by Peter's story, was alerted, and they sent their most gracious member, Barnabas from Cyprus, whom Luke had already introduced into his story, to investigate and report.

Barnabas appears to be one of those expatriate Jews who found Christ, along with such men as Stephen and Philip, in the first apostolic evangelism. He moves in and out of the story in Acts (4:36, 37; 9:26, 27; 11:22–26; 13:1–3), an unselfish, large-hearted man, always prepared to play the second fiddle well, a test of magnanimity which not everyone can pass. Verse 34 is a fine testimony to him. Such persons, like Bunyan's Mr. Greatheart, are often found engaged in forwarding the works of others. It was characteristic that he should spend some time in Antioch and that he should seek out Paul, or Saul, as he still was properly called, in his native Tarsus. Remembering how he had led Jerusalem's Jewish church to accept the notable convert, Barnabas now caught the vision of Gentile evangelism and knew assuredly that there was only one man for that task.

Luke, after his common fashion, is preparing the way for a chapter ahead. It is worth noting, to the credit of the Jerusalem church, that at this time they chose as their liaison with Antioch a man of whose liberal attitude they must have been fully aware. Paul briefly mentions the unknown Tarsian chapter in his life in Galatians 1:21, 22.

Luke notes that the word *Christian* was first used in Antioch. Some have suggested that it was an Antiochene nickname, and the Syrian city was notorious for such coinages. It is more likely that some city clerk (and bureaucracy was thorough) noted a subgroup among the Jews, picked correctly on what distinguished them, and invented the name. The Christians called themselves disciples, brethren, saints, believers, and others called them the people of the Way (John 14:6; Acts 9:2). *Christian* was used contemptuously by Agrippa (26:28); and, in the context of that occasion, we find the equally contemptuous Jewish title *Nazarene*—"this sect," as they called it (24:5; 28:22). Peter accepts it, writing about A.D. 62 (1 Peter 4:16); and Tacitus, writing about Nero's persecution of A.D. 64, speaks of "people commonly called Christians."

Agabus
(Acts 11:27–30)

It was at that time that prophets came from Jerusalem to Antioch, and one of them, named Agabus, predicted that a great famine was about to fall on the whole inhabited world. This actually occurred in the principate of Claudius Caesar. And the disciples, each as he was able, decided to send help to the brethren in Judaea. This they did, by the agency of Barnabas and Saul.

Luke has several motives for recording this cluster of events. It is difficult to guess what type of instruction was brought by the special teachers from Jerusalem. The desire of the metropolitan church was perhaps to strengthen the conservative features of the teaching in Antioch.

Agabus is to appear once more at a vital point in Paul's story, a sort of Old Testament prophetic figure of the sort that might have been not uncommon in the Jewish section of the Church. The famine of his prophecy is historically verified. The depredations of man had damaged the whole ecology of the Mediterranean world. Widespread deforestation had changed patterns of climate. Perhaps the Sahara was already advancing, as it certainly did over the coming centuries, as Roman exploitation of North Africa gave inroad to the advancing sand. Apart from man's destructive hand upon his environment, the Sahara—where the weather of Europe was made—varied under solar radiation undulating over climatic cycles and back in Mycenae-an times seems to have disastrously shifted the southern European rainbelts. But there was undoubted dearth in Claudius' day, at the close of the forties, and perhaps the Jerusalem congregation, still impoverished from the early and unwise experiment in poverty, felt the stress more than the rest.

Luke marks the beginning of this foreign contribution, the delivery of which, years later, was to lead to Paul's imprisonment. It was, at any rate, a demonstration of Gentile goodwill, which could have been more productive than its final outcome appears to have proved. Of Saul's, or Paul's, activities in the capital, we know nothing. Luke was in a mood of brevity.

12

Royal Persecution
(Acts 12:1–12)

It was at this time that King Herod laid violent hands on some members of the Church. He put to death James, the brother of John; and, seeing that this pleased the Jews, he went on to arrest Peter, also, at Passover time. Seizing him, he put him into prison, under the charge of four squads of four soldiers each, intending to bring him to trial when the Passover was finished. So Peter was kept in prison, and there was earnest prayer by the Church to God on his behalf.

On the night before Peter was to be brought out, he was sleeping between two soldiers, bound with a double chain; and sentries stood guard outside the prison. And suddenly an angel of the Lord stood there, and a light shone in the cell. He tapped Peter on the side and woke him, saying, "Up, quickly," and the bonds fell from his hands. And the angel said to him, "Belt on your tunic and put your shoes on." He did this, and the angel said, "Put on your cloak and follow me." He went out behind him and did not know that what was happening through the angel was true, for it was like a dream. They went through the first and second guardpost and came to the iron gate which led into the city, and this opened automatically before them. They went out, traversed one street, and suddenly the angel was gone.

When Peter came to himself, he said, "Now I know for certain that the Lord has sent his angel and rescued me from Herod's power and all that which the Jews were purposing to do." When he had thought it over, he came to the house of Mary, the mother of John, surnamed Mark, where a considerable number were assembled, praying for him.

Herod Agrippa, first of that name, was a grandson of Herod called the Great, the scoundrel of the Nativity story. He was a close friend of the third emperor, the insane and fortunately short-lived Gaius Caligula. He retained the confidence of Claudius, the middle-aged successor of Caligula, by that flair for diplomacy which was the mark of the Herod family, and, by Claudius' gift, received Judaea and Samaria to add to the territory inherited from his father, Antipas.

The characteristic Herodian skill had enabled Agrippa to keep the favor of Jew and Roman alike, but at this point a crisis arose. The hierarchy had not persecuted the Christians for a time, following Gamaliel's advice, but Peter's intrusion into the Roman garrison town of Caesarea alarmed both Herod and the hierarchy. Hence the attempt to deprive the Church of its leadership, particularly of James and Peter.

The story of Peter's release from prison will, of course, be summarily rejected by those who begin from the position that a miracle—in other words, an extraordinary intervention of God into the fabric of history and events—is impossible. Simply observe, however, that this is not a myth. Myths take time to grow, and they flourish in nonliterary ages. Luke, Philippian though he seems to be when we meet him at Troas, was also a man of Antioch. He must have met Peter there. He must have questioned others who knew of that extraordinary night. He also proves himself, in many contexts, to be a careful historian. Why should he cease to be so, when the events transcend common human experience? The story is factually told in a minimum of words. The intensely natural and human situation in the next episode is further evidence that it was written as a report by a man critically equipped to collect and assess evidence; and, whether the reader chooses to believe the report or not, there is no way in which it can be classified as myth or legend or by any means incorporated into an otherwise simple text. Luke must be accepted on his reputation.

Rhoda
(Acts 11:13–19)

When Peter had knocked at the door of the gateway, a servant girl named Rhoda came to listen. Recognizing Peter's voice, from joy she did not open the gate, but ran in and told them that Peter stood outside the gate. "You're mad," they said. She was emphatic that it was so, and they said, "It is his angel." But Peter stayed there, knocking. They opened the door, saw him, and were astounded. Beckoning to them, with his hand, to be quiet, he told them how the Lord had led him out of the prison, and said, "Tell James and the brethren about this." He went out and proceeded elsewhere.

The next day there was no small disturbance, among the soldiers, about what had happened to Peter. Herod searched for him unsuccessfully, examined the guards, and had them executed. He himself went down from Jerusalem to Caesarea and stayed there.

The complete naturalness of the homely little story is striking. The house obviously had a gateway onto a street, in which a panel could be opened to admit a single visitor. The porter or portress would be on duty in the passage, which led into a courtyard. It suggests a house of some size. It was common sense to seek a more secure hiding place. The heads of the Church, Herod's prime objective, seem to have been already in closer concealment. The James whom Peter mentions is the head of the Jerusalem church, the Lord's brother. Where "the other place" was to which Peter withdrew after his brief visit cannot be guessed. Those unable to resist conjecture have ranged as far as Rome.

Herod
(Acts 12:20–25)

Herod was engaged in a bitter quarrel with the people of Tyre and Sidon. By common consent they approached him, having won the support of Blastus, the king's chamberlain, and asked for peace, because their territory was dependent on the royal domains for food. A day was fixed, and Herod, putting on his royal robes and sitting on his seat of judgment, made an oration to them. The people shouted, "The voice of a god, not of a man." The angel of the Lord smote him on the spot, because he gave not God the glory. He was wormeaten and died. But the word of God increased and spread, and Barnabas and Paul, their mission accomplished, returned from Jerusalem with John, surnamed Mark.

Luke takes the reader back to the coastal garrison town of Caesarea for the grisly story of Herod's seizure and death. The two great ports of the Phoenician coast, given as they were to seagoing and maritime trade and sited on a narrow strip between the seaward Lebanon Range and the Mediterranean, depended on the hinterland for their primary produce. They always had. Witness Ahab's day and see Ezekiel 27. Herod had evidently applied some agricultural sanction; and the Phoenicians bribed ("persuaded" is common irony for this typically Eastern approach) the king's household chief, and a delegation met him in the theater at Caesarea—a strikingly sited place of assembly, very beautifully restored. The king, said Josephus, appeared in glittering silver cloth, probably a Tyrian peace offering, for such cloth is still made in Lebanon. The excitement stirred by his successful oration was evidently too much for a seriously ill man. He fell in his seat. "Eaten of worms" (KJV) is one word, a medical term familiar to Luke, which described a shockingly visible and violently agonizing intestinal malady, following some aneurism, blockage, or puncture, and rapidly fatal. He was fifty-four years of age. It was A.D. 44.

Luke prepares the way, in his last two verses, for his next outward movement of theme. John Mark was Mary's son, Barnabas was her brother. Were Mark, Saul, and Barnabas present when Peter knocked at the door of Mary's house? At any rate, Luke is serving notice that, wherever the muffled figure of Peter went as he slipped out into the darkness, it was out of his story. The great missionary outreach of the Church began with Peter, the great leader who had held the community together with the power of his personality and the firmness of his testimony to the Resurrection. He had much more to do, in Antioch, Corinth, Rome, and elsewhere, but the story is not to be told. From now on, Luke is turning to the "acts of Paul." This is a great new turning point in the book.

13

Historic Action
(Acts 13:1–3)

There were certain prophets and teachers in the Antioch church, including Barnabas, Simeon Niger, Lucius of Cyrene, Manaen, who had grown up in the household of Herod the tetrarch, and Saul. As they were at worship and fasting, the Holy Spirit said, "Separate for me Barnabas and Saul for the work to which I have called them." Then they fasted and prayed, laid hands on them, and sent them off.

In a few remarkably casual words, Luke speaks of the origin of a great movement of history. The gentle ministrations of Barnabas were behind much of what took place. He had quietly involved Saul, who had been long in his native Tarsus, in the activities of the very different Jerusalem and Antioch congregations. It was Barnabas' characteristic role. Some twelve years of Saul's life are unrecorded, save for a tantalizingly brief account of misfortune in 2 Corinthians 11:24–28. We know nothing of five condemnations of Jewish tribunals, unless one was that at Damascus. Of three Roman scourgings we know only of one, the illegal onslaught by the magistrates of Philippi. His three shipwrecks do not include Malta. The catalogue does, however, suggest a period of intense activity over a wide area, and Saul was known at Antioch. He was there for a year preceding this occasion (11:26), so it was not an unknown man on whom the Church, or its named leaders, imposed the present task of Gentile evangelism.

Cyprus
(Acts 13:4-12)

So, sent out by the Holy Spirit, they went down to Seleucia and thence departed to Cyprus. Arriving at Salamis, they began to preach the word of God in the synagogues of the Jews. They had John (Mark) as their attendant. When they had traversed the island as far as Paphos, they met a Jewish magician and false prophet, one Bar-jesus by name. He was in the service of the proconsul, Sergius Paulus, an intelligent man. He sent for Barnabas and Saul and desired to hear the word of God, but "Elymas the magician" (for so he called himself) opposed them, trying to turn the proconsul from the faith. But Saul (call him also Paul), full of the Holy Spirit, looked hard at him and said, "Full of all deceit and craftiness, you son of the devil and foe of all righteousness, will you not cease from bending the straight paths of the Lord? And now see, the hand of the Lord is on you, and you will be blind, not seeing the sun for a while." And immediately a mist and darkness fell on him, and he went round looking for someone to take him by the hand. The proconsul, seeing what had happened, believed, astonished by the teaching of the Lord.

To make for Asia Minor by way of Cyprus was natural enough. It was Barnabas' native island and a fitting point of departure for a venture of Gentile evangelization. The large island, looking on the map like a pegged-out animal hide, had shared, and was forever destined to share, the fortunes of all the northeastern Mediterranean. Settlement dates back to Minoan and Mycenaean days, and the strategic importance of Cyprus has been recognized from the Greek, Persian, and Roman empires to the British Empire. It was another meeting place of cultures and nations, like Tarsus and Antioch itself. There were large settlements of Jews (11:19, 20) there.

The importance of Cyprus was recognized by the man whom, by hindsight, we call the first Roman emperor, the great Augustus. He had professed to "restore the Republic," avoiding the error by which his adoptive uncle, Julius Caesar, had met with assassination. In the complicated system by which he kept all the republican offices in his own hands, Augustus had divided the provinces into imperial and senatorial categories. The former, which required frontier garrisons, he retained under his direct control, with a canny eye on the power of the legionary commanders and the army coups, from which, in fact, Rome was to die. The senatorial provinces were ruled by exconsuls, who still, under the disguised autocracy which Augustus so cleverly invented, controlled the ungarrisoned provinces. Augustus gave Cyprus thus to the senate in 22 B.C.; so a deputy, or proconsul, ruled. It is typical of Luke to have his titles correct. A proconsul was an exconsul.

In 1877, at Soloi, in the north of Cyprus, an inscription that is dated "in the proconsulship of Sergius Paulus," was discovered. Another, discovered ten years later, suggests a connection between an old Roman family, the "gens Sergia," and the island.

Luke assures us that Paulus was an intelligent man, although he kept in his entourage a charlatan Jew named Bar-jesus, who, for some reason over which linguists may be left to argue, called himself Elymas. Luke does not tell the story to balance Peter's Samaritan adventure with Simon. He was not that sort of writer. The scamp's discomfiture simply led to the conversion of the governor of the island, and this first recorded inroad of Christianity into the ranks of Rome's ruling class was an important matter at such a vital juncture in the narrative.

It was not unnatural that Paulus, perhaps responsibly eager to understand the religions of his province, should maintain the Jewish magician. The Romans, at this time, were intensely preoccupied with the more mystical and superstitious forms of

Eastern cults. The Emperor Tiberius maintained a band of such charlatans. He sat on Capri, says the satirist Juvenal, "With his wizard crew"; and Tacitus complained of the helplessness of legislation to rid Rome of the pests, the "Chaldaeans and sooth-sayers," who battened on credulity, as their posterity still does: "a mob faithless to the powerful, deceitful to the hopeful, which will ever be banned among us—and forever tolerated." So says the great historian. Paul, as we now, in Gentile contexts, begin to call him, was to meet the breed again (19:13–17). It seems that a type of renegade Jew specialized in such charlatanism.

Perga
(Acts 13:13)

> Leaving Paphos, Paul and his party came to Perga in Pamphy-lia. And John (Mark) left them and returned to Jerusalem.

In this verse lies a mystery. The young attendant clearly left the party including his uncle, Barnabas, following a bitter dis-agreement (15:38) that Paul remembered for years, but ulti-mately forgave (Colossians 4:10; 2 Timothy 4:11). Why did John Mark withdraw? One guess can be hazarded. Ancient writers sometimes "signed" their book by the introduction of a trivial incident in which they themselves are, or were, in-volved—after the fashion, it is said, in which Alfred Hitchcock made one appearance in his films.

In Mark's account of the arrest in the garden, there appears an unknown boy, almost involved in the incident, who fled, leaving behind him a linen cloth that was about his body. Was it Mark, a fifteen-year-old boy perhaps, who, hearing the party depart after the Last Supper, seized a sheet from the bed and followed? A tradition in the early Church spoke of Mark's having mutilated fingers. Did he receive a sword slash across his hand, and was that why Peter drew his knife?

Such a background would account for Mark, now perhaps thirty years of age and involved in a project of Gentile evangelism, but having no desire to preach to Romans. Mark had accompanied the party, apparently at Barnabas' insistence. Perhaps Mary, Mark's mother, seconded the move. If so, both sponsors were wrong. The young man was not called, or not yet called, to such service. He found at least part of his calling in later years, when he wrote a Gospel—ironically enough—for Romans. He had served in Cyprus with satisfaction, but now, in the port of Perga, he saw the drift of Paul's policy emerging.

Perga was bypassed, though evangelized on the return journey. Meanwhile Paul struck out inland for Antioch of Pisidia, the bastion of Roman power in central Asia Minor. Another reason, apart from the strategy of evangelism, could, of course, have been Paul's health. The coast was malarial, and it has been cogently suggested that Paul's mysterious "thorn in the flesh" (2 Corinthians 12:7), with its stabbing headaches and fearsome debility, was the indigenous malaria of that coast. If so, retreat to the uplands of 3300 feet, where Antioch lay, might have been essential. There the incident must be left. It is on record from Paul himself that he came to the area in the midst of severe illness (Galatians 4:13). He was exhausted, no doubt, and not acclimatized and perhaps not fit for the uphill journey of 160 miles, to where Antioch lay on the plateau behind the Taurus Range, on the edge of a wild mountain area scarcely subdued by Rome.

Antioch
(Acts 13:14–41)

From Perga they continued their journey, reached Antioch of Pisidia, and went into the synagogue on the sabbath. They took their seats, and, after the reading of the Law and the Prophets, the wardens of the synagogue said to them, "Brethren, if you have any word of encouragement to give to the people, speak."

Paul rose and, with a wave of his hand, said, "Men of Israel and adherents of the synagogue, listen. The God of this people Israel chose our fathers, and he made our people a great people while they were aliens in Egypt. With an uplifted hand, he led them out of Egypt. For some forty years he bore with them in the wilderness and, after destroying seven nations in Canaan, he divided them their land for an inheritance. Then he gave them judges for some four hundred and fifty years, until Samuel, the prophet. Afterward they asked for a king, and God gave them Saul the son of Kish, a man of the tribe of Benjamin, for forty years. Putting him aside, he raised up David for their king, about whom he spoke in truth, 'I have found David, a son of Jesse, a man according to my heart, who will do all things which I will.'

"Of this man's line, as he promised, he raised for Israel a Savior, Jesus, when John had first preached, before his coming, the baptism of repentance to all the people of Israel. As John fulfilled his course, he said, 'Who do you think I am? I am not he, but look, there comes one after me, the shoes of whose feet I am not worthy to unfasten.'

"Brethren, sons of Abraham's line, and those among you who fear God, to you the message of this salvation was sent; for the people of Jerusalem, not recognizing him or understanding the voices of the prophets read sabbath by sabbath, in judging him, fulfilled those words and, though they found no cause of death, asked Pilate that he be put to death. When they had fulfilled everything written about him, they took him from the tree and put him in a tomb. But God raised him from the dead, and he was seen many days by those who came up with him from Galilee to Jerusalem, who, indeed, are his witnesses to the people.

"And we bring to you good tidings about the promise made to our fathers, that this promise God has fulfilled to us, their children, by raising Jesus—just as it is written in the Second Psalm, 'You are my son. Today I have begotten you.' And, as to his having raised him from the dead, never to return to corruption, he has said, 'I will give you the sure and holy blessings of David.' And that is why in another place he says, 'You will not give your holy one to see corruption.' David, to be sure, after serving his own generation, by God's will fell asleep, was gathered to his fathers, and did see corruption. But he whom God raised up did not. Let it be known, then, brethren, that through this man is proclaimed to you forgiveness of sins, and that everyone who believes in him is justified from all those things from which he could not be justified by the Law of Moses. Beware, therefore, lest there come upon you what was said in the prophets: 'Look, you despisers, wonder and begone, for in your days I do a deed which you will not believe, though one proclaim it to you.' "

Antioch was one of sixteen towns named after Antiochus, son of Seleucus. In 312 B.C., Seleucus succeeded to the western and northern portions of Alexander's empire. This town named after his son became a Roman colony and military strongpoint.

A Roman *colonia,* it should be understood, bears no resemblance to what the Greeks or British called a colony. With the Romans, a colony was a device of empire: a transplanted fragment of Rome, a body of citizens—commonly demobilized veterans—settled in a militarily sensitive area as a bastion of defense. Colonies were not necessarily new foundations. For almost three centuries, since the Seleucid Empire, Antioch had been recognized as a fortress area on the plateau above the Antios River. The highlands had been a trouble spot for both the Seleucid and Roman empires, and Quirinius was engaged against the stubborn hill tribes when Augustus called on him to enforce the census in Judaea.

The Romans organized the Province of Galatia in 25 B.C.; Antioch was made a colony and rapidly Romanized, with all the appurtenances of a citizen elite, a petty senate, festivals, and all else. This would be grafted onto the Greek structure of the city populace, and the Jews would function in the Greco-Roman context, undisturbed—making their proselytes and managing life, as the expatriate Hellenistic Jew well knew how to do. Non-Jews were numerous in the composite synagogue. Paul refers to them twice, respectfully (16, 26).

Luke regarded the sermon Paul preached as a turning point in the history of the Church. Hence the deceleration of the narrative. A summary in writing was no doubt kept; for it is well to remember, in studying the Bible, from Abraham and Moses onward, that the documents came from literary ages. Babylonians, Mycenaeans, all the imperial peoples, had a passion for recording.

The style and content of Paul's address show the influence of Stephen in the historical approach and the manner of Peter in the appeal to the Old Testament Scriptures. Luke is still clearly preoccupied with the welding of both ministries. There are also distinct Pauline traits, to be paralleled in the Galatian letter to the same congregations. It is not strange that groups, intimately informed on the details of their history, should be ready and eager to hear again the story of their race. To their peril, peoples lose contact with their past; and one of the signs of a decaying culture in the West today is the increasing disregard for the history of struggle, sacrifice, and endeavor whereby familiar institutions were wrought to fullness. Paul's point, like

Stephen's, was that the history of the Jewish people is intelligible only in the consummation it found in Christ. The Law, he told them, was incomplete in that it could convict and not save (27, 32, 33, 39). Through all history, God had prepared the way for such a revelation (17–32), especially in the ministry of John the Baptist, who led a mighty religious revival (24, 25). But, in spite of all, Jerusalem's hierarchy rejected Christ (27–29), and so, alas, fulfilled prophecy and unwittingly set the atoning cross and the Resurrection into history (30–41). Is the sudden abruptness and sharp change of tone at the end of the speech an indication that Paul saw the familiar surge of disapproval ripple through the Jews of the congregation? From his personal experience, he would pick the first movement of that wave of hostility which he was to call "the offense of the cross." The reality of that opposition was soon to be seen.

Rejection
(Acts 13:42–51)

When the Jews were going out of the synagogue, the Gentiles asked earnestly that these words be spoken to them on the next sabbath. And when the congregation broke up, many of the Jews and devout adherents followed Paul and Barnabas, who spoke to them and persuaded them to abide in the grace of God.

On the ensuing sabbath, almost the whole city gathered to hear the word of God, but, when the Jews saw the crowds, they were filled with envy and spoke against what was being said by Paul, contradicting and blaspheming. Answering frankly, Paul and Barnabas said, "It was necessary that the word of God should be preached first to you, but, seeing that you thrust it away from you and judge yourselves unworthy of eternal life, look, we turn to the Gentiles. For so the Lord has commanded us, saying, 'I have set you a light for the Gentiles, to bring salvation to the end of the earth.' " The Gentiles were glad to hear this and thanked God for his word, and as many as had set themselves for eternal life believed.

The word of the Lord was spread through the whole countryside. But the Jews stirred up devout women and the leading men of the city and, raising a persecution against Paul and Barnabas, expelled them from their borders. Shaking the dust of their feet from them, they came to Iconium, but the converts were full of joy and the Holy Spirit.

Antioch showed Paul's world and the whole history of his century on one small stage. The Jews themselves were divided: those with strong Hellenistic leanings, after the fashion of Stephen, Philip, and Paul himself; and those more racially and doctrinally biased, who, like the Pharisees, rejected all but a fundamental Judaism, or who, like the Sadducees, saw their whole future in collaboration with the Roman authorities. They also ran true to form, alert for any popular movement likely to disturb the state. It was easy for the Jews, from Caiaphas onward, to stir hostile action by any mischievous raising of this consideration.

It is interesting to see a Roman colony in action, as at Philippi. That is why the book of Acts is such a unique and illuminating insight into the workings of multiracial life in a provincial town. No such evidence survives elsewhere. Observe, too, the disturbing evidence of the intrusion of a new force into a situation where Roman, Greek, and Jew had worked out some form of mutual harmony. The empire was later, in tragic error, to react as Antioch did on this occasion. Christianity could have provided that cement which Rome sought in Caesarism. Antioch is of immense historical importance.

What stirred the bitterest animosity was the turning to the Gentiles, Luke's whole purpose in highlighting this chapter. The

Jews had immense influence over their proselytes, a power illustrated by their penetration of the Christian church, as revealed in the letter to the Galatians. But, like metropolitan Jewry, here were those of the Dispersion also rejecting Christ. A sad feature was the hostility of leading women. As a Macedonian, accustomed to women's freedom, Luke must have found this very sad. The women of Galatia were not a suppressed and subjugated group. They played a free part in society and found attraction in Judaism, perhaps because of its stern moral code. And they had the ears of the city rulers.

14

Iconium
(Acts 14:1–7)

It happened in Iconium that they went together into the synagogue of the Jews and so preached that a great crowd of Jews
and Greeks believed. But the Jews who did not believe stirred up
and embittered the minds of the Gentiles against the brethren.
They went on, for some time, speaking openly of the Lord, who
bore witness to the word of his grace and granted signs and
wonders to take place by their hands. The population was divided; some were with the Jews, some with the apostles. But when a
hostile movement was made, both of the Gentiles and the Jews,
with their authorities' connivance to molest and stone them,
aware of this, they withdrew into the Lycaonian cities of Lystra
and Derbe and the surrounding countryside, where they continued their evangelism.

Iconium, today's Konja, was a city of the central plateau of
Asia Minor set in a wide and fertile tract; a Turkish headquarters, when those aliens penetrated the Eastern Roman Empire,
it became a sultan's seat and was considered a place of great
beauty. The Turks' mosques, palaces, and mansions have covered the ancient Greek city which the refugees sought down
ninety miles of Roman road. Its origins are lost in history, and
many fanciful guesses made legends about its name. But, whatever foundation lay upon the steppe, immigration of the Greek

Dispersion had turned Iconium into a Greek city. At first Rome chose Antioch and Lystra for its colony bastions, doubtless because of geographical considerations, but Iconium became a colony in Hadrian's day.

The Romans were certainly present when Paul visited Iconium, but they did not have colonists' status. Claudius, at the time, was bestowing some imperial attention on the area; according to the coinage, he had allowed Iconium to call itself Claudiconium, just as Ireland's Derry briefly called itself Londonderry. In both cases, the old name rapidly reasserted itself. The two apostles traveled along a Roman road that ran to Lystra and had a branch to Iconium. Iconium was governed by a citizen assembly, after the Greek model. Its official language was Greek.

Luke is again in one of his brief moods, perhaps because events largely reproduced the pattern of Antioch. Paul may, indeed, have remained in Iconium over the whole winter. There opposition took longer to mobilize, because there was no colonial Roman oligarchy to whom influential Jews could appeal, after the fashion of Caiaphas and Pilate. The opposition in the synagogue had to stir up the feeling of the crowd, a quite typical Greek situation. The city was divided, factions cohering as they did so often in Greek communities. It was part of a Greek attitude of mind to see all questions in sharp black and white. That is why Paul was so anxious over division in Corinth.

The situation became menacing. No formal charges were laid; but, no doubt with a church firmly founded, Paul and Barnabas judged it expedient to leave. They were to make a quiet return to Antioch and Iconium when another set of annual magistrates took over and the heat of faction had cooled. A legal expulsion would have made this impossible. Paul's experience was varied and untold. Writing his last letter to Timothy, from prison in Rome, in A.D. 66 or 67, Paul speaks of the persecutions and afflictions which came to him in the three towns, but the letter to the Galatians spoke of much kindness and happier circumstances.

A curious footnote to the story of Iconium is a second-century fiction called "The Acts of Paul and Thekla." A citizen of Iconium, Onesiphorus, heard that Paul was on his way and went to the road junction to meet him. He was told to look for "a man small in size, with meeting eyebrows, a rather large nose, bald, bowlegged, strongly built, full of grace, who at times seemed to have the face of an angel." There is no means of knowing how true the description was. At any rate, Paul became Onesiphorus' guest and taught in his house, perhaps in an internal courtyard. This was overlooked by a larger house, and so it came about that Thekla, daughter of a neighbor, overheard him and became a devoted Christian. The tale of her sufferings and persecution may or may not be true, but the story has interest for the second-century description of Paul.

Lystra
(Acts 14:8–20)

A man sat in the street in Lystra, crippled in his feet, lame, indeed, from birth; he had never walked. He was listening to Paul speaking; and Paul, looking attentively at him and seeing that he had faith to be made whole, said in a loud voice, "Stand up on your feet." And he jumped and walked. When the crowds saw what Paul had done, the cry went up in the Lycaonian language, "The gods have come down to us in the form of men," and they called Barnabas Zeus and Paul Hermes, because he was the chief speaker. And the priest of Zeus-Before-the-City brought garlanded oxen to the gates, intending to offer public sacrifice.

When the apostles Barnabas and Paul heard of this, they tore their clothes and rushed into the crowd, shouting, "Men, why are you doing this? We are only men, with the same feelings as you; and the Gospel we are preaching to you is that you should turn from such follies to the Living God, who made the heaven and the earth and the sea and everything in them; he who in past generations permitted all nations to go their own ways. Yet, in his acts of goodness, he did not leave himself without a witness, for he gave rains from heaven and the times of harvest, loading your hearts with food and joy." Even with these words, they could scarcely persuade them not to sacrifice to them.

But Jews arrived from Antioch and Iconium and won over the crowds. They stoned Paul and dragged him out of the city, thinking him dead. But the disciples stood around him, and he stood up and went into the city. The next day he departed, with Barnabas, to Derbe.

Lystra was a refuge, a Roman colony six hours journey southwest of Iconium, the farthest east of Augustus' strong points sited to control the central hill country. It was an undistinguished town with a rustic substratum of Lycaonian, that is, Phrygian Gallic, citizens. It was less cultured than Antioch, but occupied a strategic hill. An inscription discovered in 1885 at Antioch reads: "To the very brilliant colony of Antioch, her sister, the very brilliant colony of Lystra did honor by presenting the statue of Concord." The impression is that Lystra sought, rather, to honor herself.

In 14:6 it is implied that, moving from Iconium to Lystra, the travelers crossed a frontier. Geographers, following what seemed sound authority, once set this down as an error on Luke's part. It was the discovery of epigraphical evidence that Luke was correct that convinced Sir William Ramsay that Luke, whom he had discounted, was a competent historian. This was to become a theme on which the great Classical and archaeological scholar wrote abundantly.

It was at Lystra that Ramsay discovered two inscriptions dedicated to Zeus and Hermes. One was on a statue set up with a sundial and bearing Lycaonian names. The other mentions "priests of Zeus." To this we must return. Inscriptions attest the presence of Latin-speaking colonists, though Roman civic discipline was not notably in evidence in the tumultuous events of the visit, and Latin may have been little more than symbolic of Lystra's status, with the Greeks in greater evidence. Paul certainly used Greek in his sermon to the crowd—his first to a purely Gentile audience—and Paul's ready adaptation to Gentile patterns of thought is as evident here as it is, later, in Athens. There was a Jewish community, because Timothy came from it (16:1, 2); but it was liberal enough to allow such mixed marriages as that from which Timothy sprang.

The Lycaonian natives were Celts. Galatians were Gallic, a fragment of that wandering tribe that invaded Asia Minor, Greece, and Italy before settling finally in the West, in Gallia, Gaul, or modern France. Celts were volatile and excitable folk, easily led astray. Hence the emotional reaction to the healing of the cripple.

A legend of the Phrygian hill country has been preserved by the brilliant Roman poet Ovid, who wrote it down in his quite inimitable style, about half a century before Paul and Barnabas sought refuge in Lystra. Ovid told how old Philemon and Baucis entertained gods unaware:

> In the Phrygian hill-country, an oak and a linden-tree stand side by side. Nearby is a marsh, once habitable land, but now the watery haunt of divers and coots. To this place came Zeus, disguised as a mortal, and along with him Hermes . . . . To a thousand homes they came seeking lodging. A thousand homes were barred against them. But one house received them, a tiny place, thatched with straw and reeds. Poor old Baucis, and Philemon of the same age

as she, had been wedded in that same cottage in their youth, and there had grown old together. They made poverty light by owning it, and bearing it in a contented spirit. It was futile to ask for masters or servants in that house. They served and ruled together . . . .

The story is long and delightfully told, in the Roman's polished couplets. The old couple received the visitors, who stooped under the lowly door. Baucis threw a rough coverlet over the wooden bench and puffed up the dying fire, feeding it with fine-split kindling. Philemon cut a cabbage and soon had it in boiling water, along with a slice of bacon cut from a side hoisted among the blackened rafters. A tablecloth kept for high occasions was brought out, and the table was steadied with a broken bit of pottery slipped under a damaged leg. There were cheese, nuts, apples, and dried fruit.

But the wine bowl filled of its own accord, and the old folk recognized their guests and begged forgiveness for their humble fare. They had a pet goose and sought to catch it, with trembling hands, to do greater honor to their guests. The goose eluded the shaky chase and took refuge with the gods.

But, to shorten this gentle story, Zeus and Hermes took the old folk up a nearby hill, and before their eyes the land was inundated, the cottage alone remaining. The cottage itself became a temple with marble columns. The wood, hay thatch, and stubble became gold, silver, and precious stones. (Did Paul hear the story and have it in mind when he wrote to the Corinthians?) The gods granted what the old couple wished: to be priest and priestess of the temple and that neither should see the other's grave.

So it came about. When the last hour came, one became an oak and one a linden tree. And so came about a temple of Zeus-Before-the-Gate. At Claudiopolis, near Lystra, a surviving dedication records a Zeus-Before-the-Town.

This was the legend, and when Paul's gift of healing was observed, some excited Lystran proclaimed a second coming. Here they were again, the stately Barnabas, Zeus, and the wordy Paul, his messenger Hermes. Hence the tumult and the sacrifice: Lystra was not to repeat its ancient error.

Crowds are fickle. *Hosanna* readily turns to *crucify,* and the apostles soon felt the changing mood, especially when the old foes of Antioch and Iconium arrived (19). Roman authority was not strong in this remote colony, and Paul nearly died under a vicious Jewish stoning. He must have vividly remembered Stephen. Writing to the Galatians, years later, Paul says, ". . . I bear in my body the marks of the Lord Jesus" (Galatians 6:17 KJV). It was probably the scars of this vicious assault to which he refers.

Only Derbe remained as a refuge, on the very edge of the Roman province. Of that town only a few scattered stones remain, though there are one or two Christian inscriptions. Some have maintained that the 8,000-foot peak of Hadji-Baba, or Pilgrim Father, is the site, and that its name refers to Paul. The name, if anything, signifies the completeness of the Moslem victory on the plateau. But, tirelessly, they preached there.

Homeward
(Acts 14:21–28)

They preached the Gospel in that city and made many disciples and then returned to Lystra, Iconium, and Antioch, strengthening the souls of the disciples, encouraging them to stand fast in the faith, and warning that it is through many afflictions that we must enter into the kingdom of God. They appointed elders for them in each church, after prayer and fasting, commending them to the Lord in whom they had believed. Traversing Pisidia, they came into Pamphylia, and, after preaching the word in Perga, they went down to Attalia and from there

sailed for Antioch, where they had been committed to the grace
of God for the task which they had fulfilled. When they arrived,
they gathered the church together, told what God had done with
them, and that he had opened the door of faith to the Gentiles.
There they stayed, some time, with the disciples.

It no doubt required some courage to retrace the path of
persecution and danger. But administrations changed annually;
there was no recorded charge against the apostles; and they
probably made their visit as inconspicuous as possible. Their
chief task was to establish the Christian congregations (22) and
organize their government under elders. This was a sensible
arrangement that appealed to Jews, Greeks, and Romans and
that became general (Titus 1:5).

The notable success of the mission, even in remote Derbe, is
to be explained by the religious situation in those provinces.
The ancient paganism of Asia Minor—of which a spectacular
relic survived in the worship of Artemis (or Diana) at Ephesus—had been of the ancient fertility-ritual variety. It was a
morally ruinous religion that wrecked the family and, by its
"sacred prostitution," degraded womanhood. The Phrygian
highlands may have been a last stronghold of these ancient
cults, which, as Hellenism and Romanization spread, were los-
ing their hold, without anything vital to replace them.

It was at such a juncture that Christianity appeared, with its
transcendent God, its fascinating story of Christ, and its simple
brotherhood and moral purity. This accounts for what appears
to have been a remarkable spread of the faith in these provinces. Documented evidence from the second century indicates
a most powerful Christianization of the whole western half of
the blunt peninsula which we call Asia Minor. It is one of the
tragedies of history that the whole area was lost to the Moslem
Turk. The other tragedy, of course, is that Rome failed to see

the power that Christianity would have proved to be to weld the disparate mass of the empire together. Whoever or whatever the influence may have been that first used the execrable Nero to initiate persecution, the act proved to be a crime not yet expiated.

15

Delegation From Jerusalem
(Acts 15:1–11)

Certain people coming down from Judaea began to teach the
brethren, saying, "Unless you are circumcised after the custom
of Moses, you cannot be saved." Hence no small division and
debate between Paul and Barnabas and these people. They decided to send Paul and Barnabas and some others of their number up to Jerusalem, to the apostles and elders, about this controversy. Sent off on their mission by the church, they traversed
Phoenicia and Samaria, reporting the conversion of the Gentiles,
a matter which brought great joy to all the brethren.

Reaching Jerusalem, they were received by the church, the
apostles, and the elders and recounted what God had done with
them. But there arose some believers of the sect of the Pharisees,
saying that it was necessary to circumcise them and to command
them to keep the Law of Moses. The apostles and the elders
came together to consider this question.

After much debate, Peter rose and said to them, "Brethren,
you know that long ago it was through my lips God chose that
the Gentiles should hear the word of the Gospel and believe.
And God, who knows the heart, declared his acceptance, giving
them the Holy Spirit, as he did to us, and he made no distinction
between us and them, when he cleansed their hearts by faith.
Why then now put God to the test by putting a yoke upon the
disciples' neck, which neither our forebears nor we were strong
enough to carry? But through the grace of the Lord Jesus Christ

we believe we have been saved, in the same way as they are."

The last verse of the preceding chapter suggests some lapse of time. The church at Antioch was enjoying peace, in spite of the fact that some of its members must have come by way of the synagogue. At this point, an investigating delegation from James and the central church in Jerusalem arrived, a story told more fully in the second chapter of the letter to the Galatians. Small discrepancies of time and circumstance have been alleged between Paul's longer and Luke's more brief account, but it is worth remembering that the two writers knew each other intimately; Luke was informed by Paul, and it is past belief that Paul did not see what Luke wrote. In fact, unless the chronological sequence of Galatians 2:1–14 is quite unjustifiably pressed, no discrepancy arises.

The unembarrassed fellowship between Jewish and Gentile Christians at Antioch shocked the delegation (one ancient text says that they were Pharisees), and so vehement and subtle were their arguments that even Peter and Barnabas were, for a time, abashed. Peter, at any rate, separated himself from those with whom, up to then, he had been gladly associating. The whole situation shows how hardly won was Paul's battle for Christian freedom. A lifetime of deep indoctrination dies hard in any man, and Peter, as Paul says (Galatians 2:11), was blameworthy.

The line taken by the Christian Pharisees (5) was clearly that Christ was the Messiah, but was not the author of a new faith, only the consummation and confirmation of a faith that was ages old. Therefore, the Law still stood; and Gentile converts must subscribe to it, even to the sign in the flesh. The entire position of Gentile Christianity, as Paul had wrought it out, with great assent, was perilously under attack (Galatians 2:12–14). Although, from the evidence of this chapter (7–12), Paul must have rapidly won the two waverers back to his position, there must have been a great temptation to anyone with such a brilliant mind and magnificent gifts of leadership. He might have desired to repudiate the Jerusalem church, with its stultifying Pharisaism, and to base in Antioch a free Jewish and Gentile congregation with a true grasp of the meaning of Christ— one free from all legalistic requirements.

No situation could more strongly demonstrate Paul's fine statesmanship and his unassailable claim to leadership over the global Church. That Peter, and even Barnabas, should so vacillate, reveals both their lesser standing before the great apostle and the enormous power of Judaism, as the Pharisees taught it, over the lives and minds of those who were bred in its shadow. Paul resisted the urge to withdraw; and, in the end, the increasingly exclusive Jerusalem church was dispersed, with the destruction of Jewry's capital in A.D. 70.

To withdraw is often more simple than to stand and defend, and it is a testimony to Paul's rare patience and deep sympathy for those still held in a bondage from which he had broken free that he joined the embassy which went up to Jerusalem to make the situation clear. In theological insight, his keen intelligence raced far ahead of friends and opponents, but it also made it clear to him that Jerusalem was in a unique position to act as an administrative center.

Peter made magnificent amends. He recalled how, over a decade before, he had been divinely chosen to open the door to the Gentiles and how, in wisdom, he had seen fit to leave the entrance to the Church uncluttered by relics of Judaism. Peter had none of Paul's fine education or Paul's acquaintance with the Greek and Roman worlds; so his simple courage, in taking such an uncompromising lead at the apostolic conference, was fine in the extreme. With a touch of the historian's art, Luke allows him, on this high note, to take his leave of recorded history. His support of Paul at this vital point was a most significant and far-reaching action.

The Decision
(Acts 15:12–35)

The whole assembly fell silent and listened to Barnabas and Saul relating the signs and wonders God had done, through them, for the Gentiles. When they had finished speaking, James replied, saying, "Brethren, listen to me. Simeon has described how God first visited the Gentiles to take out from them a people owning his name. With this the words of the prophets agreed. Scripture says, 'After this I will set up again the tent of David which has fallen. Its ruins I will build and set up again, that the rest of mankind will seek out the Lord and all the Gentiles who call upon my name. So says the Lord who does these things.' Known to God for all time is all that which he does. Therefore my judgment is that we should not burden those of the Gentiles who are turning to God, but should write, bidding them abstain from things polluted by idols, from fornication, and from things strangled, and from blood. For Moses, for generations past, has in every city those who proclaim him in their synagogues every sabbath day."

Then the apostles and elders, along with the whole church, decided to choose men of their number to send to Antioch, along with Paul and Barnabas. Judas, named Barsabas, and Silas were chosen, leaders among the brethren. They wrote thus, "The apostles and elders and brethren, to the brethren of the Gentiles in Antioch, Syria, and Cilicia, send greeting. When we heard that some had gone out and troubled you with what they said, unsettling your souls and bidding you be circumcised and keep the Law—under no such directions from us—we have unanimously decided to send special envoys to you, with our beloved Barnabas and Saul, men who have hazarded their lives for the name of the Lord Jesus Christ. We have sent also Judas and Silas, who will tell you the same things personally. For we decided, under the Holy Spirit's guidance, to place on you no other burden than these necessary requirements, to wit: that you should abstain from what is sacrificed to idols, from blood, things strangled, and fornication. If you guard yourselves from these things, you will do well. Farewell."

Sent on their way, they came to Antioch, gathered the assembly of the church together, and handed over the letter. They read it and rejoiced over the comfort it contained. Judas and Silas, prophets in their own right, gave the brethren much encouragement by their words and strengthened them. After a short stay, they were sent back, by the brethren, to the apostles, though Silas elected to stay there. Paul and Barnabas continued on in Antioch, teaching and preaching, with a host of helpers, the word of God.

Luke set much store by this vital debate. He is observed resorting to his leisurely device of repeating vital words: here, the substance of the Jerusalem resolution. The discussion is magnificently reported. "They of the circumcision," the Pharisaic wing, rush to make their point, but these Jews were clearly a minority, abashed by Peter's noble stand and the clear arguments of Paul and Barnabas, who were backed by the events of the first foray into the Gentile world. There was nevertheless a strong feeling that deep-rooted Jewish prejudices should not be roughly flouted. Jews, after all, were numerous in the congregations; and it was nothing more than Christian courtesy to avoid that which could only stir deep disgust. The prohibition of fornication, of course, had to do with the courtesan activities centered in such cults as the worship of Artemis at Ephesus and Aphrodite at Corinth. Such centers of vice must have been a perpetual temptation in ancient cities (1 Corinthians 6:15; 1 Thessalonians 4:3).

At any rate, James, breathing authority, ably conducts the meeting and sums up (13–21). It is set forth in a decree which was a very able compromise, graciously expressed. The extremists are quite sternly dismissed as possessing no authority and harming the souls of the Gentiles. On the other hand, the prohibitions recommended are expressed quite strongly. It was a most able document and should have solved the problem.

Before passing to the more speculative theme of the fate of the Jerusalem decree, observe some marks of authenticity of the sort which might be expected in so meticulous a writer. The opening formula of the letter is found only once more in the New Testament, in the opening of James' epistle. The style of the decree has that touch of frank forthrightness so evident in James' epistle. James uses the Septuagint version of Amos 9:11, 12 in his speech to the assembly. It varies slightly from the Hebrew text behind our own versions, but, in that variation, is adapted to the point James had to make. No problem of authority is, of course, involved. Finally note his use of *Simeon,* the form for *Simon* evidently preferred by the more fastidious Hebrew of Jerusalem (Luke 2:25, 34).

What happened to the Jerusalem decree? It is evident, from the epistles, that the extremists were frustrated, but not put down; disowned, but not silenced. They dogged Paul's path, whether as envoys from metropolitan Jewry or local products. Their activities in the Galatian cities inspired Paul's letter to that church. In fact, it seems clear that Paul was soon compelled to regard the sane, promising document as a dead letter and to make new decisions. The first letter to Corinth is evidence that, in spite of the efforts of the apostles, sectarian divisions on doctrine tended to emerge in the early church congregations, and in 1 Corinthians 8:4 Paul seems to adopt an attitude more liberal than that of James' letter.

It seems clear that the Pharisaic wing in the Jerusalem church grew stronger. This could have been due to the increasing emigration of liberal and Hellenistic elements. It needed no deep awareness of events to sense the growing tensions of Judaea and the darkening political situation, as the land slid toward the momentous disaster of the Jewish War.

Paul himself seems to have felt the disapproval of this part of the Jerusalem church (Acts 21:20–26; Romans 15:31). His last visit to Jerusalem was a disastrous effort to heal the breach. The division could have continued to the point of severance; but, with the outbreak of war in A.D. 66, the Christians of Jerusalem fled to Pella, in the Decapolis, east of the Jordan. And, with the destruction of Jerusalem in A.D. 70, the Pharisaic church's base was gone. Splinters survived: There was a fourth-century Syrian sect called the Nazarenes, which seems to have practiced a Judaized Christianity. The Ebionite heresy, which also endured till the fourth century, was a Jewish version of Christianity, which repudiated Paul. It is a sad story.

Second Journey
(Acts 15:36–41)

> After some days, Paul said to Barnabas, "Let us go back and visit our brethren and see how they fare in all the cities where we have preached the word of the Lord." But Barnabas was determined to take John Mark along with them. Paul thought it wrong to take with them the one who had abandoned them in Pamphylia and did not stay with them for the work. There arose a sharp contention, so that they parted company. Barnabas, consequently, taking Mark, set sail for Cyprus, while Paul chose Silas as his colleague and set out, commended, by the brethren, to the grace of God. He traversed Syria and Cilicia, strengthening the congregations.

Luke's book is half finished. The first half showed the vast unfolding of a divine plan for the world. The great issues are Judaism and the destiny of Christianity to be a new, independent, global faith. This chapter has shown the issues joined on central ground and, in principle, settled. In something like seven hundred words, Luke has described a great turning point in which Paul's message is triumphant. That message was to be the Christianity of all the future. To be sure, battles and a rugged march await, as the letters of Paul will show, but a page has been turned.

Antioch was to be the base, and Paul's was no lonely voice (35). Paul and Barnabas were now the two recognized leaders of Gentile Christianity—backed, at least briefly, by Jerusalem. Barnabas is soon to pass on to unrecorded labors. Luke will follow Paul to the seat of the empire. And Paul has a new companion for what is to prove the invasion of another continent. We see Luke's narrative style in operation again. Just as he prepared for the arrival on the scene of Saul, and then Barnabas, so now verses 32 and 34 prepare for verse 40. Perhaps it was Paul's suggestion that Silas should stay on in Antioch, when the remainder of the Jerusalem delegation returned to Judaea.

While Luke uses the familiar abbreviation *Silas,* Paul always uses the full Roman appellation *Silvanus* (observe the opening words of the two Thessalonian epistles), no doubt in recognition of the fact that he was a fellow Roman citizen (16:37). Citizenship was no mean estate in the first century, as the ensuing chapter will show.

It is notable that Paul was not prepared to undertake his mission, which ultimately led to Europe, alone. He replaced both Barnabas and Mark (16:1–3). He was no lonely, austere man, unable or unwilling to share his task and confidence with others. His leadership was not apart and monolithic, like Moses'. Paul needed good men around him and had the capacity to find and attract them. His friendship with Luke created this book, and a considerable list of close friends could be compiled from his letters. He writes of many with warm affection. Paul seldom appears alone; and, when he did so in Athens, his unease of spirit is visible. Great leaders always need support close at hand, often yearn for it, too frequently lack it. Paul is a prime example of a great man made greater by his friends.

Hence the tragic nature of his clash with Barnabas over Barnabas' relative Mark. Conscientiously, Luke calls it a "sharp contention" and the King James Version is felicitous in supplying the adjective. The word is *paroxusmos,* from which comes our word *paroxysm.* Paul had, it must be realized, known many weeks of strain and contention. To carry his case through the Jerusalem assembly must have made heavy demands upon his resources. And, also, for all Barnabas' ultimate support in that vital controversy, there could have been a small residue of constraint after the incredible defection of Barnabas in Antioch (Galatians 2:13). As for John Mark, although Luke, writing long after the breach was healed, says nothing derogatory, Mark must, in Paul's eyes, have demonstrated serious disloyalty. Paul, too, was always sensitive to what he classed as falling short of the high standards of confidence he set (Philippians 2:20, 21).

There is slight evidence that Paul ultimately concluded that he had been hard on Mark. The "sharp contention" must have been Paul's own description to Luke—his own word. And it is curious to note that, when, in perhaps A.D. 52, he wrote his first letter to Corinth, he used an associated verb in his famous chapter on love. Love, he says, in the fifth verse, "is not easily provoked." He uses the verb *paroxunetai* and could hardly do so without remembering his description of the quarrel with Barnabas and the rejection of Mark, perhaps already recorded in

Luke's notes. Is there a touch of self-reproach over the unhappy incident? At any rate, let Colossians 4:10 and 2 Timothy 4:11 conclude the story.

The journey through Syria and Cilicia (41) probably took more months than Luke spares words in describing them. Cilicia, once the haunt of the pirate fleets destroyed by Pompey a century before, was Paul's own province, and the churches that appear to have been active there might well have been the foundations of Paul's unrecorded years at Tarsus. Luke is at his briefest, pursuing hard the goal he has: the move of the faith into Europe, where he himself became a member of the party.

16

Back to Galatia
(Acts 16:1–5)

He came to Derbe and Lystra, and there it was that a disciple named Timotheus lived, the son of a Christian Jewess, but of a Greek father. He bore a good testimony with the brethren in Lystra and Iconium. Wanting to take him out with him, Paul took and circumcised him, in deference to the Jews in those parts, for all of them knew that his father had been a Greek. As they proceeded from town to town, they gave into their keeping the rules laid down by the apostles and the elders in Jerusalem. So then were the churches strengthened in the faith and daily increased in number.

Derbe is mentioned first, because the area was approached from the southeastern and landward side, one of those small marks of authenticity so common in Luke's narrative (*see* 14:6).

In the Greek text, a particle of exclamation, which is difficult to render without overemphasis, marks the discovery and call of the gentle Timothy, Paul's "son in God" (1 Timothy 1:18). Timothy replaced Mark and was of mixed parentage. His father, from the verb and tense used at the close of verse 3, was probably no longer living. He had probably been an adherent of the synagogue, but not a circumcised proselyte. Such mixed unions were no doubt common among the Jews of the Dispersion.

Lystra was probably Timothy's birthplace, but there was

much coming and going among adjacent Christian and Jewish communities. Hence the wider commendation. In a travel-conscious world, the efficient network of communication between the Christian groups is significant. Colossae and Philippi were in touch with Paul in Rome. The Roman Christians knew of the pending arrival of Paul in Italy. Apollo, Aquila, and Priscilla were notably active migrants.

The matter which calls for further comment is Paul's circumcision of his new aide, a procedure curtly mentioned by Luke and briefly explained as an act of conciliation toward the strong Jewish minorities in the Christian churches of central Asia Minor. Paul saw the whole Jewish ritual superseded by Christ and the "sign in the flesh" without intrinsic value (Romans 2:25–29; 1 Corinthians 7:18, 19; Galatians 2:3–5; 5:2–6; 6:15; Philippians 3:2, 3; Colossians 2:11, 12). It was change of heart, not mutilation of the body, that God required; such is the import of his words.

The considered judgment of the Jerusalem Council had just laid it down, and Paul carried with him the document testifying to it. Circumcision was not to be imposed on Gentile believers. Was this, then, another example of Paul's overeagerness to conciliate the Pharisaic wing of the Church? Is this a fault for which he may, with some justice, be charged? (21:21–26). It would seem, at any rate, that the eager emissaries of a Judaic Christianity were hard on his tracks and that Paul's action in Timothy's case may have been used damagingly against him. The references, in the Galatian letter, to the churches in Timothy's own district, seem to show that his magnanimous or worldly-wise move to conciliate cost him much.

But, endeavoring to penetrate Paul's immediate motive, one must see that Timothy, for all the fact that he had a Greek father, was the child of a Jewish mother; and that made him a Jew, for it was the mother who bestowed race. In the immediate sequence of the Jerusalem decree, Paul, not anticipating its scant observance, was seeking to regard its spirit as well as its letter. In such matters, he always observed a generous attitude of compromise (1 Corinthians 9:20). All along the great trade routes which Timothy was to traverse, there were communities of Jews who were socially influential and dominated a potential mission field in the synagogues and among their adherents. As a mature man, especially with a Gentile father, Timothy could easily be accused of deliberate rejection of the Jewish rite.

Not that this, in Paul's eyes, would have been a matter of deep concern; but, in every harmless way, Paul was anxious to smooth the road to acceptance for his young companion. The Jerusalem decree drew him to gentle compromise, rather than to rigidity. It is painful that he was not met with reciprocity.

As for Timothy himself, it is from the pastoral letters addressed to him that we gain the clearest impression of his personality and character. It might be gathered that the young man was not robust in health and was constitutionally timid and somewhat dependent. He was a third-generation Christian (2 Timothy 1:5), so rapidly had the faith spread. Perhaps two devout women had played an overstrong part in a gentle boy's upbringing, but Paul trusted and loved him; and there was no "generation gap" between them. Timothy was still running well in A.D. 67, the presumed end of Paul's life (2 Timothy 4:7), and at the unknown date when a brilliant scholar wrote the letter to the Hebrews (Hebrews 13:23).

Rapidly Moving Onward
(Acts 16:6–8)

Passing through the Phrygian region of Galatia, they were restrained by the Holy Spirit from preaching the word in Asia. Reaching the borders of Mysia, they were planning to enter Bithynia, but the Spirit would not allow them. Passing by Mysia, they came down to Troas.

Luke is in his hastiest mood; and, to understand this rush of geographical description, a map is essential. The frontiers of Africa today are often ethnically unfortunate and reflect historical borderlines of imperial days. So, also, the Roman provincial system in Asia Minor sometimes distorted pre-Roman ethnic and imperial divisions.

The Province of Asia, in the southwest of the peninsula, was constituted in 116 B.C. It absorbed a large portion of the ancient Phrygian Empire. With wavering borders, it had strongly occupied the central plateau for some centuries, from the end of the second millennium B.C. Midas and Gordius were its best-known kings.

Weakening, the Phrygian Empire fell under the various imperial intruders: Lydia, Persia, the Seleucid Empire of the Greeks, and Pergamum. *Phrygian,* to the Greeks of the fifth century B.C., meant little more than "slave." After its administrative absorption into the Roman Province of Asia, a remaining part of the ethnically distinct area was attached, in 25 B.C., to the Roman Galatia, to form a "region"—one of those subordinate areas whose exact borders cause some delicate historical problems. This was "the Phrygian region of Galatia" mentioned in the text.

Mysia was a northern region of the Province of Asia, south of the Dardanelles and the sea of Marmara. They came "opposite Mysia"—that is, no doubt, to a point east of it—and could, at this juncture, have turned northwest into the Province of Bithynia, which fronted the Bosphorus and bordered on the Black Sea. Some compulsion restrained them. Bithynia was to be evangelized by others, who have left no record of their names or activities. The chance survival of two letters written by the governor Pliny in 111 A.D. shows that, half a century and more later, the province was fairly strongly Christian.

Instead, the party took a route almost due west, but its members felt no urge to pause, until they reached Alexandria Troas, on the Aegean. Years later, Paul seems to have had an active ministry in Mysia, at least around Troas (20:5–14; 2 Corinthians 2:12). His influence no doubt reached out to such important centers as Adramyttium, Assos, and Pergamum. But Luke is hurrying on, in his most clipped style; for an important new chapter is about to open.

But pause for a moment to note the ease with which Luke moves in the terminology of a large administrative area of the empire. William Ramsay's "South Galatian theory" stands firmly based in the geographical and cultural realities of the area; and epigraphical evidence demonstrates that only a first-century writer could move, with Luke's assurance, through such a narrative. His very speed, causing occasional difficulty for a remote historian, assumes that a first-century reader will easily follow the geographical patterns familiar to Luke. The day has long passed when a case could be made for a second-century date for this book.

Troas
(Acts 16:9,10)

> And Paul had a vision in the night. A certain Macedonian stood there, appealing to him with the words, "Come over to Macedonia and help us." After the vision, we set about finding a passage to Macedonia, all concluding that the Lord had called us to preach the Gospel there.

Troas is not Troy of legend and history; but that famous ruin—first unearthed in 1871 by Heinrich Schliemann's enthu-

siastic but clumsy archaeology—lies in the same fertile arc of
territory that commands the entrance to the great sea passage
of the Dardanelles, the ancient Hellespont. Early travelers—
such as William Lithgow, in 1609, and Thomas Coryat, three
years later—to the disdain of Gibbon—actually thought Alexandria Troas was the famous city of the Greek siege in the
thirteenth century B.C.

Troas, though not Troy, was historic ground, nonetheless.
Troas was built in 300 B.C. in the spate of city building that
followed the division of Alexander's empire. The kings of the
Syrian Empire—most widespread of Alexander's successor
states—held it, when their arm was strong enough to reach so
far west. Troas, like many Greek-city foundations, asserted her
freedom when Syria's hold weakened. When Pergamum controlled the area, and even under Rome, the city held a measure
of autonomy. Troas was the Asian port nearest to Europe; and
Rome's wise imperialism, here as at Ephesus, saw advantage in
allowing an important commercial gateway to enjoy the satisfying fiction of independence.

Julius Caesar, according to Suetonius, actually toyed with the
idea of transferring his capital to Troas: A project suggested, no
doubt, not only by strategic considerations, but also by the
thought that Aeneas—bringing his refugees from fallen Troy,
on the voyage to Italy and Rome's beginnings—must have embarked thereby. The project died, but Augustus made Troas a
Roman colony. This, no doubt, was agreeable to Paul, a Roman
citizen.

The goal was fairly obvious to men seeking the guidance of
God. Only Europe lay beyond. Then came the confirming vision in the night. Ernest Renan first suggested that "a certain
Macedonian," for so the phrase may be rendered, was Luke
himself. Ancient writers sometimes allowed themselves anonymous signatures. The unnamed disciple of the Emmaus road
could have been Luke; the young man involved in the arrest of

Jesus in Gethsemane was almost certainly Mark; John was "the disciple whom Jesus loved."

Then, surely of some significance, Luke did join the party at this point. *They* becomes *we* at verse 10. Here a wide and attractive field of conjecture lies open, and it may be pursued as long as it is firmly remembered that conjecture falls short of proven fact. If the pronouns are watched in the *they* and *we* sequences of the narrative, it will be seen that, at this stage of his life, Luke was a Philippian—a fact which by no means rules out the old tradition that he was an Antiochene. Many a physician, at all times, has had connection with two centers of learning and dwelt in two cities. At Antioch he could, in fact, have known Paul; and he may have sought him out at Troas, on a basis of old acquaintance.

Had he, in fact, invited Paul to come to Philippi and left the apostle undecided at nightfall? The events of a day often become the stuff of dreams, and it is psychological fact that the mind can clarify its conclusions in the hours of sleep—a suggestion which in no way diminishes the significance of Paul's vision in the night.

The phrase "a certain Macedonian" suggests that the visitant could be named, if the writer chose so to do. Macedonians had no necessarily distinctive dress. In those days, the opposing shores of the Aegean and the Hellespont were not alien to each other. The seaways only separated two Roman provinces—not two races, as they do today. One did not pass there from East to West—before the Turk thrust to the Aegean—while the Adriatic Sea divided the Greek and Roman worlds. The Greek language, in fact, crossed even that barrier. Roman imperialism and Greek culture and speech united Paul's Mediterranean area. At any rate, a sequence of puzzling events took on meaning; and, with characteristic decision, Paul set out to find a means of crossing into Europe.

To Philippi
(Acts 16:11, 12)

So, sailing from Troas, they ran straight for Samothrace and on the next day reached Neapolis. Thence to Philippi, the chief city of that region of Macedonia and a colony. And in that city we stayed for some days.

Luke drops his verbs in his haste to reach Philippi. The translation has supplied one more than he uses. It was a fast voyage. The peak of Samothrace, an island in mid-course, is a sailor's steering point, and the very wind seemed to confirm the decision to sail. In Acts 20:6, the return journey was recorded to have covered five days. The port of Neapolis is the terminal point of the great Roman artery of the Via Egnatia, the inland Roman road across Greece, between the Adriatic and the Aegean coasts.

Luke speaks with detectable pride of the importance of Philippi. It was the chief town of the region, and there is, so far, no epigraphical or historical evidence by which the exact limits of the region—assuming the term to be administrative—can be laid down. In fact, the boundary lines of the four regions into which Macedonia was divided had probably become obsolete; and if there is evidence that Amphipolis was actually the chief town of the district, its obsolescence left Philippi free to claim preeminence. Ramsay is probably right in seeing the claim advanced by Luke as a natural expression for a Philippian and an odd touch of authenticity in the narrative, of the sort so often detectable in Luke.

Philippi was the sort of center for evangelistic strategy that had long been in Paul's mind. He sought firm bases, as he had done in Pisidian Antioch. He was thinking like a Roman citizen, and it was not for nothing that Philippi had colonial status.

A Macedonian town in the plain east of Mount Pangaeus, Philippi was founded or at least refortified about 357 B.C. by Philip II of Macedon, whose splendid tomb was discovered in 1978. That ruthless militarist and subtle subverter of the free states of Greece had an eye for a strategic position, and Philippi dominated the road system of northern Greece. It is not without significance that the decisive battle in the civil war which followed the assassination of Julius Caesar was fought here in 42 B.C. Like Belgium and Palestine, like Dyrrhachium, at the other end of the Via Egnatia, the plain was one of those inevitable meeting places of hostile armies.

After Actium, in 31 B.C., Octavian (the future Augustus)— who, with Antony, was victor over the murderers of Julius— constituted Philippi a Roman colony: one of those "bulwarks of empire," as Cicero called such foundations. Octavian settled legionnaires of Antony there, thinking their presence undesirable in Italy. The Philippian jailer could have been a third-generation colonist.

Philippi's school of medicine (the occasion, perhaps, of Luke's presence there) was part of a network of such institutions and guilds, which stretched from Epidaurus to Pergamum and elsewhere in the Hellenistic world.

Luke, at any rate, seems to have been at home, as a study of the *we* passages shows, and hurried Paul straight from the port to the colony.

The Gospel in Europe
(Acts 16:13–24)

On the sabbath we went outside the city, along the river, a customary place for prayer. We sat down and spoke to the women gathered there. A certain woman named Lydia, a dealer in purple cloth, from Thyatira, who was a believer in God, was listening. The Lord opened her heart to pay attention to what Paul was saying. When she was baptized along with her household, she said earnestly, "If you have judged me faithful to God, come and stay at my house." And she insisted that we should do so.

As we were going to the place of prayer, a girl with a spirit of divination met us, who brought much profit to her masters by her fortune-telling. Following Paul and us, she would cry out, "These people are the servants of the Most High God, who proclaim to us the way of salvation." This she did for several days, until Paul, unable to endure it longer, turned and said to the spirit, "I bid you, in the name of Jesus Christ, to come out of her," which it did forthwith. Her masters, seeing that their hope of gain was gone, laid hold of Paul and Silas and dragged them before the authorities in the marketplace. Arraigning them before the magistrates, they said, "These people, Jews, are disturbing the city and proclaiming customs which we, as Roman citizens, cannot receive." The mob joined in against them. They tore off their clothes and ordered them to be flogged. After severely beating them, they put them into prison, charging the jailer to guard them safely. Receiving such orders, he put them in the inner prison and bound their feet to the stocks.

Expatriate Jews, when they were without a synagogue, seem to have established a "place of prayer" by a river. Perhaps Levitical washings were thus facilitated. There is not complete certainty that no building was involved. There was certainly none in the cameo drama of Psalm 137, where bullying Babylonians surrounded Jews assembled by the Euphrates, only to be deterred from violence by an elaborate commination. "What prayer-place are you from?" asks a drunken ruffian in Juvenal's picture of night street violence in Rome (*Satires* 3. 295).

The river, before which Luke omits the article, indicating

some familiarity (compare "to town" or "to sea" in English), was a tributary of the Strymon. Women formed the congregation, and it is a fact that women were widely drawn to Judaism and also that Macedonian women were notably "liberated." Among them was a woman from Thyatira, six hundred miles away, selling cloth dyed crimson by the juice of the madder root, a cheaper Anatolian preparation for those unable to afford the immensely expensive Tyrian purple, made from the murex shell.

That there was a guild of dyers at Thyatira is archaeologically established. Lydia may later have been the founder of the church in her hometown—a congregation that, some thirty-five years later, fell under the domination of a dangerous woman and earned John's stern condemnation (Revelation 2:18–25). Lydia became the first leader in the Philippian household congregation and thus established, from the start, that tradition of generosity for which Philippi was notable.

Lydia's household, like that of the jailer, later, shared her baptism, no doubt because they also accepted the faith. Paul would hardly have accepted less. The close-knit nature of Jewish and Roman families would certainly be a persuasive influence in all cases where the head took a strong lead.

The fact that Luke shared Lydia's hospitality is no indication that he had no lodging of his own in Philippi. He would be in no mood to be separated from the leader he had gone to some trouble to bring to Philippi.

The strange slave girl is called, in the text, a Pythia—the name given to the Delphic oracle because Apollo's slaying of a python was part of the myth on which the Delphic oracle, under Parnassus, above the Gulf of Corinth, was founded. Little is known about the glossolalia of the Delphic pythoness. Some said it was due to the cyanide in the bay leaves she chewed prior to her pronouncements. Others speak of a mephitic vapor which she breathed, but there is no evidence of such exhalations on the site. The name, therefore, is no help in the present context. Paul treated her for possession by some evil entity outside herself and so brought her to sanity. The proof of the deed, it might be said, is in the curing. There was, at least, a healthy part in her crying out for help: Nothing evil could utter the truth of her cry (17).

At any rate, a rough arrest and tumultuous trial followed. The magistrates of Philippi seemed to have called themselves "praetors," a slightly presumptuous use of the term, tolerated by Rome, whose sensible administration never bothered about harmless detail. Both Cicero and Horace express mild amusement at such titles.

It is to be noticed that the colonists were somewhat self-consciously "Romans" (21). Their victims were "Jews" (20), and Claudius' expulsion of the Jews from Rome was perhaps still news and fire for prejudice in Roman areas. Hence, the failure to note the monumental mistake they were making. To deny a Roman citizen his rights was a most serious matter and could involve the status of the city and the office of the offender, as the sequel was to show. The bench of two magistrates was expected to know the law, and the absence of proper trial and the flogging were both grossly illegal. In the general din and clamor of an undisciplined mob (22), with the streets out of proper control, the *duumviri* (who were probably intimate with the slave owners), failed to hear the protest that the prisoners must have made; so they set themselves in a perilous position.

Out of Prison
(Acts 16:25–40)

About midnight, Paul and Silas were singing hymns to God, and the prisoners were listening to them. Suddenly there was a severe earth tremor, and the foundations of the prison were shaken. Immediately all the doors were opened, and everyone's chains fell off. Awakening, the jailer saw the prison doors open; and, drawing his sword, was about to kill himself, thinking the prisoners had escaped. But Paul called loudly, "Do yourself no harm, for we are all here." Calling for lights, he rushed in and fell trembling before Paul and Silas. Bringing them out, he asked, "Sirs, what must I do to be saved?" They said, "Believe on the Lord Jesus Christ, and you shall be saved, and your household, too." And they preached the word of the Lord to him and to all of his household. He took them in that hour of the night and washed their stripes and was baptized, he and all his people, immediately. He took them into his house, provided a meal, and, having put his faith in God, was overjoyed, with all his house.

When day dawned, the magistrates sent their lictors, saying, "Let those men go." The jailer reported their words to Paul: "The magistrates have sent word for you to be let go. Go out then now and be on your way in peace." Paul said to them, "They have publicly flogged us—Roman citizens—without trial, put us into prison, and now they are putting us out secretly. No, indeed. Let them come in person and lead us out." The lictors reported all these words to the magistrates. Hearing that they were Roman citizens, they were alarmed. They came, apologized, and asked them to leave the city. They left the prison, came to Lydia's house, saw the brethren, said an encouraging word to them, and departed.

Here is a piece of vivid narrative, clear-cut in detail and characterization, in Luke's best manner. Ramsay, who, before the end of the last century, experienced earthquakes in outback Turkish towns, vividly pictures what a ramshackle Turkish prison might have been like and how a shudder of the foundations could spring both doors and shackles, without causing deadly ruin.

Paul and Silas were no doubt chanting Hebrew psalms, both

prayers and hymns, without protest; for, in such rough custody, there could have been little sleep. The paralysis of sheer fright would keep the prisoners in place. The jailer is rapidly and vividly sketched. The nature of his evangelical utterance is explained by what the slave girl had been intoning round the streets and also by the general report of what Paul had been saying in the prayer place by the river. Nor did Paul, in his reply, suggest that the faith and conversion of the father would suffice to provide every member of the household with the cover of salvation. Paul preached to all the jailer's household, they were all baptized—surely on a confession of faith—and they were all overjoyed, a reaction difficult to produce upon demand.

The magistrates must have received some hint of their grave error. Perhaps Lydia, a woman of some substance, had been active. They sent their lictors, officers bearing the axe and bunched rods—a symbol of Roman authority, which they must have arrogantly enjoyed—and gruffly bid their victims go. All they got was a frightening confirmation that they had violated two ancient laws: the *Lex Valeria* of 509 B.C. and the *Lex Porcia* of 248 B.C., which guaranteed the rights of the Roman citizen. To flog a Roman was illegal, to flog a Roman uncondemned or without trial compounded the outrage. Paul was stern with them, for the sake of the church he was leaving behind, as much as for himself and Silas. He was in no hurry to leave, but went first to Lydia's home, where the horrible damage of the lictors' blows must have received further attention; and then, with proper dignity, he went on his way. To stay might have pressed a notable moral victory too far, and Paul had no wish to provoke the praetors to find some means of staging a legitimate trial. As it was, he left a solidly founded church, some of whose members move vividly through the letter he wrote, a decade later, from his first imprisonment in Rome: the self-sacrificing

Epaphroditus; the difficult women Euodia and Syntyche. Paul appears to have visited Macedonia and, by implication, Philippi, twice on later occasions; but, in the economy of the narrative, no details survive.

17

Thessalonica
(Acts 17:1–9)

Passing through Amphipolis and Apollonia, they came to
Thessalonica, where there was a synagogue of the Jews; and, as
his habit was, Paul joined them and for three sabbath days debated with them from the Scriptures, explaining and setting before them that Christ had to suffer and rise again and that this
Jesus, "Whom," he said, "I preach to you, is the Messiah." And
some of them were convinced and attached themselves to Paul
and Silas, with a very considerable number of Greek worshipers,
including not a few prominent women. But the unbelieving Jews
in their jealousy, recruiting some bad men from the marketplace
and gathering a mob, began to set the city in an uproar. Attacking Jason's house, they tried to bring them before the people.
Not finding them, they dragged Jason and some of the Christians to the politarchs, shouting, "Those who have upset the
whole world are here, too, and Jason has welcomed them. And
all of them are acting contrary to the decrees of Caesar, alleging
that there is another king: Jesus." They disturbed the mob and
the politarchs, too, when they heard these allegations; but, taking
bail from Jason and the rest, they let them go.

Following the Via Egnatia and passing through the important
towns of Amphipolis and Apollonia, Paul and Silas found what
they sought: a Jewish synagogue at Thessalonica (modern Sal-
onici), a four-century-old city that was an important haven at

the head of its gulf. It was named after Alexander's sister, and prolific local coinage reveals its standing.

The local synagogue had attracted many Greek adherents, including—Macedonian fashion—some leading women of the town.

Paul's preaching must also have touched other levels of society than those with which he first came into contact. The fact that he made a point of working for his living, while in the city, would seem to show that his influence moved into lower classes of society, where the example of labor, diligence, and independence was of importance to his testimony (1 Thessalonians 2:9, 10; 2 Thessalonians 3:8, 9). In Thessalonica there was obviously no person like Lydia, to provide hospitality, and perhaps Paul thought it necessary to protect Jason from local Jewish hostility.

It requires an effort of the imagination to realize that the church at Thessalonica rested on the visitors' word alone. They had no New Testament; Jews and Jewish adherents among the converts had their Old Testament in Greek, but it was impossible for them to turn to a body of authoritative Christian doctrine for study, confirmation, and guidance. The fact that the little group stood firm in faith, endured persecution, and revealed the fruit of their belief in life and character is a testimony to the evangelism Paul has described in the first half of the first chapter of the first Thessalonian letter, to his genius as a preacher and teacher, and to the power of God which went with him.

From the two brief letters to Thessalonica, much information may be gathered to supplement Luke's brevity. Paul's theme must have covered a wider spectrum than the initial subject of the three sabbath synagogue discussions. A short time later, at Athens, he was preoccupied with the coming Judgment; and that must have been part of the theme at Philippi, because in both letters Paul has to speak of misunderstandings over the Second Coming of Christ.

His concern over clarifying his teachings points to a hasty withdrawal from the city. For example, in 3:6 of the second letter, as though he had left some essential words unsaid, Paul urges discipline in the community. Some, misusing the doctrine of the Second Advent and forgetting Paul's own example, were living on their more active and energetic brethren (2 Thessalonians 3:10, 11). An idle and work-shy community is no commendation of the faith it professes. "In the name of the Lord Jesus Christ," says Paul, "we appeal to such people—we command them—to quiet down, get to work, and earn their own living" (2 Thessalonians 3:12 LB).

Then, in the anxiety of love, Paul bids his Christians not close their hearts because some had been found to abuse generosity. Necessary discipline is to be exercised by the church, without rancor or bitterness (2 Thessalonians 3:15), for redemption and peace are the aim. Rebuke loses all its moral meaning if a taint of personal hostility invades it. An ancient rabbinical comment on Deuteronomy 25:3 suggests that, after punishment, the offender should be expressly addressed as *brother* or *sister*. Paul obviously has this generous precept in mind.

The two letters give a very clear picture of the members of a church community; some ardent, self-sacrificing, loving; some puzzled by death that had visited their group, by prophecy, by persecution; and some finding occasion to live on the work of others and using the society of Christ for personal advantage.

Trouble came and had its usual origin (1 Thessalonians 2:14–16). Observe that the Jews who sought to stir up riot found their support not so much among the educated, as among the "bad men from the marketplace" (5); the unemployed (Matthew 20:3); and the proletarian associates, no doubt, of the Jewish business houses. This is one of many pieces of evidence that refute Gibbon's once-accepted opinion that Christianity made its first appeal to the dispossessed and the ignorant. It also shows, like Ephesus, that the first public opposition came from the working-class people in the Mediterranean cities.

Proceedings here were more regular than at Philippi. As was the custom, voluntary prosecutors set the law in motion, and a charge of treason (7) was one which "the rulers of the city" (KJV) had to treat with the utmost seriousness. Luke twice (6,8) calls these officials politarchs. Since the term was unknown elsewhere, the critics of Luke once dismissed it as a mark of ignorance. Sixteen epigraphical examples now exist in modern Salonica, and one is located in the British Museum, on a stone which had formed part of an archway. It was evidently a Macedonian term. It was Luke's general practice to use the term in commonest use in educated circles, and it is a mark of his accuracy.

The charge of treason was dangerous. The politarchs could not possibly overlook it, and merely to take "security" (KJV) from Paul's host must be regarded as mild action on their part. On the other hand, it put Paul under a strong obligation. As later, at Ephesus, he could not easily go back. From 1 Thessalonians 2:18 this seems clear; and from 1 Thessalonians 2:13, 14 and 3:3, it also seems obvious that local persecution continued. But a strong church had been founded during Paul's stay— probably from December A.D. 50 to May A.D. 51. It was active in evangelism from the beginning (1 Thessalonians 1:8, 9) and reached out—north and south—with the Gospel, in the manner Paul intended.

Berea
(Acts 17:10–15)

Without delay, the brethren dispatched Paul and Silas to Berea, by night. On their arrival, they went to the synagogue of the

Jews. These were more generously minded than those in Thessalonica and received the word with all eagerness, daily studying the Scriptures to see whether what was told was true. Many of them became believers, including prominent Greek women and not a few men. But as soon as the Jews of Thessalonica learned that the word of God was preached by Paul in Berea, they came there, too, rousing the crowds; so the brethren promptly sent Paul off as if to proceed to the sea, but Silas and Timothy stayed behind there. Those who escorted Paul brought him as far as Athens. Receiving a message for Silas and Timothy to join him as soon as possible, they departed.

Evangelism had been hard, so far, in Europe, but two churches had been founded; and Paul, along with Silas—refugees once more—again found themselves on the highway to the south. It was sixty miles to Berea; and, as was his dogged habit, Paul began with the synagogue. He found there a better type of Jew, "more noble," as the King James Version renders Luke's phrase, more generous in outlook. He meant that they were more free than their nearest neighbors from the endemic jealousy of their contemporaries—their racialism, in a word. There is no nobility in prejudice, in self-esteem, in vain claims to superiority, in ignorant refusal to listen to a contrary opinion.

Paul, after long meditation during those hidden years in Arabia, had concluded that the Old Testament was laced and filled with foreshadowings of the faith and the Gospel he had found. This was the burden of his message to the Jews. Instead of shrinking from a reappraisal, the Jews of the Berean synagogue studied the Scriptures in an earnest endeavor to discover the truth. It is implied that they were prepared to accept the truth they found. Paul found them satisfying.

Cicero describes Berea as "off the beaten track." It was here, curiously enough, on the eastern slope of the Olympus Range, that an unpopular Roman magistrate, retreating from Thessalonica in a storm of popular protest, found refuge in the town's comparative seclusion; and so, for how long Luke does not choose to say, did Paul's party. The Roman magistrate's enemies picked up his trail, and Berea proved no hiding place (Cicero *In Pisonem* 36 end). So did Paul's determined foes.

At what point in the Bereans' salutary searching of the Scriptures the envoys from the Thessalonian synagogue arrived, it is impossible to say. Paul must have made progress within Berea and found friends, because there were those who cleverly extricated him from yet another situation of peril. So far, from Damascus to Greece, Paul had left six cities in flight, in haste, in danger, or under the menace of judicial action. Luke reports it all without emotion. Perhaps Paul viewed it all as nonchalantly and so narrated it to him.

Athens
(Acts 17:16–34)

While Paul was waiting for his friends in Athens, he was deeply stirred to see the city given over to idols. And, so, in the synagogue he debated with the Jews and their adherents, and in the marketplace every day with any he chanced to meet.

Some of the Epicurean and Stoic philosophers met him, and some of them said, "What is the purpose of this picker-up of oddments?" And others said, "He appears to be a preacher of foreign deities," for Paul was preaching the Gospel of Jesus and the Resurrection. So they brought him urgently to the Hill of Ares, saying, "May we know this new teaching of which you speak? For you bring to our hearing matters quite strange to us. And so we want to know what these things mean." (All the Athenians and the strangers residing there spent their leisure in nothing else but talking and hearing about something new.)

Paul stood in the middle of the Hill of Ares and said, "Athenians, I observe that in every way you are uncommonly religious; for, going about and looking at the objects of your worship, I even found an altar inscribed TO THE UNKNOWN GOD! That which you worship, therefore, in ignorance, I am making known to you. God, who made the universe and all that it contains, he, the Lord from all time of the heavens and the earth, does not dwell in temples which hands have made; nor is he served by human hands, as though he needed something—giving, as he does to all, life and breath and everything. And he made of one blood every race of men, causing them to dwell upon all the face of the earth, marking out for them their boundaries in time and their place of habitation and prompting them to seek God, if perhaps they might grope for him and discover him—though, indeed, he is not far from any one of us. For in him we live and move and, indeed, exist, as some of your own Stoic poets have said, 'For we are also his offspring.' Being, therefore, by the nature of things, God's offspring, we ought not to think that the divine is like gold or silver or stone, carved work of man's devising. Well, then, the times of ignorance God overlooked, but now calls on all men everywhere to repent, because he has set a day in which he purposes to judge the world in righteousness, by the Man whom he has appointed, giving assurance to all men by raising him from the dead." Having heard of a resurrection of the dead, some scoffed. Others said, "We shall hear you again about this." So Paul came out from their company. But some men remained with him and believed: among whom was Dionysius, a member of the Court of the Hill of Ares, a woman named Damaris, and others along with them.

Paul, somewhat troubled and anxious, had come alone to the great city. Northern Greece had seen stormy experience. In Athens, suffering some reaction, Paul was a prey to that sharp loneliness felt by sensitive spirits amid an alien throng, and in

an environment which disturbs and repels. In the summer of
A.D. 51, it seems clear that—for all his deep understanding of
the Greeks—Athens appeared, to Paul, to be a hostile place.

The reasons are not far to seek. Today, those who view with
wonder the magnificence of Athens' ruined heart are without
the Jew's deep loathing of idolatry. He who climbs the steps
through the Propylaea and sees the breathtaking majesty of the
shattered Parthenon—mellow in its golden marble and superbly
placed—has no thought of Athene, who once stood in the dim
interior, the object of man's devotion. In the precinct, he may
trace the base of another colossal image of Athens' patron goddess. It stood with spear upraised so high that sailors off Sun-
ion, forty miles from Athens, caught the sun's glint on its point.
When the Goths intruded, at the beginning of the dark fifth
century after Christ, they scattered in flight at the first sight of
the image. The modern visitor, standing on the flat foundation,
regrets the destruction of a great statue. The reverence of the
Athenian, the terror of the Goth, the repugnance of the Jew for
blasphemy in bronze and stone, mean nothing to him.

Perhaps the Christian can still touch the edge of that sensa-
tion only in the revolting presence of the phallic image. Some
intricately carved fragments on Delos reveal the gross mingling
of carnality and religion that stirred the wrath of the Hebrew
prophets and that evoke a Christian's disgust. The sculptured
sensualities of some Eastern temples rouse the same nausea.
Athens must have had examples enough of this baser use of
Greek art. *Athene Promachos* and the *Wingless Victory* were not
its only creations. There were the crude phallic herms of every
common street; and, if evidence is needed to prove that these
rough cult images were something more than decorations, there
is the famous case of 415 B.C., in which their wanton desecra-
tion provoked a serious crisis in Athenian political and judicial
history. So real was idolatry.

The remedy for loneliness and oppression of spirit is work. With his usual dexterity, Paul adapted himself to the Athenian environment of endless talk, discussion, and public argument. Along with the synagogue, Paul sought the agora (excavated in the last generation) and went to work, after the fashion of Socrates.

To gather an audience was no difficult matter. The great Greek city once led the world in its intellectual achievement: It held a people who, once, in an ardent, unparalleled fifty years of human history, produced great works of literature that are still unsurpassed; art and architecture that still astonish; poetry, philosophy, and all else that betoken the finest flowering of the human mind. Yet, in Paul's day, Athens lived on the greatness of her past.

Teachers great and small, worthy men or charlatans, gathered there to turn wisdom or cunning into cash. It might be called the university city of the Mediterranean. The mighty age of Pericles was five centuries past. Weariness and decadence were in the air—an alien atmosphere which, along with the ubiquitous idolatry, daunted Paul's spirit.

An ancient court, once the highest court of justice in the state, still functioned and, at this time, seems to have had some jurisdiction over what visiting teachers had to say. Hence the polite summons to appear before it, on the Hill of Ares, an outcrop of stone beneath the Parthenon. There Paul spoke to the assembled philosophers: Stoics and Epicureans, who seem to have shared the court's tasks of adjudication. Hence the Areopagus address, a triumph of Paul's adaptability and a supreme demonstration of his familiarity with Greek ways of thought; Greek literature; and Stoic philosophy, which, after all, had its beginnings in his native province of Cilicia.

To understand the speech, the schools must be understood. Zeno, the founder of the Stoic school, came from Citium in

Cyprus. A second Zeno, who was head of the school in 204 B.C., actually came from Tarsus. It was he who gave Stoicism the practical turn that so attracted intelligent Romans such as Seneca and Marcus Aurelius. Aratus, scientist and poet, who is quoted by Paul in the speech before the Areopagus, was a Stoic of the first vintage, born at Soli in Cilicia, and converted to Stoicism in Athens, a few yards from where Paul spoke. Cleanthes, whose hymn to Zeus also uses the words of Paul's quotation, was a man of Assos, in Asia Minor. As second head of the school, he infused a deeply religious element into Stoicism.

Zeno, first founder of the Stoic school and, it appears, a Semite, came to Athens about the year 320 B.C., at the very time when Epicurus was finding delight and relief in the atomic theory of Democritus, in Colophon, across the Aegean. Two questions confronted Zeno, as they confront all seekers after truth: what to believe and how to live.

Nothing but goodness is good, Zeno asserted. Rank, riches, health, race, and pleasure are incidentals. Epicurus might argue that pleasure is good and find the bulk of the world to support him. But does history ever praise a man because he was happy, healthy, long-lived or rich? No, indeed. What lives in memory is a man's goodness, virtue, or heroism. History is obviously groping after some form of ultimate justice. A man, therefore, possesses all good in his person. What matters is what he is, not what he has or what happens to him. No earthly power can make a man bad outside his will. It can rob him of freedom, possessions, and health, but not goodness.

The Stoics conceived of their god as a mighty life force surging through all things and thrusting toward perfection. It was a near pantheism not unlike the Ultimate Reality or the Ground of Being of some philosophic theologians. Hence Stoicism propounded a way of life that was toilsome, enduring, and defiant of an evil world.

It is easy to see why Paul then addressed himself to the Stoics of his audience. He, too, believed in a Purpose working to a vast consummation and the need for man to cooperate with it. He, too, believed that what a man *was* mattered supremely, not what he possessed. He, too, sought self-sufficiency and superiority above circumstances. His God, too, was transcendant and beyond the patronage of man. There were points of sympathy and contact, a bridgehead of persuasion. It is Paul's Jewish and synagogue approach, applied to Greek Stoic philosophers.

Look now at the Stoics' rival school. The Epicureans, a philosophic school founded by Epicurus, who lived from 342 to 270 B.C., were materialists. Paul had no point of contact with them. Basing their world view on the atomic theories of Democritus of Abdera, they sought to explain all phenomena on physical principles. It was a philosophy born in a time of stress, and it sought to banish tension and anxiety by explaining away the sources of such disturbances. The soul was, they taught, atomic in structure and therefore died with its host. There were gods, for men saw such beings in dreams, and dreams had a material explanation in films of atoms penetrating the brain, but the gods were not involved in life.

Epicurus' passionate quest was for peace of mind. He saw religion; the hope or fear of survival; the expectation of judgment; a power which punished, cared, or interfered, as disturbances for the soul and poisons of its peace. Let man seek only happiness, and happiness could only be pleasure.

The true sage, Epicurus taught, curbed passion, scorned excess, lust, ambition, for all have an aftermath of pain. He narrowed desire; that disappointment, anxiety, and apprehension, all desire's by-products, might not ruffle his calm, he sought health, quietness, and simplicity, for all are part of the unseen, unenvied way. He pursued, in short, a species of quietism without much doctrine, save the view of physics on which so much

162 of the Church

depended; his philosophy rejected mystery. Virile souls may
have turned more readily to Stoicism. The timid men of a disil-
lusioned age found more obvious escape in Epicureanism.

There is no means of knowing the color of the Epicureanism
held by the philosophers of Paul's audience. They were academic types; sound, no doubt, in their doctrine; virtual athe-
ists; contemptuous of all belief in divine care for human virtue,
human sin, or human life. Josephus, who described the Epicureans as the Sadducees of the Athenian philosophic world,
touched the truth. The worldly Jewish sect that held doctrine
lightly and denied another life, resurrection, and judgment, was
not dissimilar to the Epicureans. Significantly, Paul disregarded
both groups in two notable addresses. It is idle to speak to those
with whom there is no point of contact, no overlap of experience.

The address itself must next be considered. The approach
was conciliatory and courteous, but perhaps just touched with
that irony which was the common fashion of Athenian speech.
". . . Athenians," said Paul, "I observe that in every way you
are uncommonly religious." Here was Athenian *parrhesia,*
"freedom of speech," of the first order: tactful, yet challenging;
polite, yet without sacrifice of the speaker's position. ". . .
going about and looking at the objects of your worship," Paul
continued, "I even found an altar inscribed TO THE UNKNOWN
GOD." Thus it must be translated. He was not deceived about its
meaning, but, like any perceptive preacher, sought an illustration and a point of contact in a known environment. The device
captured attention and anchored the theme in experience.

It was convenient to Paul's approach and simple to slide
from the altar's dedication to the Stoic god who needed nothing
from any man. Or was it quite the Stoic god? Not, perhaps, in
the more austere significance of their belief. Paul's Creator was
still his own personal God, the great I AM. Indeed, he snatches

a remembered phrase from a speech which had burned into his brain. It was Stephen, on trial before the Sanhedrin, who had protested in Paul's hearing that "God does not dwell in temples made with hands."

Stephen spoke of Solomon's shrine. Paul quoted the words under the great stone altar of Greece, the Acropolis. Whether he spoke on the traditional site, the lower outcrop of stone below the greater, called "the Areopagus" or "the Hill of Ares," or whether the hearing took place in the Royal Porch in the agora—as others, without proof, contend—the magnificence of the temples on the height was in full view: the glorious Parthenon; the Erechtheum; and the fairy-light shrine of the *Wingless Victory,* on its promontory beside the entrance portal. And wherever he deprecated the thought that deity could be set forth in ". . . gold or silver or stone, carved work of man's devising," the commanding statue of *Athene Promachus* lifted its bright-tipped spear above him, and the gold and ivory figure of the same Athene listened from the religious light of her sanctuary in the great temple. Paul was a bold man and his listeners amazingly tolerant.

He proceeded to quote two Stoic poets, dexterously applied. Indeed, in this report of masterly brevity, several allusions to Greek literature are discernible. Paul's educated allusiveness is impressive. Then, having spoken in the language of his hearers, within the context of their thought, and with amazing adaptation, Paul thrust home with his point and his appeal.

The Areopagus speech was Paul's first major exposition of the Gospel to an audience without any background of Old Testament thought.

Note that he was grappling with the thought of mankind's unity before God, which had been his theme of bitter controversy with the Jews. It is a mark of the greatness of his mind that he could contest the same point in another context, in another framework of thought. It was the boast of the Athenians that they had "sprung from the soil"; and, though men of Stoic coloring or conviction, like Seneca and Epictetus, had glimpsed the thought of mankind's unity, it was left to Paul, in two racial and religious settings, to give the concept lifting power and application.

Toward God, says Paul, mankind had ever "groped." The word he uses would raise echoes in the minds of every listening Greek. Homer and Plato were familiar reading. Every educated man would remember that the verb is used in the *Odyssey* to describe the blinded Cyclops, groping for the entrance of his cave, and in the *Phaedo,* Plato's most moving dialogue, for the very search for truth which Paul here envisages on its highest plane: the quest for God. The word, it is true, is used four times, in the Septuagint, to mean "groping in the dark," but Paul must have had familiar Greek contexts in mind. His easy allusiveness is the impressive point.

So far, so good. With astonishing intellectual dexterity, the Jew of Tarsus, the Pharisee of Gamaliel's school, met the cream of Athens' intelligentsia on their familiar ground; shrewdly discerned the portion of the audience open to his argument; and, with polished persuasion, in their common speech, put his concept of God before them. With fine audacity, he swept the Acropolis of its divine significance, dismissing the magnificence of the grandest Greek art as irrelevant in the search for God. It is Athenian free speech at its boldest—exercised and also tolerated—for the broad-minded acceptance of Paul's argument is as remarkable as his courageous use of it. He spoke appropriately for the time and place and couched his message, as the Church is ever and rightly urged to do, in the thought forms of the day.

But where Paul's example parts company from the professed efforts of some theologians to follow it, is in the sequel. The message, in the same process, must not lose content and tradition. There are those today who profess a search for an elusive God—greater and higher than "the God of revelation." They end bewildered, with something not unlike the Stoic *phusis*—some ancient pantheism dressed in modern words, an impersonal or scarcely personal Force. Paul made no such disastrous mistake and sought no easy compromise. He met his audience where he could, sought by all means to graft his teaching onto accepted ideas and to express it in acceptable and comprehensible terms. But he knew that a point of challenge had to come. It came with his introduction of Christ and the divine authentication of his Person. In the act, he lost the bulk of his audience. The Epicureans had listened impatiently throughout. They were those who scoffed. The Stoics dismissed him with more polite formality. The true Stoic, the Wise Man of their famous concept, needed no repentance, feared no Day of Judgment, looked for no resurrection or reward.

A question of some importance remains. From Athens Paul moved on to Corinth, the cosmopolitan city of two seas. Writing, some four years later, to the contentious church which he founded there, he remarked upon the studied simplicity of the Gospel he had preached among them. Are those right who see in this attitude a repudiation of the intellectual approach which marked the Areopagus address? By no means, even if it be correctly assumed that the argument before the philosophers was commonly pursued in the agora—a reasonable assumption, if the sermon at Lystra is evidence. There, too, Paul had a Gentile audience, unversed in Judaism or Old Testament imagery.

The remark to the Corinthians must be seen in the context of the restrained irony that characterizes the first four chapters of the epistle. With the shallow intellectualism of the Corinthians, Paul was disposed to waste no time. He was not prepared to give them a Christianity diluted with their pseudophilosophical ideas or necessarily expressed in their attenuated terminology. Nor had he been prepared to do that in Athens, as the confrontation of his address amply demonstrates.

The audience dispersed. If the function of the Areopagus was the informal or formal investigation of new teachings, they no doubt regarded their function as fulfilled. The newcomer had nothing pernicious to disseminate, only the stock-in-trade of the religious enthusiast the world over; and Athens could absorb such trivialities and survive. Only one member of the court found conviction and Christ as did some of the bystanders—for there was, no doubt, a listening circle.

The whole address remains a model for those who seek to present the Christian faith in such circles. In addition, it is a warning to those who, in misguided moments, have seen a virtue in crudity and a loyalty to truth in a disrespect for the views, habits of thought, and attitudes of intelligent people who fail in all points to follow them. Confrontation there must be, but with a preamble of courtesy, with the tolerance which is not incompatible with earnestness, and with the sincerest of efforts to see good where good has found a place.

It is not known whether any Christian group cohered in Athens. It is strange that no mention is made of any wide synagogue ministry, though surely Paul would have sought his usual point of entry. And it would have been interesting to meet the Jews who had formed a congregation in the intellectual center of the world. It seems that Paul set off fairly promptly for Corinth, round the curve of the Saronic Gulf. His companions were to meet him there.

It has been necessary to deal with the chapter as a coherent whole. Luke's splendid reporting seems to demand such treatment. It will be appropriate, however, to pick up one or two details of language and interpretation.

First, observe that the word used in verse 16 about Paul's spirit being "stirred within him" (KJV) is related to the noun used of the difference between Paul and Barnabas in 15:39. It is *paroxuneto* and indicates a most vehement emotional disturbance. Such was the effect of idolatry on a Christian.

Second, the word in verse 18 which is translated "babbler" (KJV) is *spermalogos,* which means "seed picker" and is used, by both the comedy writer Aristophanes and the naturalist-philosopher Aristotle, of small granivorous birds. It became a slang word for the eclectic "picker-up of trifles"—one who took oddments of learning and set them forth as his stock-in-trade of teaching or the sum of education.

Third, the word *superstitious,* equally ill-rendered in the King James Version, reveals Paul's distinguished command of Attic Greek. Aristotle uses the word *(deisidaimonesteros)* for a genuine religious attitude, the "fear of the Lord." Admittedly Theophrastus used it in a sense near that of the King James Version, but it is remarkable how Paul deftly and ironically combines the two meanings.

Fourth, the correct translation of the altar inscription is "to the unknown god." There is plenty of evidence for the existence of such altars with plural inscriptions.

What did the inscription mean? Plato preserves a tradition that Epimenides, the Cretan religious teacher and miracle worker, was in Athens about 500 B.C. Some said it was 600 B.C., but dates are neither here nor there in a half-legendary situation. The story was that, to combat an epidemic, Epimenides directed the Athenians to loose sheep from the Areopagus and, wherever they lay down, to build an altar "to the unknown god" of the place and to make sacrifice. Perhaps the story is an etiologic myth, a tale invented to explain a visible phenomenon. Perhaps the altars merely represented a scrupulosity that, in a city full of deities from all the Eastern Mediterranean, sought to avoid offense to any, in this slightly naive fashion. It is impossible to say more.

18

Corinth
(Acts 18:1–11)

Departing from Athens, Paul came to Corinth; and, finding a Jew named Aquila, born in Pontus, but lately arrived from Italy, with his wife Priscilla, following Claudius' banishment of all Jews from Rome, he lodged with them and labored with them, for they were workers in tent cloth.

In the synagogue, every sabbath, he debated and tried to persuade both Jews and Greeks. When Silas and Timothy had come down from Macedonia, Paul was absorbed in teaching the word [following the preferable reading, *word* for *spirit,*] earnestly testifying to the Jews that Jesus was the Messiah. When they set themselves in opposition and blasphemed, shaking his garments, he said to them, "Your blood be upon your heads. I am clean, and henceforth I go to the Gentiles." And he moved to the house of a man named Justus, who was a worshiper of God and lived next door to the synagogue. And Crispus, the leading man in the synagogue, believed on the Lord with his whole household, and many Corinthians heard, believed, and were baptized. And the Lord spoke to Paul, in a dream at night, "Do not be afraid, but speak, and go on speaking, for I am with you, and no man shall attack you to do you harm, for I have many people in this city." He stayed there a year and six months, teaching among them the word of God.

To found and establish a Christian church in the cosmopolitan seaport on the isthmus was a major achievement of Paul's life. The congregation, volatile, divided, prone to heresy, and yet eager and beloved, was always a burden on the apostle's heart.

As he wrote to them four years later, from Ephesus, he pictured the apricot-colored roofs on the low ridge between the twin gulfs and the great crag of the Acrocorinthus above. He saw the crowded marketplace, with the high platform where Gallio sat at its far end and Apollo's temple dominated the other. And he remembered, no doubt, the strangely varied experience of his first crowded year in Greece. Philippi had provided stormy adventure and had widely awakened the apostle's consciousness of his Roman citizenship. Athens, with its talkative marketplace and its challenging philosophers' court, had demonstrated the supreme value of the Greek education won at Tarsus, that confluence of East and West.

When he found the synagogue of the Corinthian Jews and a home and haven with that much-traveled and cosmopolitan couple Aquila and Priscilla, Paul must have felt very much a citizen of three worlds. He was no less, thanks to his superbly varied background and education. Nor would Corinth herself allow any sojourner to forget the tumultuous Mediterranean world of which the isthmus formed a hub of communication and commerce, with a dozen nations jostling in the streets, a dozen tongues a hubbub in her market.

Paul no doubt remembered that he had arrived somewhat heavy in spirit—the victim, perhaps, of one of his periodic illnesses. The "weakness, fear, and trembling" (1 Corinthians 2:3; 1 Thessalonians 3:7) with which he went to work in that noisy, riotous, and ruthless environment may have been the reaction of a brain overworked and ravaged with malaria—if that, as Ramsay so cogently suggested, was his "thorn in the flesh" (1 Corinthians 4:10; 2 Corinthians 10:1–11; 12:7). The disease would have marred his presence and appearance among the aesthetically minded Greeks.

But Aquila and Priscilla, of whom more presently, were firm friends; and good news came, with Silas and Timothy, from the north. Paul left the hostile synagogue, was vindicated in a Roman court, and gathered a congregation from the motley community. The city treasurer, the ex-rabbi of the synagogue, the rich lady Chloe, were among its many members. But so, too, were the nameless, rootless horde, the contentious Jews and Greeks, the self-styled philosophers so ironically dealt with in the first four chapters of the letter, the ill-bred dregs of dockland, temple girls, those who formed the horrific list of the sixth chapter (1 Corinthians 6:9, 10): in short, the tumbled multitude of the most notoriously licentious city in the Greek world. (To "act the Corinthian" was, in Greek slang, to play the part of an immoral rake.)

Hence the stern battle for stability, integrity, balance, purity, and a clean, clear testimony in the Corinthian church. It is a patent fact that cities have a color and a character and that the Christian community, for both good and ill, demonstrates, in its corporate life, facets and aspects of its time and place. The factious moods, the pseudophilosophical preoccupations, the divisive loyalties, the emotional extravagances of the Corinthian church were nothing more than a reflection of the faults of the community from which it was drawn. This is not to say the church was an unsanctified replica of the society in which it found itself. It is merely to assert that, then as now, the local Christian group often retained some flavor and rendering of the population at large. It is the task of leadership to promote the good and to quench the bad in that collective character. Paul sought no less.

Hence the famous chapter which forms a climax in his first epistle: the poem on Christian love. It was a harassed, divided, stumbling, and sadly tormented church which first heard the moving words of chapter thirteen. The writing of them and their dispatch across the Aegean were the measure of the author's optimism, of his confidence and his care. He had not despaired of his Corinthians, and he addresses them with irony, appeal, sternness, tenderness, and yearning love. He was not aware of how wide a world he was writing for and of the long vista of history down which his words would move with passion and with power. They search the soul.

But, to turn to greater detail, Corinth, was, in fact, a different experience—unlike Philippi, Thessalonica, or Athens. Beyond all other Mediterranean cities, except perhaps Rome itself, it was cosmopolitan and without deep roots. Its history had, in fact, suffered a traumatic interruption. Athens' old naval rival of the fifth century had lived until 146 B.C., when the Romans ruthlessly destroyed it.

Julius Caesar, exactly a century later, seeing the inevitable importance of the site, had rebuilt the city; and, save for the ruins of Apollo's temple on the ridge, the remains which so impress the visitor today are what is left of Caesar's city. But it may be guessed that it was difficult for Corinth to resume a strong thread of history. The people of Paul's Corinth—a century after the restoration—were the victims of events; philosophically pretentious, in jealousy of Athens; and too ready, with the facility of all immigrant communities, to adopt the vices, rather than the virtues, of their hosts. Faction, morality, social conduct, the Christian ethical code, and death, all formed problems for their brash and shallow philosophy.

No common habit of thought gave a multilingual community a coherence of outlook or some unity of standards. A strongly based synagogue community, for all the opposition Paul had met from the Jews, certainly gave this. His religious and ethical language was understood. Perhaps the Jews in the newly formed church, those who had left the synagogue, were far from being an important section. It was, in fact, a church situation which has much to teach this century, which, in so many ways, again encounters all the problems of the first century A.D.

In the first letter that he wrote to Corinth, Paul recalls that he had approached the city with misgivings. He had understood Athens and had even sensed a kinship with the Stoics of his notable audience. The pseudophilosophic pretentions of some of the Corinthians he despised. Hence the deep irony which infuses the first four chapters of his first epistle to Corinth— perhaps lost on those to whom he wrote—and his determination not to pander to the group by "preaching the Gospel in philosophic terms" (*see* 1 Corinthians 2:4). This is what his resolve to "know nothing else" (1 Corinthians 2:2) but the simplicities of his message means. It is by no means a repudiation of the Areopagus address. In both Athens and Corinth, he refused to compromise on the fundamental historic facts of revelation.

This, presumably, was the theme of the weekly debate in the synagogue (part of whose door lintel has been discovered in the city's ruins). As at Athens, these debates may also have been in Greek contexts. At any rate, he seems to have made wide contacts with society at large, had Silas and Timothy to encourage him, and had the remarkable benediction of two new friends. There had been some uproar in the Roman ghetto, "over one Chrestos" says Suetonius. If some scraps of historical evidence can tentatively be put together, notably the Nazareth Rescript of Claudius, it would seem that the intrusion of Christianity and Jewish protest over the Resurrection had impelled Claudius to expel all the Jews. There is evidence that such drastic acts were seldom widely enforced and not long maintained, for Paul's friends were soon in Rome again (Romans 16:3, 4). Thanks to Claudius, Paul met Aquila and Priscilla.

Fortunately for him, they were in Corinth on his arrival. Prisca (or, in the diminutive, Priscilla) and her husband, a man of Pontus, were a much-traveled pair. They seem to have accompanied Paul to Ephesus, where they instructed the preacher Apollos from Alexandria in the emerging Pauline theology. Prisca and Aquila kept open house, the home of a "household church," and formed a noble link in European Christianity.

There is still the Church of Saint Prisca, on Rome's Aventine Hill; and there is a cemetery which bears her more affectionate and familiar name, Priscilla. This cemetery was the burial ground of the ancient family of the Acilii; one of its members, Acilius Glabrio, became a Roman consul in A.D. 91, but seems to have died a martyr's death as a Christian, five years later. If the Priscilla of the catacomb cemetery is the Priscilla of this story, Aquila may have been a freedman of the family of the Acilii, an ex-slave, perhaps a Jew. But this can be no more than intriguing speculation. And since Prisca is a common name of the Acilii, there could be, in their partnership, a moving illustration of the faith breaking through the barriers of caste and station and uniting a Roman lady with a freedman of her house. It is a curious fact that, in four of the six passages in which the pair are named, Prisca, contrary to custom, is named before her husband.

Picture a house with a shop front, opening, Roman fashion, onto the street; this was an unconventional but intimate point of contact with the local population and, so, for Christians, a preacher's pulpit. Paul and his hosts, as some Jewish custom decreed, had a trade. Paul had, no doubt, inherited his father's expertise—one very proper to his province, where a strong, coarse, goat-hair fabric, called Cilician cloth, or cilicium, was produced. It was the fashioning of the already-woven material which formed Paul's handicraft, and, since it was commonly a material for tents, the craftsmen were called tentmakers.

The cloth must have had many and varied uses, especially among seafaring men. It is highly unlikely that an established Cilician industry should not have discovered many diversifications for its products. So Paul found a livelihood, until his preaching became all-absorbing (5), as he appeared to have similarly done in the other seaport, Thessalonica. The work load he customarily carried was immense.

Paul's eighteen months of Christian preaching, having begun in the synagogue (4), again encountered the pride and nationalism of the Jewish minority, and so the evangelist moved next door, to the house of an adherent, Justus. The rabbi of the synagogue left with him, a notable convert. The imperfect tenses of verses 4 and 8 give an insight into Paul's patient teaching: "He used to debate in the synagogue every sabbath, and press his message on Jews and Greeks . . . and many of the Corinthians who heard him would believe and be baptized."

Paul must have deeply felt the vital nature of his task. Corinth was a crossroad of trade. From that point the faith could be disseminated down the sea-lanes of the Mediterranean world. He felt the urgency of the Gospel on his heart. The brevity of time, the magnitude of the task, a sense of weakness, and overwhelming responsibility: all these, together with a consciousness of God's indwelling power, led to a change of method. Instead of "reasoning (4)," Paul now "testified" (5). Exactly what this means is difficult to say. Personal experience is certainly the keynote of the later speeches in the book. Perhaps 1 Corinthians 2:1–4 refers to this simplification of his message.

The Corinthian Christians were a varied mixture. A few of the converts, some, indeed, "wise men after the flesh" and "noble" (1 Corinthians 1:26), are known to us by name: Crispus, the ruler of the synagogue; Erastus, the city treasurer (Romans 16:23. Perhaps also Acts 19:22; 2 Timothy 4:20); Stephanas and Gaius, who seem to have been in a position to exercise generous hospitality; and the lady Chloe, who had a large household. Also mentioned are Fortunatus; Achaicus; Quartus; and Tertius, who acted as amanuensis for the epistle to the Romans. A strong Latin element appears likely, and Justus, probably a *colonus,* might be a "Roman," like Paul.

It was to prove a difficult congregation, as the two letters to Corinth show. The turbulence and spirit of faction, an old Greek vice; the fundamental skepticism; the deplorable relapses; the undue tolerance toward sins of impurity; the intellectual arrogance and philosophical posing; and the very abuse of the gifts of the Spirit for self-display, which seem to have marred the Christian community, were reflections of the life of the restless Greek city itself. But a climax was looming.

Gallio
(Acts 18:12–17)

> And when Gallio was proconsul of Achaia, the Jews made a concerted attack on Paul and brought him to the judgment seat, saying, "This man is seducing people to worship God contrary to the law."
>
> Paul was on the point of answering, when Gallio said to the Jews, "If this were a case of misdemeanor or plain viciousness, Jews, I should have given you a proper hearing. But if it is a dispute about some form of words and titles and your own law, see to it yourselves. I have no intention of being a judge in these matters." And he cleared them from the judgment place.
>
> And all the Greeks laid hold of Sosthenes, the leader of the synagogue, and began to punch him, before the judgment seat. And Gallio paid no attention to these matters.

Ramsay was right in regarding this incident in Corinth as a

turning point in Paul's career. Gallio appears to establish for the Christians a freedom of speech which Paul accepted with delight. It implied no special favor or recognition, only freedom to propagate. Had it not been for the tragic events of just twelve years later and Nero's descent upon the Church, after the Great Fire of July A.D. 64, the path ahead seemed to lead where Paul so passionately desired it to lead: to the imperial acceptance of the faith. But first look at the remarkable person who, on this dramatic occasion, was the spokesman for Rome in the city of Corinth and the Province of Achaia.

Junius Annaeus Gallio, the proconsul, was the brother of the Roman philosopher, dramatist, orator, and tutor of Nero, Lucius Annaeus Seneca, one of the most cultured and noble figures of that age. They were members of a Spanish family, two of many men—writers, senators, emperors—whom the great Romanized Iberian peninsula sent to Rome to be leaders in politics and culture. An inscription, discovered at Delphi in 1905, indicates that Gallio was proconsul of Achaia in A.D. 52, thus providing a fixed dating point for Paul's activities in Greece.

Gallio, according to both the Roman poet Statius and Seneca, was a gentle and amiable person, and the Jews obviously misread both the magistrate and the situation. He was not the man to yield to noisy demonstrations and violence, a strength of such characters which not infrequently surprises those who seek to take advantage of what they imagine to be weakness. The Jews, with arrogant confidence, also thought to profit by the new magistrate's inexperience and phrased their charge to look like one of treason. So they had done before Pilate. So they had sought to harm Paul in Thessalonica. Perhaps, too, they forgot the fact that, with Claudius' recent expulsion of the Roman Jewish colony, the nation was somewhat under a judicial cloud, and not likely to obtain, even from the most impartial

Roman court, anything more than their bare due. Gallio proved quite capable of distinguishing between matters of serious political significance and charges relating to minutiae of Jewish law. Incidentally, Seneca, Gallio's brother, calls the Jews "a most scoundrelly race."

It is possible, in Corinth today, to picture the scene. The old agora has been excavated, with its row of shops overlooked by the remaining eight pillars of the temple of Apollo, on the northwestern ridge. The vast bulk of the acropolis—the Acrocorinthus—topped by the temple of Aphrodite, whose host of priestess-courtesans did much to give Corinth its notoriously rank flavor of moral corruption—stood high above the town. At the end of the marketplace is the massive stone platform on which Gallio sat, the *bema,* and in front of it the wide pavement on which the angry leaders of the synagogue crowded round their victim. There are few places where it is easier to imagine the drama of the ancient scene.

Paul must have met the magistrate's brusque intervention with some amazement. He had not even found it necessary to appeal to his Roman citizenship. He had never been so promptly silenced (14). As for the Jews and Crispus' successor in the rabbinate, Sosthenes, their general unpopularity prompted the turbulent Corinthian mob to assault them. This was deplorable, but Gallio, annoyed at the presumptuous and arrogant attitude of the synagogue, took no action.

Paul never forgot the moment. As he turned to retire, with sensible promptitude, the first sight that met his eyes was the temple on the ridge. It was one of those moments which forever stamp some reality on the mind. Is that why, in both letters to Corinth, he seems to picture Apollo's temple, sole survivor of the Roman vandalism of 146 B.C., and work it into a telling metaphor? (1 Corinthians 3:16, 17; 2 Corinthians 6:16).

Paul's Vow
(Acts 18:18–23)

Paul still stayed on for some time, and then, saying good-bye to the brethren, set out to sail to Syria, accompanied by Priscilla and Aquila, after he had shaved his head, in pursuance of a vow, at Cenchrea. And they put in to Ephesus, where Paul left them. He went to the synagogue, where he debated with the Jews. When they asked him to stay longer with them, he declined, saying good-bye to them with the explanation, "I must definitely keep the forthcoming festival in Jerusalem. I will return again to you, God willing." And he set out from Ephesus. Landing at Caesarea, he went up and, after greeting the church, went down to Antioch. He spent some time, set out again, and passed successively through the Galatian and Phrygian regions, strengthening all the disciples.

Luke's brevity over the rapid visit to Jerusalem is quite disconcerting. It is just grammatically possible to take it that Aquila made the Nazirite vow. But almost universally it is assumed that it was part of Paul's preparation for another visit to the Jerusalem church. Perhaps he was preparing himself for some ministry with the Pharisaic wing of that assembly, which dominated the church and which Paul longed to bend to his point of view. To this the theme will later return.

There is much between the lines which it is difficult to read. What was the reason for Aquila's and Priscilla's move to Ephesus, unless it was in preparation for a period of evangelism there? And, if so, why does Paul seem to have made his customary initial visit to the synagogue, alone? He was under a strange urgency, and we would gladly know why he set such store by the coming festival of Jewry.

It is quite difficult to avoid the feeling, in this rapid itinerary, that, whatever Paul had in mind, the visit to Jerusalem was a disappointment. Perhaps Luke mentions it, in his preparatory fashion, because of the space he must needs devote to the long and tragic journey that dominates the last eight chapters of the book. The name of Jerusalem is actually not mentioned. He simply "went up" and then "went down" to Antioch. Even there, little mention is made beyond that he spent "some time" there; and he was on the road again, this time, contrary to his custom, alone, for another sweep through the churches of central and western Asia Minor.

The quite difficult question of Paul's unusual Nazirite vow must be considered in this context.

The Scofield Bible, published over seventy years ago, sadly heads this section of Luke's story: "The author of Romans 6:14; 2 Corinthians 3:7–14; and Galatians 3:23–28 takes a Jewish vow." It is, in fact, an inconsistency difficult to reconcile in one so clear in his doctrine and so decisive in his way of life. How is it to be explained?

Cenchrea, the modern Kichries, lay some seven miles east of Corinth, on the Saronic Gulf. It was the isthmus city's outlet to the Aegean Sea. Phoebe, who is commended to the Roman church, first of all the list in Paul's letter (Romans 16:1), came from Cenchrea, where a church functioned in her home. It was probably here that Paul found shelter during the period of his vow.

It was a Jewish ritual of gratitude to take a Nazirite vow. The whole proceeding is set forth in Numbers 6:1–21. Paul may have wished to thank God for the blessing and preservation he had known in Corinth. It may also have been prudent, after the ironical outcome of the prosecution in the proconsul's court, to withdraw from sight for a time, and Cenchrea was a convenient place of retirement. Nor, indeed, was a man with a shaven head without some useful semblance of disguise. The normal proceeding was to withdraw from the common pursuits of life for thirty days, while hair and beard grew again, to abstain from meat and wine, and in the end make certain offerings in the temple at Jerusalem.

Nonetheless, the full story of what Paul had in mind eludes us. Apart from the convenience of the Nazirite withdrawal, there is no doubt that, after his arduous time earning his own living and founding and instructing a church in Corinth, a weary man needed rest and time for prayer and meditation. It may, on the other hand, have been a proceeding not without somber consequences. The sequel is perhaps found in a later chapter (21:18–26), where Paul is persuaded by the Pharisaic wing of the Church to demonstrate his continuing loyalty to Judaism by meeting the charges of four men who had undertaken precisely such a vow. Perhaps Luke is thus preparing the way. The Jerusalem Christians, unsure of their Christian liberty, must have heard of Paul's act of compromise at Cenchrea or observed its continuing evidence on his head and seized upon it as a concession to them. It led to serious trouble.

Apollos
(Acts 18:24–28)

A certain Jew named Apollos, an Alexandrian by birth, a gifted preacher, and an authority on the Scriptures, came to Ephesus. He had been instructed in the way of the Lord and, with spiritual fervor, talked and taught carefully about the Lord, though he knew only John's baptism. He began to speak openly in the synagogue; and Aquila and Priscilla heard him, took him in hand, and explained the way of God to him more carefully still. When he expressed a wish to go over to Achaia, the brethren encouraged him and wrote to the disciples to receive him. When he arrived, he was a great help to those who had believed through the grace of God. He forcefully refuted the Jews in open debate, demonstrating, through the Scriptures, that Jesus was the Messiah.

Luke has the important episode of the long and influential Ephesian ministry in view and, with his hasty travelogue, has temporarily dismissed Paul from his carefully ordered story. Lest, however, he should give the impression that Corinth was not a continuing work, at this point he introduces a remarkable newcomer. It is an intrusion into the story of a notable missionary, which can only make us realize how many large, rich tracts of the early history of the Christian Church are unknown to us, for lack of a chronicler to record and pass the story on.

The world's largest colony of expatriate Jews was in the great Egyptian city of Alexandria. Two-fifths of its million-strong population were Jews, many of them rich and cultured, most of them turbulent and powerful. A papyrus letter from the emperor Claudius, dated A.D. 42, rebukes both Jews and Gentiles for riotous behavior and seems to suggest that the trouble in the city was due to "immigrants from Syria"—perhaps Christian missionaries. It is a curious fact that the clever and eccentric Claudius seems to have been well informed about the religions of the empire.

The Jews of Alexandria, proud of their cultural and literary heritage, had given the world the Septuagint, the Greek version of the Old Testament. The Alexandrian synagogues were also the proponents of varied allegorical interpretations of the Old Testament, not unlike exaggerated forms of typology sometimes still found in Christian contexts.

Apollos (the name is probably an abbreviation of Apollonius, and his Jewish name was, no doubt, Abel) was brought up in this tradition. He was accurately informed about Jesus, either by the "visitors from Syria" mentioned in the memorandum of

Claudius, or from some early written account; and the whole drift of papyrology suggests that written information of this sort was of an earlier date than was once thought possible. The verb in verse 25 suggests that Apollos was orally instructed, but it is just possible that at least parts of Mark's Gospel could have been in circulation. Apollos, at any rate, was a man of natural gifts and received the message with enthusiasm. He set out, in true Christian fervor, to propagate the truth he had discovered and humbly received the deeper teaching given him by the devoted Priscilla and Aquila. The diligent couple was perhaps exercising the ministry prescribed for them by Paul.

Apollos moved from Ephesus to Corinth, where he showed a truly Pauline ability in dealing with the informed Jews of the synagogue. His teaching must have had some characteristic features of Alexandrian scriptural interpretation for a group to gather round him and exaggerate his distinctiveness, as the references in the first Corinthian letter imply (1 Corinthians 1:12; 3:4, 5). Paul saw it as a genuine contribution to understanding: "Apollos watered." Perhaps, on the other hand, this particular Corinthian faction had no firm center in teaching, but was merely a personality cult. Apollos was eloquent, perhaps fervent in spirit, and attractive.

Perhaps Apollos' desire to dampen such unnecessary controversy lay behind his reluctance to return to Corinth as Paul had requested (1 Corinthians 16:12). Years later, he was still active and in Paul's confidence (Titus 3:13). The suggestion that he was the author of the epistle to the Hebrews is based on the allegorical exposition common in that book. It is a suggestion as old as Luther's days, but, possible though it is, has no certain evidence to back it.

19

Ephesus
(Acts 19:1)

> While Apollos was in Corinth, Paul arrived at Ephesus, by the
> hill-country route. . . .

Thus, in one brief sentence, Luke introduces what must be
the greatest triumph of Paul's life—the evangelization of the
Province of Asia—for that was virtually what the foundation of
the great church of Ephesus was.

The city lay at the mouth of the Caÿster River, between the
Koressos Range and the sea. Like all the valley plains round the
blunt end of the Asian continent's western coasts, the Caÿster
was a highway into the interior. It was one terminal of the trade
routes that, linked with other roads, converged and branched
toward the far civilizations of continental Asia and the steppes.
That is why Athens' early Ionian colonists settled there. It was
a "way in," and that is what the word *emporion,* the Greek for
such coastal foundations, meant. From their *emporia* and the
city-states which grew from them, the Greeks commercially
penetrated the interior. They were entrances, not like Roman
colonies.

It is difficult to plot Paul's route on this occasion. The decline
of Ephesus' seaborne trade had been going on for some time;
and the Caÿster road may have been less used and consequent-
ly more convenient for a lone traveler, than, say, the frequented
highways of the Lycus Valley, through Colossae, Laodicea,

Hierapolis, Aphrodisias and the rest. It was an area Paul had not yet visited, and perhaps haste to reach his principal goal of evangelism may have suggested the less preoccupying route.

Ephesus' decline as a place of seaborne trade was due to the silting of her harbor. Miletus had a similar problem, but one not yet so far advanced. Deforestation has been man's ancient folly, only now meeting tardy diagnosis and remedy; and no part of the Mediterranean world suffered more than the peninsula we call Asia Minor. The quest for timber and charcoal and the destructiveness of that Mediterranean curse, the omnivorous goat, denuded the hinterland. Topsoil slipped from the bared hillsides; streams became swamps; and the storm waters, reaching the sea loaded with silt, choked the harbors. The harbor installations, still visible in Ephesus today, are miles from the sea. A reedy plain occupies the ancient roadstead and haven for ships.

The city, over several generations, was fortunate in her engineers, who did more than Miletus was able to do to keep some form of useable waterway open. From the days of the kings of Pergamum (from whose last ruler, Attalus III, Rome inherited the Province of Asia in 133 B.C.), to Domitian, at the end of the first century A.D., valiant attempts were made to keep the port open. The city was called, in Roman days, The Landing Place, a title found on a coin as late as the third century A.D. It derived from the fact that the incoming proconsul of Asia traditionally landed there. But it is perhaps significant that the third-century coin bears the impress of a small oar-propelled boat, an official's barge, not the deep-hulled merchant ships that marked the city's pride in her maritime trade on the coinage of earlier centuries.

Ephesus had some centuries of history yet to live, for it was not until Justinian's day, in the sixth century A.D., that the city was demonstrably falling to ruin in a swampy terrain. It was, nonetheless, even then of sufficient significance for that emperor to found a church to Saint John on the site—perhaps in partial compensation for his looting of columns from the temple of Artemis, for Saint Sophia's basilica, in his capital. There they may be seen in Istanbul today. John gave his name to part of the site. The apostle John was called the Holy Theologian, *Hagios Theologos,* and from that the Turkish name for the local village Ayasoluk derives. For the huge ruins, the name Efes is still used.

Like Athens, Ephesus was, in many ways, living on her past. Deepening economic decline had made the presence of the worship of Artemis and her mighty temple a major, indeed vital, asset for the city. When the half-legendary Codrus, king of Athens, first founded a colony there, he had planted his migrant Dorian Greeks near the shrine of an ancient fertility goddess of forgotten name. Following the religious syncretism common in the Greek and Roman world, the intruding Greeks called the goddess Artemis. This was, perhaps, as far as it is possible to date events so remote, toward the end of the second millennium before Christ. So began the Artemis cult, with its fertility rituals, orgiastic rites, and religious prostitution.

One peculiar feature in Ephesus was "the image which fell down from Zeus"—the *diopet* or "god fall"—mentioned in the official's speech (19:35). This was probably a piece of meteoric iron in the rough shape of a human body. The object could still lie somewhere in the vicinity, unless Charles Seltman—who suggested that it is a stone "pounder" from Ephesus, now in the Liverpool City Museum—is right.

Artemis appears in art and on coins as an ornamented female figure accompanied by a shrine, basket, or battlements; on her head is a veil decorated with animal forms; she wears long necklaces and embroidered sleeves; her legs are sheathed with panels of animals; and above her waist are what look like multiple breasts or, more likely, clusters of grapes or dates, symbols of the goddess's function as the nourishing spirit of nature.

Croesus, most famous of the kings of neighboring Lydia (560 to 546 B.C.), promoted the building of the first temple. This building was maliciously burned in 356 B.C., on the night, it was said, that Alexander was born; and it was Alexander who contributed richly to the new temple, which was to be numbered among the Seven Wonders of the World. It was four times the size of Athens' Parthenon. The ruins are inconsiderable. A marsh had claimed them, where, the water now drained away, the foundations of the huge shrine may be seen.

The temple was widely depicted on coins, one form of its promotion, and the guild master's claim about the wide spread of the Artemis cult was not without justification. Its hordes of visitors brought demand for services and the manifold commercial activities which internationally regarded institutions engender. Paul's ministry in Ephesus was, therefore, attacking not only a clutter of magic cults and their charlatan purveyors, not only one of the principal shrines of heathendom in the Eastern Mediterranean, but also an aspect of the city's commercial prosperity that, with the slow erosion of her other means of livelihood, she could ill afford to see damaged.

And yet Ephesus proved to be a successful diffusion point for churches up the valley trade routes. Since, at the head of the Lycus Valley, Colossae, Laodicea, and Hierapolis lie within easy walking distance of one another, it is highly likely that there were scores, perhaps hundreds, of such congregations set up during Paul's sojourn. "A great and effectual door is opened to me," he wrote, "and there are many adversaries" (1 Corinthians 16:9). A ministry so successful could hardly lack opponents, and the last half of the chapter tells the story of one concerted attack. When it came, Paul's foundations had been most well and truly laid.

John's Disciples
(Acts 19:1–7)

> . . . Finding some disciples, Paul said to them, "Did you re-
> ceive the Holy Spirit when you became believers?" "No," they
> replied, "we have not even heard whether the Holy Spirit exists."
> He asked, "Then what baptism did you receive?" "John's," they
> said. Paul answered, "John, indeed, baptized a baptism of repen-
> tance, bidding the people believe on one who should come after
> him, namely Jesus the Messiah." When they heard, they were
> baptized in the name of the Lord Jesus, and when Paul laid his
> hands on them, the Holy Spirit came upon them, and in ecstatic
> language they spoke the deep truths of God. In all they num-
> bered about twelve men.

It is difficult to account for Luke's careful inclusion of what
seems a comparatively unimportant incident in this important
account of the Ephesian ministry. Luke emphasizes that the
group which roused Paul's curiosity or concern was small (7).
Perhaps they were a remnant of Apollos' less-mature ministry
in the city (18:24, 25), and Luke is at pains to deprecate any
personal responsibility on the part of the Alexandrian visitor at
the time (1). Apollos had a striking personality and a distinctive
message that, even after his frank acceptance of Paul's Gospel,
Paul's acceptance of him, and the ministrations of Aquila and
Priscilla, was powerful enough to collect a distinctive following
(1 Corinthians 3:4). We know nothing of such parallel streams
of witness, which were flowing along with Paul's, but they must
have been many. It was, nonetheless, Paul's Gospel which prevailed among the Christians of the Gentile world; and one purpose Luke had in mind in making this report may have been to
demonstrate the readiness with which those who held an inadequate view of Christianity saw the force and logic of the full-

orbed presentation of the faith for which Paul stood and, without hesitation, embraced it.

It is not so much "signs" and special manifestations of the Spirit's benediction which are in view here, for, in his first letter to the Corinthian Christians, Paul is obviously anxious not to overemphasize the more unusual phenomena. The group of a dozen Ephesians caught Paul's attention because of their sad inadequacy. They were living in the days of repentance, which, initially necessary though such confession is, cannot be permitted to shadow life and, perhaps, promote a toilsome asceticism like John's own. They probably lacked "assurance" and the sense of emancipation proper to the presence of the indwelling Christ. They knew nothing of the Comforter. The Old Testament taught the existence of the Holy Spirit, so the apparent emphasis of their reply should not be too heavily stressed. They had not heard, they imply, whether the Spirit of God was active in a special way in the new faith.

Tyrannus' School
(Acts 19:8–12)

Paul went to the synagogue and for three months spoke out fearlessly, in debate and sermon, about the things of God's kingdom. But when some of them grew hard and would not believe, speaking evil of the Way, in public, he abandoned them and withdrew his disciples and daily held debate in the school of one Tyrannus. This went on for two years, so that all in the Province of Asia heard the word of the Lord, Jews and Greeks. God did unusual deeds of power through the hands of Paul, so that some would even take home, to the sick, handkerchiefs and aprons which had touched his body; and their diseases left them, and spirits of evil went out of them.

Paul was painfully accustomed to the sequence in the synagogue: attention; response, especially from the non-Jewish elements; the hardening and mobilizing of a coherent opposition that, becoming vocal and publicly hostile, ended the Jewish ministry. Sad experience lay behind the intensely Jewish chapters (9–11) of the letter to the Romans. But Luke seems to be anxious to record that, as in the ministry of the Lord, the synagogue was given priority, and its assembly was offered patient explanation, before Paul ever "turned to the Gentiles."

According to the commonly accepted text of Acts 19:9, Paul taught in the afternoon in ". . . the school of one Tyrannus," which, since school instruction was commonly given in the morning (Martial 9:68; 12:57; Juvenal 7:222–6), would be vacant for his use later in the day. If this reading is correct, Tyrannus was a living Ephesian schoolmaster. If another well-supported reading is followed, the text would run ". . . in the school of Tyrannus." This could indicate a public building traditionally named thus or a school founded by Tyrannus. The name was common enough.

The response was tremendous and in accordance with the spirit of the place, for Ephesus was a hotbed of oriental magic. The extraordinary practices that Luke mentions (12), common enough at the heated edges of all deep movements of evangelism, receive no word of promotion or commendation from the narrator or the apostle himself. It happened. It included some salutary phenomena. It is therefore reported. There were also extravagances beyond the pale of reason or acceptance, which are recorded in the next section.

Sceva's Sons
(Acts 19:13–22)

Some itinerant Jewish exorcists took it upon themselves to pronounce the name of the Lord Jesus over those who were held by evil spirits, saying, "We command you by Jesus whom Paul proclaims." Seven sons of Sceva, a Jewish high priest, were practicing this. Replying, the evil spirit said, "Jesus I recognize, Paul I am acquainted with, but who are you?" And the man in whom was the evil spirit leaped on them and so completely mastered them that they fled the house, stripped and wounded.

This story went round all the Jews and Greeks who lived in Ephesus; fear fell on everybody, and the name of the Lord Jesus was venerated. Many who had found faith came, confessed, and admitted what they had been wrongly practicing. And a considerable number involved in occult arts collected their books and burned them in public. They reckoned up the price and found it totalled 50,000 pieces of silver. So remarkably grew and triumphed the word of the Lord.

After this, Paul conceived the plan of proceeding to Jerusalem, after a circuit of Macedonia and Achaia, saying, "After I have been there, I must also see Rome." And he sent into Macedonia two of his aides, Timothy and Erastus, while he himself stayed on in Asia for a time.

Just as both genuine and charlatan philosophers were drawn to Rome, so to Ephesus—with its varied paganism, cults, and strange heresies—came preachers of religion: magnificently true men, like Paul, and corrupt and vicious deceivers, like Sceva. There are cities today where charlatans—men like Simon, Elymas, and the sons of Sceva—haunt the edges of genuine religion and lead the simple astray. Twice already, in Luke's story, we have met such figures from the darker fringes of Jewry, who turned the high reputation of the better types of Jew to corrupt gain. The Roman world was a superstition-ridden environment. The capital, as Rome's great historian Tacitus and the satirist Juvenal bitterly complain, could not purge itself from the wizards and magic mongers who battened on the credulous and even invaded the imperial court. It is not, therefore, surprising to find the breed in the cult-ridden city of Asia, along with the veneration of Caesar and the vicious worship of Artemis. Such creatures of the night still nibble at the edges of the faith.

The discomfiture of the Sceva brethren was evidently a prelude to an immense rejection of occult and magic arts in the city and is, for that reason, told by Luke. It is also a prelude to the next major incident, a narrative of deep historical significance.

Riot
(Acts 19:23–41)

At this juncture, a considerable disturbance arose about Christianity. One Demetrius, a silversmith who made souvenir shrines of Artemis, provided plenty of work for his craftsmen. He gathered them together, along with workmen in associated trades, and, addressing them, said, "Men, you are aware that our prosperity depends upon this business; and you see and hear that, not only in Ephesus, but through almost all of the province, this Paul, by his preaching, has turned away a great host of people— telling them, as he does, that you cannot manufacture gods. Not only is our trade in danger of falling into contempt, but the temple of the great goddess Artemis will cease to be respected, and her majesty, whom all Asia and the civilized world worships, will be heading for destruction." When they heard these words, they were filled with rage and shouted, "Great is Artemis of the Ephesians." And the whole city was a scene of confusion. They surged, with one accord, to the theater. The Macedonians, Gaius and Aristarchus, who had come with Paul, were caught in the moving crowd. Paul wished to face the multitude, but the Christians would not allow him, and some of the Asiarchs, who were well-disposed toward him, sent and urged him not to risk an

appearance in the theater. All this time, some were shouting one
thing and some another, for the assembly was in confusion, and
most of them had no idea why they were all there. Some of the
crowd explained it to Alexander, and the Jews put him forward.
Alexander, waving his hand for silence, tried to make a speech;
but when he was seen to be a Jew, all voices merged in a chant
which they kept up for two hours, "Great is Artemis of the Ephesians." When the city clerk had quieted the crowd, he addressed
them, "Ephesians, what human being is there who does not know
that the city of Ephesus is temple warden of the great Artemis
and the Thing Which Fell from Zeus? These facts are beyond
dispute, and it befits you to show restraint and not act recklessly.
I say this, for you have brought forward these men who are
guilty neither in act nor speech of offensive behavior toward our
goddess. If, therefore, Demetrius and his fellow tradesmen have
a complaint against anyone, courts are set up, and there are
proconsuls. Let those concerned go to law. If you have any other
matters to enquire about, they will be aired in the regular city
meeting. In fact, we risk being called to account for today's civil
disturbance, there being no valid reason we can give for this
uproar." With such words he broke up the assembly.

The historical importance of this passage can hardly be exaggerated. The facets of life and history, which glint in the plain
and well-told story, are worth examining. The characters stand
out: the two Macedonians, recognized as friends of Paul and
hustled down the street (so nobly visible in the ruins of the city
today) on the wave of the moving horde; Paul, cool as ever in a
crisis; the provincial custodians of the Caesar cult, not sorry
perhaps to see some damage to the religion of Artemis; Alexander, probably a Hellenistic Jew anxious not to be exposed to
unpopularity or pogrom because of the conduct of a splinter
sect. Observe, too, the germs of what was to become, in the next

half-century, a conflict with the proletariat. (This conflict was noted by Tacitus and Pliny in their secular accounts of Christianity.) The metrical chant is almost audible as it takes the place of reason in the collective mind of an excited mob, and Luke describes it with a phrase of classic irony.

Note, too, the sure touch of Luke's plural, which slips like a remembered phrase into his report of the city official's politic speech. "There are proconsuls," he reminds the promoters of the tumult. A province had only one proconsul; but, see the plural in the context of the speaker's anxiety over the privileged standing of his city before the watchful imperial authorities, and another convincing mark of historicity emerges. The plural could, grammatically, be generalizing. But it is much more likely to convey a touch of obsequious respect for the two imperial stewards, who—having murdered the proconsul of Asia, M. Junius Silanus, the great-grandson of Augustus—must have been left with the administration of the province on their hands, pending the appointment of a successor. The crime was of the vicious Agrippina's devising, shortly after Nero's accession, in the autumn of A.D. 54. She was clearing all possible rivals away. Tacitus takes occasion to make a bald account of it the preamble to the terrible story of Nero's principate. The tactful plural in the official's speech could be evidence, in one letter, of the aftermath of a political assassination.

Ephesus was a sensitive point in the imperial network. There were other corners of the empire where Rome could afford to overlook some measure of disorder, especially where local and responsible diagnosis could judge its incidence as harmless or salutary. Hence the significance of the story of Gallio's judging of the Jewish tumult in Corinth. In that cosmopolitan city, the Jewish minority presented no peril, as it did in Alexandria; and a magistrate could afford an exhibition of Rome's liberal disregard of laws other than her own. Claudius' edict of expulsion was also a recent memory, and the ghetto, swollen by immigrant malcontents, may have been due for a rebuke. With a breath of anti-Semitism in the air, Gallio judged it wise to allow a brief outlet for emotion, as long as it was in full view and under his control.

Not so with Ephesus. It was too politically vulnerable, and the chief official of a free city within the Roman system was not of the standing of the proconsul of a province. The historical and literary value of this narrative has attracted the attention of historians. Ramsay regarded it as:

> . . . the most instructive picture of society in an ancient city which has come down to us. . . . We are taken direct into the artisan life of Ephesus, and all is so true to common life, and so unlike what would occur to anyone writing at a distance, that the conclusion is inevitable: we have here a picture drawn from nature.

The terse account reads, says Charles Seltman, who had no sympathy for Paul's "puritanical" and Christian invasion of the Asian city, "like a modern press report." And Luke's book—writes A. N. Sherwin-White, in wider and more general terms, stressing the exactitude of the historical framework, with its precision of detail of time and place—conveys the feel and tone of provincial-city life, seen through the eyes of an alert Hellenistic Jew. Acts, he writes: "takes us on a conducted tour of the Greek and Roman world with detail and narrative so interwoven as to be inseparable."

For the Christian historian, it is a strong, clear light on the manner in which the new faith was cutting across established forms and patterns of pagan life in the first century. So it came about that Paul "fought with beasts at Ephesus" (1 Corinthians 15:32 KJV). Paul was catching up a phrase of Plato, picked up, perhaps, in his student days in Tarsus. Plato likened the mob to wild animals.

Two matters require some final word of notice or explanation. The story of the riot in Ephesus was Paul's first recorded encounter with the trade guilds, or *collegia*, a theme which was to cause deep problems for the Church, as is evidenced by Paul's first letter to Corinth and by passages in Peter's second letter, in Jude, and in Revelation.

These societies were not like today's trade unions. Their functions were primarily social, and they were multitudinous in ancient society. Records exist of guilds of bankers; doctors; architects; producers of woolen and linen goods; dyers; workers in metal, stone, or clay; builders; carpenters; farmers; gardeners; fishers; bakers; pastry cooks; barbers; embalmers; and transport workers. Their ramifications extended to such convivial groups as the Late Sleepers and the Late Drinkers, who have left their scribblings, in jest or earnest, on the walls of Pompeii. The collegia satisfied a need for the pleasures of social intercourse and self-expression.

On the other hand, the tumult at Ephesus is clear evidence that the social club, under adroit leadership, could become a political weapon in the hands of those whose economic interests coincided. Hence the sensitiveness of the Roman administration toward their institution. This is vividly illustrated by Trajan's prohibition of the formation of a fire brigade at Nicomedia; it is found in the letters of the Roman governor of Bithynia to the emperor in A.D. 111.

The situation in Ephesus was full of portent. Demetrius secured his prime objective: Paul withdrew. Although the tradition of Roman law stood firm, Paul no doubt clearly saw that a watchful State was likely to deal as severely with the Church as with its persecutors. He was, in fact, witnessing something sinister. A decade later, Nero was to canalize the dislike of the proletariat for the Christians, in a shocking persecution of the Church. The trade guilds were the first base of this hostility; the rank and file of common society turned on the Christians before organized authority struck out at them.

We must also look at the Asiarchs (31). This honorary assembly was a body of substantial citizens who were called upon to finance public spectacles and games in the Province of Asia. Perhaps such a festival was at the moment in train, with a vast influx of pilgrims and tourists providing more ample fuel for Demetrius' fiery speech. In such a case, the presiding Asiarchs would be most reluctant to have their great occasion spoiled by a riotous situation in the city. The Roman government, by whose grace and favor they held the honor, was most sensitive to any disturbance of the peace; and Ephesus, as a so-called free city, was anxious to avoid all cause of offense to the imperial authorities.

Asiarchs were elected for a fixed term of four years or less; and, when that term expired, the incumbent permanently retained the honorary title. It might be that several such men lived at Ephesus. Seeing they were (among other duties) the presiding priests of the imperial cult (the formal worship of the spirit of Rome and the empire, which later occasioned the disastrous clash between State and Church), they might not have been sorry to see the rise of any religion which weakened the influence of the prevailing cult of the Ephesian Artemis.

It may therefore be guessed that the Asiarchs passed a word of warning to Paul, not so much out of acceptance or regard for his Christian message, as because they approved of the social consequences of his activities. The Christian sometimes finds friends in unexpected places. It may also be true that they added a word of advice, if not a firm direction, to leave the city and not risk further mob action on the part of the silversmiths. Paul seems to have made a fairly prompt withdrawal across the

Aegean; and he never entered Ephesus again. A strong church had been founded, and of that church we are to hear more in the later pages of the New Testament. Paul was becoming accustomed to such retreats.

20

A Year's Work
(Acts 20:1–6)

When the tumult was over, Paul gathered the disciples together, said good-bye, encouraged them, and left for Macedonia.
Passing through those regions and with many words of encouragement, he came to Greece. Here he spent three months, and
when a plot was staged against him, as he was about to depart by
sea for Syria, he decided to return by way of Macedonia. Sopater
of Berea went with him as far as Asia; Aristarchus and Secun-
dus, both of Thessalonica; with Tychicus and Trophimus of
Asia. There were also Gaius of Derbe and Timotheus. These had
gone on ahead to wait for us at Troas. We set sail from Philippi,
after the Passover, and joined them in Troas after five days'
journey and stayed there seven days.

In 20:31 the period of the ministry in Ephesus is named as
three years. Those unnecessarily preoccupied with mathemati-
cal exactitude in a casual remark of Paul add up the three
months of 19:8 and the two years in 19:10 and allege inaccura-
cy. Defense is hardly necessary; but it might be remarked that,
in ancient enumeration, parts of three years could be legiti-
mately called "a space of three years," the term which is actually employed.

At any rate, after the "tumult" in Ephesus (Luke again uses
the word of 21:34 and 24:18), Paul, probably under the
Asiarchs' firm insistence, left Ephesus—possibly, again, with

Aquila and Priscilla, who appear in Rome later (Romans 16:3–5). Paul remarks in his letter that they risked much for his sake.

There follows a rapid account of almost a full year's activity, which Luke passes over with the utmost brevity. He was hastening on to his long account of "the passion of Paul," perhaps with the format of his first book in mind and seeing a similarity between the Lord's ascent to the city of pain (Luke 19:41–44) and the tragic journey to Jerusalem, which so interrupted the career and preaching of the apostle. Paul was heavily preoccupied with organizing the Gentile churches' collection for the impoverished community in Jerusalem. He had set high hopes on this, for it was of deep concern to him to heal an emerging rift between the mother congregation and the Christian assemblies of the non-Jewish world; and the westward sweep through Greece had this object, as well as evangelism and confirmation, in view.

Some reasonable attempts have been made to reconstruct, from other documents, the story that Luke so swiftly bypasses. From the most highly autobiographical of all the epistles, the second letter to Corinth (which may be a single communication or a conflation of two or three communications), it seems that Paul left Ephesus for Troas (or the associated region of the Troad) in some distress—not for peace, but for considerable affliction, as he says in his second letter, written, it appears, from Macedonia in the fall of A.D. 56, a year and a half after 1 Corinthians. (The problems are complex over both dates and events, and those interested are referred to detailed commentaries on the epistles.)

At any rate, Paul found abundant opportunity to evangelize a region where he had earlier been unable to exercise his ministry (Acts 20:6; 2 Corinthians 2:12)—a stay marred by his acute anxiety over the nonarrival of Titus, who had been sent on a vital mission to sort out and report upon the troubles which were assailing the Corinthian congregation. He interrupted his work and journeyed, no doubt over his old route, to Philippi (2 Corinthians 2:13). Perhaps he had heard that Titus was proceeding, by land, in that direction. Paul was relieved at the encouraging news that Titus brought to Macedonia (2 Corinthians 7:5–16), and it was in the mood of such relief that the apostle wrote the first seven chapters of his second epistle to the turbulent congregation on the isthmus.

He must have felt some welcome sense of confidence in them, if he could make so bold as to write the next two chapters, which take up a certain dilatoriness in the Corinthian response to his appeal for active participation in the Jerusalem collection (2 Corinthians 8, 9). Titus may then have been sent with the second letter and with him, as support, the brother "who is praised for his preaching of the Gospel in all the churches" (*see* 2 Corinthians 8:6, 16–18, 22). It is suggested that this was Luke himself, characteristically refraining, in his own book, from any reference to an important role he played. A third brother, who had "again and again been proved zealous in many ways," was also a member of the delegation.

The notably abrupt opening of chapter 10 of 2 Corinthians, with a theme which is followed to the close of chapter 13, seems to indicate that a further piece of news from Corinth spoke of a personal attack on Paul himself. Perhaps the Judaizing missionaries, after doing damaging work in Galatia, had arrived on the isthmus. There seems every indication that this pursuit of Paul was carefully organized—by whom, if not elements in the Jerusalem church? They seem already to have made the Jerusalem decree a dead letter. It might have been expected that Paul would conclude that his forthcoming personal conveyance of the Gentile gifts to Jerusalem was unlikely to alter for the better a most lamentable situation, but Paul was not a man to be easily deterred from a project upon which he had long set his heart.

So, it seems, a summer and an autumn passed—anxiously,

for such was Paul's temperament, but with much preaching and organizing activity. He went through "those parts," says Luke vaguely (2) and penetrated westward to the borders of Illyricum (Romans 15:19). This indicates no more than that he followed the Via Egnatia to its western terminal, on the coast of the Adriatic Sea, which touches the southern border of the provincial area of Illyricum, covering modern Albania and parts of Yugoslavia. Apart from the Greek settlements on the coast, this was a wild and mountainous area, which, as a vulnerable frontier, Augustus had long since brought under imperial control. The prince, assuming his function and office as *imperator,* or supreme commander of the armed forces, had judged it wise personally to control the legions allotted to the difficult task of stabilizing that part of Rome's defenses. It was not Paul's type of country at all, and there were none of those bases that his evangelical strategy always chose to visit. True, the Gospel seems to have penetrated Dalmatia (2 Timothy 4:10), but probably by diffusion from the Via Egnatia or the coast. Dalmatia was the name of the Illyrian province.

With the onset of the hard winter, which made northern travel difficult, Paul, along with Timothy and others, moved south on his promised visit to Corinth (1 Corinthians 16:6). Here, for a space of three months (3), he lodged with Gaius (Romans 16:23) and wrote his massive letter to the Roman Christians. It may be possible to infer, from the comparative serenity of this famous document of the faith, that Paul had personally triumphed over his detractors in Corinth and enjoyed a period of solid ministry.

But his Jewish enemies in the surviving synagogue of the port, still resentful over their discomfiture in the court of the proconsul, were bitterly vindictive; and news leaked out of a plot to murder Paul aboard the pilgrim ship which he proposed to board at Corinth. Recent Jewish scholarship, notably that of

Professor A. Fuks, of Jerusalem, has demonstrated the world-wide nature and, indeed, the international organization of the Jewish opposition in the empire—a fact revealed in blood and misery over the next eighty years. Jewish feeling was concentrating, at the time, to the flash point of the Great Rebellion. One, who, like Paul, was not only a Roman citizen by right of birth, but openly claimed his Roman rights in a context of imperial evangelism, must have been a prime target for Jewish resentment. He was the living symbol of a renunciation of the rising temperature of Jewish nationalism that was to find a climax in Jerusalem. On a pilgrim ship, the opportunities to be rid of such an enemy might have been many. Against this menace, Paul had recently asked for special prayer (Romans 15:30, 31), and it is the measure of his cool courage that he knew and faced such a threat.

The Gentile Christians, assuredly in close touch with Jewish feeling, did their utmost to dissuade Paul from such a perilous journey (22), but could do no more than make him change his itinerary and choose the safer detour through Macedonia (6). He was, however, determined to make a last attempt to cement a bond of love and trust between the Gentile and Jewish wings of the Church. It was a ministry he set above life itself (24), and so he turned resolutely from the warnings of "every city."

And was he impelled by some mystic urge to repeat, in some fashion, the Lord's last ascent to Jerusalem, to ". . . supplement [in his own person] the afflictions endured by the Christ . . . ," as he was to write to the Colossians? (1:24 TCNT). Or was he, in pursuance of this noble motive, in fact moving contrary to the revealed will of God? The warnings were to be further multiplied, and whether Paul was right to take the course he did is beyond others' decision. It certainly ended what appeared to be an expanding and a richly fruitful ministry, but produced the "prison epistles."

The first-person-plural pronoun in the narrative (5) indicates that Luke himself, with the considerable delegation which the convoy of a large sum of money demanded (if indeed it was carried in cash), joined Paul at Troas. It was one of his busiest years of Christian activity—all, in the economy of the record, confined to half-a-dozen verses.

Troas
(Acts 20:7–12)

On the first day of the week, when the disciples were gathered to break bread, Paul was speaking to them, for he intended to move out on the morrow. Paul continued his address until midnight, and there were a goodly number of lamps in the upstairs room where they were gathered. A youth named Eutychus was sitting in a window and, slipping into deep sleep as Paul went on and on preaching, at last, completely overcome by his drowsiness, fell from the third story and was picked up for dead. Paul went down, bent over him, and, folding him in his arms, said, "Do not fear, for his life is in him still." They returned to the upper room, broke bread, had a meal, and talked together until dawn. And so Paul departed. They brought the young man in alive and were not a little comforted.

The section gives a fascinating picture of an early church group in its common activities. They were probably Paul's recent converts, and their zeal to hear all they could about their newfound faith is humbling. All they had had come to them by personal testimony, and the conviction which animated the words of such evangelists as the great apostle must have been overwhelming. He had one night to spare, on his Jerusalem journey, and he used it all to instruct them.

They met on the first day of the week, which seems, as the

day of resurrection, to have been thus early set apart for the business of God (1 Corinthians 16:2). They met in the home of some member who was able to provide such accommodation—in this case an upper room, like the scene of the Lord's Supper, in a house pretentious enough to be three floors high. In the ruins of Herculaneum, such a third-level room may be seen, with the charred remains of a cross on the wall, to all appearences the meeting place of the local congregation. It could have belonged to Paul's hosts, perhaps, when he landed at Puteoli (28:13).

The occasion in Troas was an evening gathering, including a common meal or *agape,* the institution that proved the occasion of much abuse among the cruder elements of the Corinthian congregation. It might be inferred from this story that Paul had, as a result of the misconduct at Corinth, taken steps to separate the more formal observation of the Eucharist from the more general and social activities of the common meal. An upper room was often used as a dining room, and the words are rendered *cenaculum,* or "dining room," in the Latin versions.

The lamps have no ritual significance. Their rising fumes of oil were the reason for the deterioration of the atmosphere. The windows would be high in the wall, for more effective ventilation; and Eutychus had secured a vantage point on the sill, only better to expose himself to the stale air which rose and found exit there. Something in the nature of a coroner's verdict that concerns the death of a slave boy survives among the Egyptian papyri. The boy leaned too far out of such an alcove, to watch a passing troupe of musicians, and fell to his death on the street below.

Luke was a physician and appears, in his terse report, to confirm the fact that, on first observation, the youth was dead. It was a horrifying experience for Paul. Immersed in his long theme, he saw the poor boy, no doubt weary from a long day's work, fall from the alcove. In an agony of love, he rushed down, gave what today is called the kiss of life, and the victim breathed again. A congregation so earnest, staking faith on the apostle's word, would be mightily encouraged by such a miracle. Perhaps the people of Troas quipped on the boy's name— first belied, they would say, and then vindicated—for *Eutychus* means "lucky."

On to Miletus
(Acts 20:13–16)

We, going ahead to the ship, set sail for Assos, intending there to pick up Paul, for so it was arranged, while he purposed to go on foot. When he met us at Assos, we took him aboard and came to Mitylene. Sailing thence, we put in at a point opposite Chios, on the following day, and on the next arrived at Samos. With a stop at Trogyllium, we came the next day to Miletus. Paul intentionally sailed past Ephesus; for, in his haste to be in Jerusalem, if possible, for the day of Pentecost, he did not wish to spend time in Asia.

With a few rapid words, Luke takes us through seaways and places loaded with ancient history. Only a few miles from the port of Troas, Alexander's foundation, was Homer's Troy—the fortress of the great siege of Greek legend and Aegean history. Paul, for some reason that he may not have shared even with his traveling companions, chose to walk the twenty miles to Assos, a strategic strongpoint on the Gulf of Adramyttium in Mysia, facing south to the historic island of Lesbos. Mitylene was Lesbos' capital, home of the early poets "burning Sappho" and the fiery Alcaeus, whose meters were turned into Latin form by the Augustan poet Horace. Assos was a fortified port below a terraced hill that would make Paul's landmark as he trudged the long road with his thoughts. The island of Chios is as likely a place as any, amid the eight claimants, for the honor to have been the birthplace of Homer. Samos was the island of Polycrates, the dictator, whose fleet brought wealth and a golden age of art to a lovely island. Polycrates, a figure legendary for good fortune, sponsored poets like Simonides and Anacreon, until the Persian governor of Sardis murdered him. Trogyllium was a promontory some score of miles south of Ephesus and north of the mouth of the Maeander. It formed a narrow channel, barely a mile wide, between the mainland of Asia and Samos, but thus provided a protected roadstead in which a prudent shipmaster might anchor for the night, before running across the open gulf, to Miletus. Mitylene and Miletus were tangled with long tracts of Athenian and Ionian history. They had fathered colonies and participated in Aegean history from its beginnings.

Paul would know all this pageantry of history. He could hardly fail to remember that Cleanthes, the Stoic poet whom he quoted in Athens, was born at Assos. He had lived in the intellectual climate of Tarsus and was aware of the culture which was part of his heritage.

At the same time, he had much to ponder over the amazingly successful years of work in the Province of Asia. If Colossae, Laodicea, and Hierapolis lay within a few miles of each other, far up the Lycus valley, it is a fair guess that the whole frequented river plain was reticulated with churches. The seven to which John was to write, some thirty years later, were only a few of the successful foundations that Paul and his successors in the work had so firmly founded. They could be viewed with deep thankfulness and hope.

And was there, too, a quest for loneliness? Was he, in picturing the Lord's last visit to Jerusalem, seeking his own Jericho road? Christ trod it in spiritual solitude, his disciples bunched, disputing, in the rear. He ". . . set his face steadfastly to go to Jerusalem." Was Paul playing out a similar role? Christ knew what would happen there. Did Paul think that he knew, too, and faced it in the same way, to be like his Master?

Miletus
(Acts 20:17–38)

And from Miletus he sent to Ephesus and summoned the elders of the church. When they arrived, he spoke thus: "You know, yourselves, from the first day I set foot in Asia, the kind of life I lived with you throughout, serving the Lord with all lowliness of mind, and how, with many tears and the trials which I encountered from the plotting of the Jews, I shrank in no way from telling you what was good to tell or from preaching and teaching in public and in homes, witnessing to Jews and Greeks, repentance toward God and faith in our Lord Jesus Christ. And now, look, I go, bound in spirit, to Jerusalem, not knowing what will come upon me there, save that the Holy Spirit makes it clear to me from city to city that prison and tribulations wait. But I make nothing of this, nor hold my own life dear, if so be I may finish my course with joy and fulfill the commission I received from the Lord Jesus: to declare the Gospel of the grace of God. And now, look, I know that all of you, among whom I have gone about proclaiming the kingdom of God, will never see my face again. And that is why I call you to witness on this very day that I am clean of the blood of all men, for I have not shrunk from declaring to you the whole will of God.

"Be watchful, therefore, over yourselves and the whole flock over which the Holy Spirit has made you overseers, to shepherd the Church of God which he bought with his own blood. For I know this, that, after I am gone, savage wolves will enter, who will not spare the flock; and from your own number men will arise to seduce the disciples to follow them, with perverted words. Watch then, remembering that for a space of three years continually I counseled each one of you, day and night, with tears. And now, brethren, I commend you to God and the word of his grace, which is able to build you up and give you an inheritance among all whom he has sanctified. I have not sought, from anyone, silver, gold, or clothes, for you know yourselves that these hands have served my own needs and my companions', too. I have in every way shown you how that by so working you must support the weak and bear in mind the words of the Lord Jesus: 'It is more blessed to give than to receive.' " This said, he knelt down with all of them and prayed. There was lamentation from them all, and, embracing Paul, they kissed him, sorrowing most over his saying that they would not see his face again. They went with him to the ship.

Paul had bypassed Ephesus, and the harbor at this time was in no condition to accommodate ships of any size. We have no information concerning the draught of Paul's vessel or whether the master's routing dictated the port of call. At the same time, his firm insistence to the elders of Ephesus that they would never see him again does reinforce the suggestion, already made, that he had undertaken not to visit the city again. Miletus almost served as a port for Ephesus, and a stay there to take on or unload cargo gave Paul the opportunity to meet the elders of Ephesus. It is suggested by indomitable critics that the evident firm organization of the Ephesian congregation demands a date twenty years later. Certainly, writing a few years later, to Timothy, in Ephesus, Paul has much to say on church government. This merely elaborates rules which require little invention, and the leaders of the Church were men who lived in ordered societies with systems of leadership manifest everywhere: the free cities, provinces, trade guilds, and the rest. An eldership was no outstanding novelty.

Paul's perceptive warning, from his long acquaintance with

the city, spoke of tensions to come. They came, and a letter of John is the witness. John became the leader of the Ephesian church. When he was in Patmos, during Domitian's persecution, he addressed cryptic letters to seven of the churches of Asia. It was prudent to write in the style of Hebrew apocalyptic literature.

Ephesus, as was proper, was the first church John addressed. The letter reveals that Paul's forebodings were well-founded. There was much to commend the church, which is thus glimpsed a generation from its foundation. Three years in the school of Tyrannus had laid a firm base. But the weariness of a declining city had seeped into the church; and the spirit of compromise, which had been an instinct in the city's artificial and curiously mingled religious life, had produced the group known as the Nicolaitans, who sought for some means of accommodation with the pagan environment. Of this group we should gladly know more. They were probably Greek converts who saw their own mystery cults as a species of preparation for Christianity and looked, with a kindlier eye than either Paul or John would have sanctioned, on the practice and ritual of pagan cults.

Perhaps the Nicolaitans had some such preoccupations. Perhaps, too, they were those who saw in the Caesar cult only a harmless ritual of loyalty and not an issue of man worship on which a Christian need stake life and livelihood. Ephesus, at any rate, taught by two apostles, had rejected such compromise. On the other hand, the hothouse intellectual life which was inseparable from Ionian Greece, first seedbed of Greek thought, had produced its crop of false teachers, even as Paul had forseen; and the Christian community's first glow of enthusiasm had cooled. It is the fashion of a church, as Ramsay brilliantly demonstrated, to interpret in its attitudes the defects and the qualities of the society in which it functions; and Ephesus, old in history, past its glory, and economically stagnant, was weary.

It is a notable fact that this is the only speech reported by him which Luke actually heard in person. This in no way diminishes the authenticity of the rest. Paul and his companions were highly literate men, and there is nothing more likely than that a record would be kept of highly important utterances.

The speech to the elders rings with truth. Pauline words, expressions, sentiments, which find identical form in his epistles, can be noted throughout. The man, too, appears in full-length portrait: independent, no seeker after popular approval, consciously responsible for those to whom he spoke or ministered, urgent in his faithfulness, indefatigable in his evangelism, wise, penetrating in his insight. He had never "trimmed his sails in preaching," he says, using in verses 20 and 27 a word for reefing sail, suggested perhaps by the crowded port and his own ship nearby. He knew there was no other message, and he presented it unmodified; but he knew life, and he knew history, and that trouble would undoubtedly come. It came, indeed, but as far as a man could build a wall against it, Paul had done just that.

And there is a small glimpse into his mind and some indication why he disregarded so many warnings not to continue on to Jerusalem. He does seem to be convinced of God's command and, in the light of such convictions, might regard all dissuasion as a testing of his determination.

As he said, he never returned to Ephesus. It seems clear that, after his Roman imprisonment, Paul had a period of liberty and visited Troas, possibly the place of his arrest, in A.D. 66 or 67, but in Ephesus Timothy and John took over.

21

Voyage Continued
(Acts 21:1–9)

When at last we had parted from them and had set sail, we made a straight run to Cos, the next day to Rhodes, and thence to Patara. Coming across a vessel bound for Phoenicia, we went aboard and set sail. Sighting Cyprus, we left it behind on the left, and, making for Syria, docked at Tyre, where the ship was to unload. Having sought out the Christians there, we stayed a week with them. They kept urging Paul, through the Spirit, not to go up to Jerusalem. When our visit was over, we set out on our way, and they all came out to see us off, women and children, too, outside the city, where we knelt on the beach and prayed. When we had bade each other farewell, we went aboard, and they back home. Continuing our voyage from Tyre, we came to Ptolemais, where, greeting the brethren, we stayed one day. The next day, we of Paul's party set out, went on to Caesarea, and found hospitality in the house of Philip, the evangelist, one of "the Seven." He had four unmarried daughters, who spoke God's word.

The journey through islands and coasts rich in legend and history continues. It appears that, given a measure of good fortune with the weather, a well-appointed ship could make a series of straight runs eastward before the Zephyrs, the west winds that blew down the Mediterranean.

Cos was one of the centers of Jewish life in the Aegean and

had ancient contacts with the Jews, as references in the books of the Maccabees and Josephus show. The island was some forty nautical miles from Miletus. It was the birthplace of the painter Apelles and—perhaps a point of special interest to Luke—was also the birthplace of the great master of Greek medicine, Hippocrates. There was still a medical school there.

Rhodes (the word means "rose") lay south of Caria, a sun-drenched, large island, chief of the Dodecanese, whose coins boasted, on one side, a radiant head of Apollo and a rose on the other. It is unlikely that Paul put into the port where the mighty colossus, another of the Seven Wonders of the World, lay, at this time, prostrate, after an earthquake; but he could have put into Lindos, in the northwest, where a snug little harbor under the high acropolis actually bears Paul's name. Rhodes was once a considerable nation in its own right, a naval power, and the ally of Rome. The books of the Maccabees speak of Jewish residents here, too.

Patara was on the Lycian coast, a city of some splendor. Ships in large numbers plied this route; and the party found, without delay, a larger vessel bound for Tyre. It must have been of some size, for it took a week to discharge its cargo. Cyprus was evidently one of its marking points, and Luke uses a seaman's term (3), "showing up Cyprus." It was a straight run from here down to the age-old port of the Phoenician cedar trade. Tyre was a place of consequence and ancient history and was, along with Sidon, an imperial capital of old Phoenicia. From here ships had sailed to Cornwall for tin and had circum-navigated Africa, hundreds of years before.

A moving little picture of the Tyrian congregation follows, with all of them, women and children, too, escorting the party back to the dock and kneeling in prayer on the sand.

The warnings about Jerusalem continued, but Paul was un-moved and went on to Ptolemais (today's Acco, which was also a maritime stronghold of the Crusaders). Thence they came down to Caesarea and lodged with Philip, who had worked in the Roman garrison town for twenty years. Here Luke may have acquired his material for Philip's story in chapter eight. Four unmarried daughters had an important ministry in the Church. They were "prophetesses," as the King James Version puts it—the Elizabethan word for "preachers." (Jeremy Taylor's work on the "Liberty of Prophesying" was not written to uphold some freedom to predict, but freedom to preach.)

Up to Jerusalem
(Acts 21:10–16)

> We had stayed there for some days when there came down a prophet from Judaea, named Agabus. He came to see us, took Paul's belt, and, binding his own hands and feet, said: "Thus says the Holy Spirit: 'So shall the Jews of Jerusalem bind the owner of this belt and betray him into the hands of the Gentiles.' " Hearing this, both we and the local Christians begged him not to go up to Jerusalem. Paul replied, "What are you doing, weeping and breaking my heart? For I am ready, for the name of the Lord, not only to be bound, but even to die at Jerusalem." When he could not be persuaded, we fell silent and said, "The Lord's will be done." Then we loaded our baggage and set out for Jerusalem. Some of the disciples of Caesarea went with us, including one Mnason of Cyprus, an original disciple, with whom we were going to stay.

Agabus of 11:27, 28 appears again with symbolic warning reminiscent of the Old Testament prophets (1 Kings 22:11; Isaiah 20:2; Jeremiah 13:1; Ezekiel 4, 5). Luke had never met him before; but, apart from any special enlightenment, Agabus knew the state of the capital and the growing bitterness of the Jews. The great clash with Rome was looming.

Paul's obstinacy before what seems such obvious guidance is

difficult to understand. In a minor way, he had taken a few precautions. The swift voyage east from the Aegean had left him time to spare, and he used that time in Caesarea. Perhaps he had the Lord's example in mind (John 7:1–10); on that occasion, the journey to Jerusalem had been concealed, by Jesus, from even his brothers. It was sixty-five miles up to the city, and Paul gives the appearance of so timing his arrival as to leave no spare days into which the danger might be extended. Perhaps, too, if he was in the grip of some mystic parallelism, he saw Caesarea as his Gethsemane. The Lord spoke of his coming passion three times. Paul was three times warned—a point not to be pressed too far.

James' Mistake
(Acts 21:17–26)

When we arrived at Jerusalem, the brethren gave us a warm welcome, and the next day Paul went with us to visit James. All the elders were there, too. After greeting them, he told in detail all that God had done among the Gentiles through his ministry. When they heard it, they glorified God, and James said, "You observe, brother, how many tens of thousands of Jews believe, and all of them are zealots for the Law. But they have been informed of you that you teach all the Jews among the Gentiles to forsake Moses, telling them not to circumcise their children or to observe the customs. What then must be done? It is quite certain that a crowd will gather, for they will hear that you have arrived. Do, then, what we suggest. We have four men who are under a vow. Take them, undergo the rites of purification with them, and meet their expenses, that they may have their hair cut and all may know that there is no basis for the reports about you and that you yourself live in obedience to the Law. As regards the believing Gentiles, we have sent word deciding that they

need observe no such thing, save to abstain from what is sacrificed to idols, from blood and things strangled, and from fornication." So Paul took the men, and the next day, sanctifying
himself, went into the temple to give notice of the fulfillment of
the days of purification and until an offering should be made for
each of them.

Luke may have been in one of his moods of brevity in the
first verses of this revealing passage, but it is not easy to explain
why he should be. When he handed the solid evidence of the
Gentiles' goodwill over to the metropolitan eldership, Paul
reached a climax of years of earnest endeavor and anticipation.
Had it won any measure of success, one might have expected
some clear word from the historian.

A reasonable reading of the situation might be this: James
and the elders received Paul cordially enough, but his arrival
was highly embarrassing to them. Hence the haste with which
they turned from his account of the success of his Gentile evangelism to the "myriads" of Jews in the Church, all of whom,
they hasten to add, are "zealots for the Law." In other words,
the Jerusalem church's leaders had a situation beyond their
control and, having accommodated the Gentiles by what they
regarded as the most magnanimous of concessions, were now
disposed to recognize, if not two grades, at least two species of
Christians: those who had not been brought up to recognize the
Law and those who, having once apprehended it, were bound,
in conscience, to graft their Christianity on to it.

The Judaizing emissaries who so dogged Paul's steps, may, in
fact, have justified their activities with the thought that all they
sought to do was ensure that Jewish Christians in a Gentile
environment did not claim emancipation to which, as enlightened ones, they had no right. The whole attitude of the Jerusalem church had evidently changed over the years. The strong

presence of Peter and other apostles was removed; they were busy with remote evangelism. The Herodian persecution had scattered the original clear-thinking and liberated Christians. Pharisees were moving into the Church in numbers, and the epistle to the Hebrews is evidence that it was their Jewishness that prevailed and tended, in many, to immerse their essential Christianity.

James understood Paul, but his own epistle is clear evidence that he thought Paul expressed freedom in Christ in terms too downright and needed a gently restraining hand.

He was an anxious man, doing his best to avoid a split in the Church and seeing hope in such endeavor only if Paul would make some slight gesture of reconciliation—as if the large sum of money which Paul had handed him was not in itself some contribution to this end. In the minds of the bigoted, all such munificence weighed little, beside the petty observance of "the customs," which Paul had long since repudiated, in spite of his strange act at Cenchrea. Was he trying to show, by his still relatively short hair, that he did, in fact, function as a practicing Jew? If so, James unreasonably wanted more. He mentions, or the elders mention, with scant tact, the shaky reputation Paul had, after all his mighty work in two continents, among the narrow-minded members of the Jerusalem congregation.

This is the situation into which Paul, overly anxious about his old associates, had betrayed himself. And, after all, what had he written, in so many words, to the church at Corinth? (1 Corinthians 9:19–23). Let him now put such noble principles of compromise into salutary action! Paul still saw the Jerusalem church as the rightful and original head, and he was not to know that the storm of the next decade was to sweep the Jerusalem church, with its hesitations and reservations, into the limbo of history. Imprudently, he obeyed James' and the elders' directive. It was disaster.

Riot
(Acts 21:27–40)

And when the seven days were over, the Jews from Asia, catching sight of him in the temple, stirred up the whole crowd and laid hands on him, shouting, "Men of Israel, help. This is the man who is teaching everyone, everywhere, against the people, the Law, and this place; and, what is more, he has brought Greeks into the temple and profaned this sacred place." (They had seen Trophimus, the Ephesian, with him in the city, and surmised that Paul had brought him into the temple.) The whole city was in an uproar, and a crowd quickly gathered. Laying hold of Paul, they dragged him out of the inner temple area, and the doors were closed. As they were trying to kill him, word came to the tribune in command of the cohort that all Jerusalem was in a tumult. He immediately took troops, with their centurions, and charged down upon them. Seeing the tribune and the troops, they stopped beating Paul. The tribune came up, arrested Paul, and ordered him to be bound with two chains, asking who he was and what he had done. Some among the crowd cried one thing and some another, and, unable to find the truth amid the din, the officer ordered him to be taken into the fort. When Paul reached the stairs, he was actually being carried by the soldiers, because of the violence of the crowd, for the whole mass of them were following, yelling, "Away with him." As Paul was about to be taken into the fort, he asked the tribune, "May I have a word with you?" "You know Greek?" he said. "Are you not that Egyptian who recently roused a riot and took out into the desert four thousand of the Knifemen?" Paul replied, "I am a Jew of Tarsus, in Cilicia, a citizen of no mean city. I am asking you to allow me to speak to the people." Turning about, as he stood upon the steps, Paul signed with his hand to the people. There was complete silence, and he addressed them thus in the Hebrew tongue.

This is a piece of reporting as vivid as the story of the riot in Ephesus. Paul had forgotten the Jews of Asia, from whom he had precariously escaped, but they had him now. There is nothing more insanely dangerous than a mob substituting slogans for truth, and the Jews of Ephesus had been ready pupils of their Greek hosts in rabble-rousing and disturbance.

The foursquare Tower of Fort Antonia, occupying the present site of the Convent of the Sisters of Zion, was attached to the corner of the common court of the temple, to keep watch for exactly this type of disturbance. A cohort of picked troops always garrisoned it at times of Jewish festival, when such riotous elements as the Ephesian Jews were in town. A stairway led down to the court, for quick access to deal with precisely this eventuality.

It is interesting to see a Roman riot squad in action. A tribune was equivalent in rank to a colonel in a modern military force, and he led the rescue operation personally. Here is a well-told story, focusing on the strong efficiency with which the troops, apparently reinforced by a number of tough centurions, snatched Paul from a murderous mob.

Paul made no attempt to reveal his Roman citizenship at this early stage, and his commanding presence is quite evident in the whole story. In the midst of a violent task of riot control, the senior officer pauses to listen to him, battered half to death though he was. Paul actually persuades him to allow him to speak to the raving crowd; on the steps, he was behind the soldiers' barricade of spears. He lifts his hand, and the tumult dies, to be replaced by deep silence. The stamp of reality is over the whole story, but what a triumph of supreme self-control in the chief actor in the scene. Did Paul remember Agabus?

22

Paul's Speech
(Acts 22:1–22)

"Brothers and fathers, hear now my defense which I make before you." (When they heard him addressing them in the Hebrew tongue, they kept the greater silence.) And he said, "I am indeed a Jew born in Tarsus, a city of Cilicia, but educated in this city, at the feet of Gamaliel, and taught according to the strict manner of our fathers' Law—as zealous for God as all of you here today. And I am the one who persecuted this Way to the death, chaining and handing over for prison both men and women. For that the high priest is my witness and all the eldership. Receiving letters of introduction to our Jewish fellowship there, I set out for Damascus, to bring those who were there back to Jerusalem for punishment.

"As I came near Damascus, on my journey, round midday, suddenly a great light from heaven shone round me. I fell to the ground and heard a voice saying to me, 'Saul, Saul, why are you persecuting me?' I replied, 'Who are you, Lord?' And he said, 'I am Jesus of Nazareth, whom you are persecuting.' They that were with me, although they saw the light and were alarmed, did not hear the voice which spoke to me. I said, 'What shall I do, Lord?' And he answered, 'Get up and go into Damascus, and there you shall be told about everything which has been set out for you to do.'

"Since I could not see for the glory of that light, led by my company, I reached Damascus; and one Ananias, a devout man and obedient to the Law and of good standing among all the Jews resident there, came to me and, standing there, said, 'Brother Saul, see again.' Then and there I looked up at him. And he said, 'Our fathers' God has chosen you to know his will, to see the Righteous One, and hear the words of his mouth, for you shall be his witness to all men of what you have seen and heard. Now why delay? Arise, be baptized and wash away your sins, calling on the name of the Lord.'

"And, one day, after I had returned to Jerusalem and was praying in the temple, I lost awareness of all else and saw him saying to me, 'Hurry, and get quickly out of Jerusalem, for they will not receive your witness about me.' I answered, 'Lord, they themselves know that I was imprisoning and flogging round the synagogues those who believe in you, and when the blood of your martyr Stephen was shed, I, too, was standing and approving of his murder, even looking after the clothes of those who were murdering him.' And he said to me, 'Depart, for I shall send you afar off to the Gentiles.' "

They listened to him up to this word, but now raised their voice, saying, "Away with such a fellow from the earth, for he does not deserve to live."

Paul's defense is a pure statement of experience. Somewhere on the Damascus road, perhaps somewhere near where the highway over the Golan Heights bends northeast beyond Kuneitra, Paul met Christ. This was no hallucination. The power of Paul's mind had been demonstrated in two continents, where he had already loosed forces which were to change the course of history. In more situations than the present one on the Fort Antonia stairway, he had demonstrated the iron control he had over mind and body.

Luke is telling the familiar story again, because it is vital to his purpose. Paul was not anti-Jewish; he was not a leader of sedition. He was a man called to a task; he harmed no one by fulfilling it and did only good. The foes of the faith, as three procurators saw, were not good men, but entrenched leaders, at all costs determined to hold to their position. Rome found it expedient, in the interests of peace on a difficult tract of frontier, to work in with such people; but Luke wishes to make it quite clear that Christianity and its chief global proponent, Paul, were no peril to the administration.

A few difficulties of chronology between this and the earlier account of Paul's conversion have been imagined. Since Paul must have seen Luke's narrative, since Paul personally told Luke about the Damascus road and what followed, and since Luke witnessed the present incident, vital discrepancies are impossible. If some appear, it is due to some vital fragment of information or circumstantial link being missing, and it is of no consequence at all.

The mob is frightening. The Romans should have taken more careful note of the tempest of passion the very word *Gentile* roused. Matters, as the next few chapters show, were almost out of hand in Judaea, as the nation lurched, as though under some strange compulsion, toward the awful tragedy of the First Jewish War. Jewish nationalism throughout the world was reaching a volcanic explosion point; this was a most sinister portent.

Paul and Lysias
(Acts 22:23–30)

While they were shouting, tossing their garments about, and throwing dust into the air, the tribune ordered Paul to be brought into the fort and questioned under the lash, to find out the cause of their outcry against him. And as they were stretching him out with their bonds, Paul said to the centurion standing by, "Is it permitted you to scourge a Roman citizen, without trial?"

On hearing this, the centurion approached the tribune and

said, "Look at what you are going to do, for this man is a Roman." The tribune came up and said to him, "Tell me, are you a
Roman?" "Yes," he replied. The tribune replied, "I acquired this
citizenship at great expense." Paul said, "I was even born a Roman." Those who were about to examine him drew back from
him, immediately, and the tribune was alarmed when he found
that he was a Roman and that he had put him in chains.

The next day, desiring to know the facts and what charges
there were from the Jews, he released him and commanded the
high priests and all the Sanhedrin to appear. He brought Paul
down and set him before them.

The disgraceful exhibition of mob hysteria at the foot of the
stairway does no credit to the Jews. The tossed dust was symbolic of the stones they would gladly have thrown, and it was
only one word which had released the storm of hate. In spite of
the nerve-shaking violence to which he had been subjected,
Paul had sought, in complete command of himself, to conciliate
the crowd. He postponed, as far as possible, any reference to
the Gentiles, even, at one point, modifying the very words of
Christ to do so (15).

It was too late, and, when the door of the fort closed behind
him, Paul was truly in the custody of the Romans. He was to
remain therein for five years. Within the fort there was dis-
played a remarkable exhibition of Rome in action. The tribune
in command of the garrison was a career soldier; that he was a
Greek is shown by his name, Lysias. He had taken the name of
the emperor Claudius when, by a bribe—probably to the notorious freedmen Pallas and Narcissus—he acquired the Roman
citizenship, still a valuable asset in the world. It was a guarantee
of a fair trial; it carried the right of appeal to a higher court, as
Paul's action was soon to demonstrate. Lysias seems to have
been a vigorous and capable soldier who had easy relationships

with the officers on his staff (26). The centurion was eager that his commanding officer should not make a mistake.

Paul made a great impression upon him. At a word, Paul could still infuriate a dangerous crowd. Lysias had felt it safe to allow an unidentified prisoner to do so. And now he discovered that, by right of birth, Paul was a Roman citizen. It is an interesting demonstration of the "first European" in action. Paul was the first person known to history who visibly bore in his own person the integrated heritage of the three cultures—Hebrew, Greek, and Latin—from which European civilization has, over the centuries, sprung. It was his speaking Greek which first caught the attention of the Roman tribune. He tamed the crowd with a speech in the Hebrew dialect of Aramaic. He quietly claimed, and was granted, his rights as a citizen of Rome. Lysias probably could not follow the Aramaic speech. Most of his spell of duty in Judaea was spent in the garrison town of Caesarea, where Greek and Latin were the common languages, and he may have felt a little irked by the fact that a great concession accorded the prisoner had ended in a renewed uproar. He would not have been assigned to his command in Jerusalem in the explosive days of festival time, had the high command not judged him capable of the required standards of tact and expertise; most Jewish situations demanded increasingly delicate tasks of race relations.

And now, for the fifth time, the supreme religious court of Jewry was about to adjudicate on the Christian Church. Lysias was probably well briefed. Rome was handling the deepening menace, on this vital frontier, with delicacy and care. The tribune was eager to leave no cause for complaint in the hands of the collaborating hierarchy; and—in pursuance of a policy toward the Jews, which Pilate's heavy-handed conduct of his procuratorship had shown to be necessary—Lysias set Paul before the senior tribunal of his own people.

23

Sanhedrin
(Acts 23:1–10)

Looking steadily at the Sanhedrin, Paul said, "Brethren, with a good conscience toward God I have lived as a citizen until this day. . . ." At which the high priest Ananias told those standing by him to hit him across the mouth. Then Paul said to him, "God shall strike you, you whitewashed wall. And you are sitting there to judge me in accordance with the Law, and you bid me be smitten, contrary to the Law?" Those standing by said, "Do you revile the high priest thus?" Paul replied, "Brethren, I did not know that it was the high priest, for the Scripture stands: 'You shall not speak evilly to the ruler of the people.' "

Observing that half of them were Sadducees and half Pharisees, Paul cried, "Brethren, I am a Pharisee, like my father before me. Concerning the hope of the resurrection of the dead I am called to judgment." When he said this, a dissension arose between the Pharisees and the Sadducees, and the assembly was divided; for the Sadducees say that there is no resurrection, nor angel nor spirit, while the Pharisees believe in both. There was general uproar, and the scribes of the Pharisees' faction were on their feet, contending, "We find no evil in this man. If a spirit or an angel has spoken to him, let us not fight a battle with God." When the dissension became intense, the tribune, fearing lest Paul be torn apart by them, ordered a squad of troops down to snatch him from their midst and take him to the fort.

The tribune, watching—it might be supposed—from the stairway, must have been astonished at the turbulence of the high court of the Jews. Paul evidently misread the occasion. The Sanhedrists saw it as a trial in which he was not to speak unless called upon to make defense. He regarded it as an opportunity for an apologia. He did not know the high priest, hence his rather grudging apology. It had been a generation since he had seen that court in session.

Ananias is not the Annas of the Gospels and Acts 4:6. He was a Herodian appointment, quite recently in office, and one confirmed, for their own reasons, by Rome. He seems to have held office until the departure of Felix. His strong support of Rome earned universal hatred, and Josephus has a good deal to say about his atrocities. When the land exploded in A.D. 66, he was a prompt victim of mob violence, was dragged from a sewer, and was knifed by the murderers he had not scrupled to use during his ascendancy. To describe Ananias, Paul uses a word of Christ (Matthew 23:27). Tombs were whitewashed to guard against accidental contact at sacred festivals—a mischance which might preclude participation in the ceremony.

Paul had meanwhile been getting his bearings. Few faces were familiar to him, in the gathering, but he remembered how the worldly Sadducees and the legalistic Pharisees had formed a brief alliance to destroy Christ. He may also have been conscious that it was the Resurrection which had formed a point of contact with the Pharisees in the first teaching of the Church. The Pharisees seem to have turned Gamaliel's advice (5:39) into an item of policy. He saw that ordered discussion was impossible and proceeded to exploit the situation. The disciplined action of the Romans in the whole context of events stood in strange contrast with the passionate division in the great court of the Jews; and it so angered him that he cleverly added fuel to the smoldering fire. How much of the whole occasion would be comprehensible to Lysias is impossible to say.

Paul could see, at any rate, that constructive argument would be fruitless and so appealed to his own group, the Pharisees, with whom he at least had a point of contact. The worldly, venal, heretical Sadducees were, in any case, beyond all argument of piety or reason. F. W. Farrar, one of Paul's early great biographers, condemns Paul for thus dividing the assembly, but W. M. Ramsay has a convincing reply, if one is necessary:

> His defence was always the same, and therefore carefully planned: that his life had been consistently directed towards one end, the glorification of the God of Israel by admitting the Nations to be his servants, and that this was true Judaism and true Pharisaism.

Hence the relevance of the defense before the Sanhedrin. "If one party," Ramsay continues, "was more capable of being brought to a favorable view of his claims than the other, he would naturally and justifiably aim at affecting the minds of the more hopeful party." That is exactly what Paul did at Athens, when he addressed himself, almost exclusively, to the Stoic element in his audience. He was claiming, moreover, to represent the true line of development in which Judaism ought to advance.

For the second time in two days, a Roman military riot unit was forced to rescue Paul from the hands of a murderous Jewish assembly. The conduct of the priests must have not a little amazed the Roman officers.

The Plotters
(Acts 23:11–15)

> The following night, the Lord stood by him and said, "Take courage, Paul, for as you have borne witness about me in Jerusalem, so you must bear witness in Rome." The next morning,

some of the Jews got together and bound themselves by an oath
not to take food or drink until they had killed Paul. There were
more than forty in the plot. They approached the chief priests
and elders and said, "We have taken a solemn oath not to eat or
drink until we have killed Paul. Now we want you, along with
the Sanhedrin, to indicate to the tribune that you want him to
bring Paul down to you tomorrow, as though you were going to
make a more precise judgment on him. Before he gets near you,
we are ready to do away with him."

It was a mad plot. If the officers, of whom we know five
centurions and one tribune, give the impression of being men of
exceptionable caliber, picked for service in Rome's most difficult province, it can also be certain that the centurions concerned picked the men for their own centuries. For a band of
fanatical Jews to imagine that they could murder Paul before he
was presented to the assembled Sanhedrists and after he had
left the fort involved a direct attack on a platoon of the best
men in the Jerusalem detachment—those up from Caesarea on
a special assignment and therefore alert for trouble. The plotters had small chance of success.

Their pledge not to eat or drink until they had effected their
purpose was without much meaning. They missed the first meal
of the day—no more. And, in any scribal or Pharisaic situation,
there were abundant formulas of discharge or absolution available, to make it quite certain that none of the frustrated plotters
unfortunately died of thirst or hunger. Sophistic devices could
circumvent any of the inconveniences which their absurd med-
dlings had loaded onto the grand Mosaic laws.

The central figure in the whole sorry drama most claims our
attention: the great man himself, who, but a few days earlier,
had arrived in Jerusalem, so full of hope. Now, a prisoner of
Rome and the old foes of his Lord, he was receiving no re-

corded help—if help, indeed, were possible—from the Christians of the capital of Jewry. Picture Paul's state of mind. He had passed through days of terrible mental and spiritual stress. He had escaped a plot against his life and was about to hear of another. He had been twice rescued, by force, from the insane violence of his own people. He must have been deeply hurt by the narrow-minded group of his own fellow Christians who had demanded a demonstration of formal agreement with their erroneous prejudices and, in so doing, had opened the path to catastrophe.

He must also have been overwhelmed by misgivings, for he had battled his way to Jerusalem and this disastrous suffering, against roadblock after roadblock of advice to retreat. Like Abraham, who had flung his hastily armed shepherds against an invading force from the Euphrates Valley and had faced, in the outcome and with time to weigh the consequences, a painful collapse of confidence, Paul needed a word from God (1). The great Abraham was Paul's hero. He had pondered deeply over the life and adventures of the patriarch. It seems not by accident that, in his moment of crisis, in those somber hours of the night when the darkness of heaven seems to penetrate the soul, he received a word from the Lord which is almost an echo of the word which came to Abraham (Genesis 15:1).

The encouragement sets no seal of divine approval on Paul's journey to Jerusalem. The wisdom of that enterprise still stands open to question. But it is like God, in such dark hours of the soul, to show some token of his love.

Paul's Nephew
(Acts 23:16–22)

But Paul's nephew, hearing of the plot, went into the fort and told Paul. Summoning one of the centurions, Paul said, "Take this young man to the tribune. He has something to report to him." The centurion took him to the tribune and said, "The prisoner Paul summoned me and asked me to bring this young man to you, for he has a matter to talk about to you."

The tribune, taking his hand and drawing him aside, asked him what it was he had to tell him. He answered, "The Jews have plotted to ask you to take Paul down to the Sanhedrin tomorrow, as though intending to make more detailed inquiry about him. Do not be persuaded by them, for more than forty of them are going to lie in wait for him, men who have bound themselves by an oath not to eat or drink until they have made away with him. They are all ready at this moment, awaiting your consent."

The tribune dismissed the young man with the caution, "Talk to nobody about what you have revealed to me."

The plot, quite unexpectedly, throws a ray of light on Paul's family, the only scrap of information we possess. Paul's nephew was his sister's son. If the secret plotting of the fanatics became known to Paul's sister, the family must have had the highest connections in the city. It was, moreover, an act of no small courage thus to lay information. The deference with which Lysias treats the boy is also notable. Had the Tarsus family moved to Jerusalem, or was the boy studying, like his uncle, and was his mother there on a visit or to make a home for him?

Loyalty is a pleasant sight; and, after his night of darkness, Paul must have seen in his sister's and nephew's love yet another token of God's continuing care for him. And it would come with greater sweetness to him if such loyalty was seen against a background of family repudiation. John Pollock, commenting on Paul's home circumstances, remarks, "My personal reading of the scanty extant evidence is that Paul was . . . a widower, or, more probably, had been repudiated by his wife when he returned to Tarsus a Christian—he suffered the loss of all things for Christ." Was Pollock wrong, or was repudiation not complete? However this may be, Paul's sister and her son saved Paul from danger.

To Caesarea
(Acts 23:23–35)

The tribune called two centurions and ordered, "Get ready two centuries of troops, and go to Caesarea, with seventy horsemen and two hundred auxiliaries, to start after the third hour of the night; and provide horses for Paul to ride and bring him safe to Felix, the governor." And he wrote a letter, somewhat as follows, "Greetings to his excellency, the Governor Felix, from Claudius Lysias. This man was seized by the Jews and was on the point of being killed by them. Coming on them with a detachment of troops, I rescued him, having found out that he was a Roman citizen. Wanting to know of what they were accusing him, I brought him to their Sanhedrin. I found the charges had to do with controversial matters of their own law and nothing meriting death or imprisonment. But when I was informed that a plot was being put together by the Jews against him, I sent him to you promptly, charging his accusers also to state their case before you. Farewell."

The soldiers, according to their orders, took Paul and brought him by night to Antipatris. The next day, they left the cavalry to escort him and went back to the fort. When the cavalry detachment reached Caesarea, they delivered the letter to the governor and set Paul before him. The governor read the letter and asked of what province he came. Learning that he was from Cilicia, he said, "I will hear your case as soon as your accusers are come." And he ordered him to be kept in Herod's praetorium.

Lysias' special arrangements reveal a man prepared to take

no chances in a quite difficult situation. Imagine the desperate state of the country, illustrated by the revealing fact that it required a detachment of 470 troops to ensure the safety of one political prisoner traveling down the descending road to Caesarea. This was probably the highroad down to the coastal plain, where, today, the shattered trucks and jeeps lie in the scrub, as a memorial of another guerrilla-haunted year. The situation in Palestine must have been grave indeed, and it seems clear that firm Roman control was practically confined to the cities.

The chapter closes with a last glance at the tribune. He takes a small liberty with the truth, if Luke's précis does the letter justice, when he advances the hour of his concern for Paul's status as a Roman. It was a neater story, sets Lysias in a somewhat more favorable light, and is quite in character. He was a good officer, and his efficiency reinforces the suggestion that the imperial government set some store by the type of man chosen for service in a difficult land.

Paul was now at least safe. The garrison port of Caesarea, Rome's bridgehead and base, was completely secure. There was a church community there. Philip lived there, and there was no safer stronghold in all the land. Paul was free to write and Luke to pursue his researches through the land. The third Gospel was the result, and the "acts of Peter." The extensive ruins of Caesarea, visible today, are of immense Christian significance.

24

Trial
(Acts 24:1-9)

After five days, Ananias, the high priest, came down, along with the elders and an orator named Tertullus, who formally stated their case against Paul to the governor. When Paul had been called, Tertullus began the accusation thus: "Seeing that we enjoy great peace through you, and on all sides wrongs are righted for this nation, we accept it, most noble Felix, with all gratitude. But, not further to weary you, I beg you, of your kindness, to hear a few words of us.

"We have found this man a pest and a stirrer of faction among all the Jews through all the world, the ringleader of the heresy of the Nazarenes, and who even tried to desecrate the temple. We arrested him and were ready to judge him according to our law, but the tribune Lysias, with great violence, snatched him from our hands, commanding his accusers to come before you. Examining him yourself, you will be able to know the truth about the charges we bring against him." The Jews, too, kept joining in insisting that these things were so.

The high priest cuts a somewhat ludicrous figure, coming to the procuratorial court armed with the orator Tertullus. He had badly misjudged the atmosphere of a Roman tribunal and thought, no doubt, thus to impress Felix. Tertullus was possibly a Roman Jew, superficially trained in the principles of rhetoric fashionable in the capital. Roman oratory—the branch of literature in which Rome and the Latin language would have excelled, even without the stimulus of the Greeks—deprived of its political significance with the establishment of the imperial autocracy, flourished in the schools and the courts. It became a staple of Roman education. In the late sixties, the orator and writer on oratory Quintilian returned to Rome from Spain, and his writings on rhetoric are one of the few surviving relics of Latin literature from the first century.

Tertullus, in fact, was clearly no great orator. Felix, scoundrel though he was, seems to have been quite unimpressed by the suggestion that a case of treason was on his hands. The prosecution made a serious mistake in directing a side blow against the capable commander of the Jerusalem garrison. Felix knew that his covertly corrupt rule depended on the efficiency of such officers as Lysias. Nor, in fact, was the plausible Tertullus well trained in his corrupt art. In oratory, the greatest art is to conceal art; and Luke seems to take a subtle pleasure in reporting the prosecutor's too obviously elaborate flatteries, an obsequious approach no doubt somewhat dimmed by the sour presence of the high priest.

In fact, the Sanhedrin thoroughly misread the situation. They failed, probably because of Felix's regard for Lysias, whose further advice he thought it prudent to await (22). It is fairly obvious that, when the tribune came to Caesarea, he counseled prudence. It is to be hoped that Tertullus was not paid his fee. The world has had enough of those who use words to hide the truth.

Felix, like Pilate, was a lamentable mistake. All sorts of crimes and irregularities disgraced his governorship. He was the brother of Pallas, the notorious freedman and senior minister of Claudius, an upstart of whom Tacitus, the greatest of Roman historians, speaks with blistering scorn. He is no less contemptuous of Felix, who, he said, ". . . thought he could commit every sort of iniquity and escape the consequences." He felt secure under his powerful brother's shadow. Nothing could be more untrue than the opening gambit of Tertullus' artificial oratory. The parlous state the country was in is clear from the fact that Lysias detached the major part of his cohort to secure the safe arrival of Paul in Caesarea. From Felix onward, the path to the great disaster of A.D. 66 did not pause on its way downhill.

Such was the man before whom Paul preached of righteousness, self-control, and judgment and who put off consideration of such things until a more convenient season. Tacitus mentions Felix again in describing the events which immediately preceded the rebellion. He describes him as ". . . a master of cruelty and lust, who exercised the powers of a king in the spirit of a slave." Nero recalled him in A.D. 56 or 57, and he passes from the scene.

Ironically, the man on whom so much of the world's future history hung was standing in chains, while a reprobate was on the judgment seat.

Reply
(Acts 24:10–21)

At the governor's nod, Paul replied, "Knowing that for many years you have been a judge among this people, I the more gladly offer my defense. You can verify the fact that it is not more than twelve days since I went up to Jerusalem to worship, and they neither found me arguing with anyone in the temple; nor creating a disturbance among the people at large, in synagogue or city; nor can they sustain the charges they now make against me. I do confess this to you that, according to the way which they are calling heresy, I worship the God of my fathers, believing all things according to the Law and such as are written in the prophets. And I have the hope toward God, which they also share, that there will be a resurrection of the dead, the good and the bad alike. This being so, I always strive to have a good conscience, toward God and man, continually.

"After an absence of many years, I came to bring gifts and offerings to my people, and while I was busy with this, some Jews of Asia found me performing a rite of purification in the temple, not with a crowd about me, nor any disturbance of the peace. And they should have been present before you to make their charge against me, if they have one to make. Or else let these men say if they found any misdemeanor in me when I stood before their Sanhedrin, unless it be that, as I stood among them, I cried, 'It is concerning the resurrection of the dead that I am being judged by you today.' "

Paul's reply is a model of clarity, which Luke takes some pleasure in setting against the artificial oratory of the hired prosecutor. As before Pilate, the Jews had not prepared this case. Not an Asian visitor, the instigators of the whole tumult though the Asians were, was produced as a witness, as Paul damagingly points out.

He deals first with the charge that he was a damager of Rome's peace (11–13). This dangerous allegation he had met before at Philippi and Thessalonica, and he met it with plain facts, challenging his accusers to produce their evidence (12, 13). He had simply appeared in Jerusalem on a notable errand of goodwill and, in the temple court, was in no way a center of interest, ill-feelings, or faction, until the Asian Jews inflamed the mob. Where were they? Equally, it might be asked, where were the Christians of the Jerusalem congregation, whose supporting testimony might have been useful on this occasion? It was a situation he was to know again (2 Timothy 4:16).

True, he was a Christian, but that involved no loss of reverence for the old heritage of Israel. He also admitted that he had annoyed the high priest by alleging that the real cause of their hostility was that he, Paul, like all good Pharisees, believed in the resurrection, a doctrine abhorrent to Ananias. It was a brilliant defense without a wasted word—a demonstration of Paul's ability to meet any challenge and, equally, of Luke's ability as a reporter.

Reaction
(Acts 24:22–27)

> When Felix, who had a fairly accurate knowledge of Christian matters, heard this, he adjourned the inquiry, saying, "I will go thoroughly into your case when the tribune Lysias comes down." He told a centurion to take Paul in charge, to allow him some liberty, and not to prevent any of his friends from looking after him or visiting him.
>
> Some days later, Felix appeared with his Jewish wife, Drusilla, and, sending for Paul, listened to what he had to say about faith in Christ. As he discussed uprightness, self-control, and judgment yet to be, Felix became afraid and said, "You may go now. When I have a suitable opportunity I will send for you." He had hopes, too, that he might be bribed by Paul, to set him free, and so he sent for him and talked with him more often. But, after two years, Porcius Festus succeeded Felix; and, to gratify the Jews, Felix left Paul in custody.

Drusa (Drusilla is a pet name, as Priscilla is for Prisca) was one of the daughters of Agrippa I. About A.D. 53, she married Azizas of Emesa, who was king of an independent principality in the north of Syria. In the following year, still only about sixteen years of age, she was seduced by Felix and became that scoundrel's third wife, a situation which provoked contempt even in Rome. After Claudius' death and the consequent passing of Pallas' protection, it was probably the influence of Drusilla's sister, Bernice, and Agrippa II that secured the recall of Felix from his mismanaged governorship. Pallas did not long survive the ascendancy of Agrippina and her son, Nero, in A.D. 54.

According to Josephus, who, as Vespasian's secretary and a Jewish historian, is likely to have been in possession of factual information, Drusilla bore Felix a son, whom she named Agrippa, after her father. She survived her husband's recall and subsequent death, and lived in the Campanian town of Pompeii, until August A.D. 79. On the twenty-fourth of that month, Vesuvius exploded in the famous eruption which Pliny vividly describes in two letters to his friend the historian Tacitus. Drusilla and her son could have perished under the ash which sealed Pompeii for the discoveries of another age. Was it some Jewish slave who wrote *Sodoma Gomora* on a wall, possibly as doom descended? Could it have been Drusilla's house? She was thirty-nine or forty years of age at the time of the disastrous eruption.

Drusilla must have had some knowledge of her father's unfortunate relations with the Christians, hence perhaps some desire to hear a leader of the group. She had thus the immense privilege of facing a direct appeal from the most famous Christian preacher of her day. She heard Paul preach of "righteousness, self-control, and judgment to come." It is intriguing to imagine what words from that distant courtroom she may have remembered when the great mushroom cloud "like a pine tree," said Pliny, referring to the umbrella pines of his land, rose about the shaking land on that hot August day and the mephitic vapors began to roll, under dense darkness, on the seaside towns and villas of the Naples bay.

Like Felix, whose importunity had seemed to open such vast possibilities of romance, excitement, and social standing, she, too, came to the end of the road.

Felix, returning to Rome in apprehension, needed friends whenever he could find them. Hence his illegal detention of Paul. The Jerusalem Sanhedrin had failed to prove their case, but it suited them to have Paul out of the way.

25

New Procurator
(Acts 25:1–12)

When Festus succeeded to the province, after three days he
went up to Jerusalem from Caesarea. The high priest and the
Jewish leaders laid information before him, against Paul, asking
as a favor (designed against Paul), that he should send for him to
Jerusalem. They intended to ambush and kill him on the way.
Festus answered that Paul was in custody at Caesarea and that
he himself was going there soon. "Therefore," he went on, "let
those with authority among you come down with me and lay a
charge, if there is anything against this man."

After some ten days among them, he went down to Caesarea
and the next day, taking his seat on the bench, commanded Paul
to be brought. When he appeared, the Jews who had come down
from Jerusalem gathered round and brought many serious
charges against Paul, which they were unable to sustain. He replied in defense: "I have committed no offense against the Law
of the Jews, nor against the temple, nor against Caesar." Festus,
wishing to gain the goodwill of the Jews, answered Paul, "Are
you willing to go up to Jerusalem and there be judged on these
charges before me?" Paul said, "I am standing at Caesar's judgment seat, where I have a right to be tried. I have in no way
wronged the Jews, as you yourself know well enough. For if,
indeed, I am a criminal and have committed a capital offense, I
make no appeal against death. But if there is no truth in the
accusations of these people, no man can make a present of me to

them. I appeal to Caesar." Then Festus, after consulting with his assessors, replied, "You have appealed to Ceasar; to Caesar you shall go."

The Romans knew well enough the difficult people they had to govern in the Jews. The passionate little nation was, however, a problem which could not be disregarded, because the two areas of administration—Samaria and Judaea—lay across vital communication lines and constituted a frontier problem not to be lightly set aside. Willing always to improvise and use ready-made organs and instruments of authority, as we have observed in the story of this book, the Romans were served well by the Herod family, whose skillful diplomacy aided the empire for almost a century, and by a collaborating priesthood which exacted a high toll in crime in return for its support.

As much as it could, Rome sought to keep the evidence of occupation and the iron fist of authority out of sight. From the deposition of Archelaus, in A.D. 6, save for a few brief years under Agrippa I, the land was under the rule of procurators. Some fourteen of them are known—heavy-handed civil servants, for the most part, and men of no great brilliance. They were a mistake, but Rome was in a dilemma. The principal legionary force was as far away as Antioch, in the command of the legate of Syria, and Rome was seeking to make the occupation of the land as inconspicuous as possible. Half a legion at Caesarea was a force quite inadequate to police such an area.

The procurators, in fact, faced a task beyond their means, and the Jewish hierarchy, from the time of Pilate onwards, more than had the measure of the situation. The word *procurator,* in its original sense meant a steward, a trusted subordinate in an aristocratic society—one who was directly responsible to his chief. In the political sense, the word really meant no more. Procurators governed smaller provinces, such as Thrace and

Judaea, which were in the emperor's control; and these men were immediately responsible to him for the conduct of their office. Hence Pilate's final capitulation before the Jews' threat of a new complaint to Tiberius and the studied respect of Festus for Paul's appeal to Nero.

It was a mistake, perhaps, on the part of the Roman central administration to give such power to petty governors and yet to leave them in such uncertainty over the risks they should take in enforcing order and the manner in which they should handle difficult collaborators. The whole area loosely known as Palestine should, perhaps, have been placed under a special commissioner, after the model of the governor of Egypt—a man with proconsular powers and an occupation force strong enough to enforce peace in a land amply provided with the background for guerrilla war.

These chapters of Luke's narrative are fascinating insights into the problems of the procurators and their inevitable feeble handedness in dealing with a determined, fanatical, and clever people. Luke's preoccupation is evidently to show that, in the eyes of the Roman authorities, Christianity, in the person of its greatest protagonist, was not a seditious movement. In court after court Paul is vindicated, and the real authors of disturbance and breaches of the peace are exposed. And yet Felix, for his own reasons, does not set Paul free, nor, for his own reasons, too, does Festus.

In point of fact, reflected in the story may be seen the drift of imperial politics. It was in A.D. 54 that Agrippina became a widow. This clever and wicked woman had, rumor had it, cleared the way for her son by a previous marriage by murdering Claudius. A boy of eighteen years, Nero became prince, but Agrippina had no intention that he should function independently from her. She had the aid of Afranius Burrus, prefect of the Praetorian Guard, the city garrison that, by Rome's misfortune, could never again be disregarded in the choice of the succession. The great Seneca, philosopher, sage, dramatist, orator, and one of the finest literary figures of the century, functioned as Nero's tutor. He and Burrus were an efficient partnership.

For five years, until Nero at last rebelled and murdered his evil mother, Seneca and Burrus governed Rome and its provinces. The *Quinquennium Neronis,* "Nero's Five Years," became a legend for good government. Determinedly, the soldier and the statesman sought to set the world in order. Along with Agrippina, who saw her own advantage in the situation, they broke the power of the freedmen, especially Pallas and Narcissus, who, by the misfortune of Claudius' illness and weakness, governed too much of the world. Hence Felix's recall. He was one of the smaller pieces of flotsam which was swept away, as an able government, using well the civil service which had functioned since Augustus, sought to set the world aright and make the system function.

New appointments, of whom we have a most interesting glimpse in Porcius Festus, were seeking to gather up the reins of office, to understand the local forces with which they were required and trusted to work, and above all to make no initial mistakes. Under the brief years of sound government, perhaps up to A.D. 59, it behooved a provincial official to watch his steps and to know that, for the moment, there was no corrupt grace and favor at the central seat of government, on which he could fall back. This is what makes the next two chapters of the Acts and the drama at Caesarea so deeply interesting. We are privileged to see such a man feeling his way, baffled, seeking help where he could find it, and relieved to find a frustrating problem neatly lifted from his hands by the action of the central character involved.

Porcius Festus succeeded to the mismanaged procuratorship

in A.D. 57 or 58, and the brief episode of his examination of Paul and his consultation with Agrippa II are our only glimpse of him in action. Festus had inherited from Felix a lamentable legacy of trouble. There was wide lawlessness in the countryside and armed rivalry between the factions of the hierarchy. Events were in full flow for the disaster of eight years later. Festus simply could not afford to alienate collaborating elements, and the determination of the priests to make away with an obviously innocent man was a problem which required the most careful handling. It was the situation of thirty years before, repeated with other actors and on a wider stage. Festus, however, was a luckier man than Pilate. He found a way of escape through the prisoner's own action. He had offered Paul an acquittal on the charge of sedition and added the proposal, not unreasonable, from his point of view, that the ex-Pharisee should face a religious investigation before his peers. He had not yet measured the iniquity at Jerusalem.

For Paul, however, it was a crisis. He knew the perils of Jewry. He grasped the realities of the political situation, the growing tension, and the deepening local anarchy better than the procurator himself. If Festus found himself inhibited, by official policy, from refusing and frustrating the Jerusalem hierarchy, Paul proposed to cut the knot. By exercising a Roman citizen's right, he could save himself and free the governor from all embarrassment. He therefore appealed to Caesar.

The process to which Paul had recourse was the act by which a litigant disputes a judgment, with the consequence that the case is referred to a higher court, normally that of the authority who had originally appointed the magistrate of the court from which the appeal originated. Caesar had appointed Festus. He was Caesar's steward, theoretically; and so he was obliged to accept the appeal and refer it on, accompanied by relevant documents and a personal report, the framing of which must have presented considerable difficulty. He saw no fault in Paul by any standards of Roman law and justice familiar to him. Newly arrived in Judaea, he found both Jewish law and Jewish religion unfamiliar. In his difficult office, he was not free to sweep such matters aside with a Gallio's contempt. Festus had his career to make. His difficult province was a hard testing ground, and the lucidity and correct terminology of a document over his signature, in a court so exalted as that of Caesar himself, must have been a matter of anxious concern to him. Hence the alacrity with which he availed himself of the help of Agrippa II. He acted with propriety and may, perhaps, be regarded as the best of the procurators. It is a pity that he died about two years later.

Agrippa and Bernice
(Acts: 25:13–27)

A few days later, King Agrippa and Bernice arrived at Caesarea to pay their respects to Festus, and after they had been there a few days, Festus put Paul's case before the king, saying, "There is a man here left in custody by Felix, concerning whom, when I was in Jerusalem, the high priests and elders of the Jews laid information, demanding judgment against him. I answered them that it is not the Roman way to hand over a man to death, as a favor, before the accused has met his accusers face-to-face and he receives opportunity to answer the charge. So when they had foregathered here, without any delay, I took my seat, next day, on the bench and ordered the man to be produced. The accusers stood up and brought no sort of charge as I had in mind. They had certain controversial matters against him relating to their own religion and one Jesus, who was dead, and whom Paul said was alive. For my part, perplexed how I should investigate the matter, I asked whether he would go to Jerusalem for judgment about it. Paul having entered an appeal to be reserved for Augustus' judgment, I ordered him to be detained until such time as I could send him to Caesar."

Agrippa said to Festus, "I, too, have been wanting to hear this man." So, on the morrow, when Agrippa and Bernice were come, with great ceremony, into the audience hall, with tribunes and leading men of Caesarea, at Festus' command, Paul was brought in. And Festus said, "King Agrippa and all here present, you see this man about whom the mass of the Jews have made representations to me, in Jerusalem and also here, clamoring that he should live no longer. I, convinced that he had done nothing worthy of death and, pursuant to his own appeal to Augustus, determined to send him there. But I have nothing definite to write to my master about him. That is why I have brought him before you all, and especially before you, King Agrippa, so that, when examination has been made, I may have something to report. For it seems to me absurd to present a prisoner and not to indicate the charges against him."

Festus, in the whole of this interchange, makes a particularly good impression. It was lamentable that Pilate had not his view of "the Roman way." He had given the Jewish leaders no cause to complain of cavalier dismissal, but left no doubt that he found their case—as seen, at least, by a Roman judge—quite absurd and as irrelevant to Roman law and justice as Gallio in Corinth had found it. However, Paul had relieved him of the task of decision, and his problem now was whether the imperial court would regard their procurator as absurd or illogical for failure to put the case forward in proper legal terminology.

(Observe that the honorary title *Augustus*, conferred on Octavian in 27 B.C., had become, like the family name *Caesar*, a dynastic term. "Master," or "Lord" of verse 26 might have been proper for a procurator in reference to his appointing authority, but it was a term which was to become sinister in its connotations.)

Agrippa turned it all into a state occasion (23). It was in the same city that his father had died amid such pomp and circumstance (12:21–23), and the taste for such display would seem to have descended to his son. It was Herodian pomp and circumstance, harmless in Roman eyes, if it served a purpose.

Agrippa undoubtedly was a man of ability, of wide knowledge of Judaism, and of more than a nodding acquaintance with Christianity. He must have known the long-standing policy of his house. Paul's attitude and careful apologia show that he valued the opportunity afforded, doubtless as much for the sake of the Church and its freedom as for his own sake. It was of prime importance to the prisoner, as well as to the procurator, that the report to Rome should be accurately phrased and properly documented with detail. It is an interesting situation. The careful governor, obviously anxious not to make a false step amid the growing perils of the province; the care of Rome's representative to honor the client-king, so true to official policy as old as Augustus; Paul's dogged battle for justice, so often to be repeated; the background of menace outside the safety of the garrison town: Where else in all ancient literature is so authentic a record of the empire in action to be found?

There is little more to say of Herod's house, but it may be interesting to finish the story. Agrippa makes one or two brief appearances in later history. Josephus shows him actively and despairingly at work in a hopeless endeavor to preserve the peace when the great rebellion was looming. With the sure diplomatic instinct of his family, he was active in support of Vespasian, the successful survivor of the troubled year of civil war which followed Nero's death. He was actually in Rome, whither Vespasian had sent him, to salute Galba, the first of that year's ill-fated emperors. In Tacitus' brief phrases, it is possible to catch a glimpse of the old decision and sure choice characteristic of others of his house, when it was obvious that the year A.D. 69 was to see more than one claimant:

> Soon after, Agrippa, informed by private message from the East, left Rome before Vitellius received the news, and hurried back on a fast ship. With equal spirit Queen Bernice espoused Vespasian's cause. She was in the bloom of her youth and beauty, and had made herself agreeable to Vespasian, old though he was, by the magnificence of her gifts.

It was not a Herod's first bold voyage across the sea between Italy and Judaea. Agrippa took an active part in the war in Palestine, was wounded at Gamala, and was with Titus at the siege of Jerusalem. From the safety of Caesarea, he watched the final ruin of the country he had sought to save. With Agrippa II ended the Herods, an astonishingly able family, whose pro-Roman policy went far to postpone the clash between Rome and the Jews and played, in consequence, an unwitting but significant part in holding the peace during the formative years of the Christian Church.

The remarkable woman, his sister, who accompanied the king, is also worth consideration. She was a daughter of Agrippa I, sister to both Agrippa II and Drusilla, and was born in A.D. 28. Her first husband was Marcus, a Jewish official of Alexandria, who died soon after marriage. Herod Agrippa I then betrothed her to her uncle, also a Herod by name—the ruler, under Claudius, of the little kingdom of Calchis. Of this marriage there were two sons. Herod of Calchis died in A.D. 48.

As a widow, Bernice lived in close friendship with her brother, and there seems to have been a strong bond between them,

with the inevitable result that rumors of an incestuous relation-
ship were rife. Of this allegation there is no concrete evidence
whatsoever, nor evidence of the actual marriage of brother and
sister—an arrangement not uncommon in the East, especially
in Egypt.

Bernice was present in Jerusalem when the procurator Florus
pillaged the temple, in one of those last tragic acts of Roman
folly which preceded the outbreak of revolt. She risked her life
in begging him to show sense and desist and was almost killed
by Florus' undisciplined troops. She wrote to the proconsul
Cestius, in Syria, to complain of Florus, and stood, in superb
courage, by her brother's side, when he personally appealed to
the Jerusalem crowd to abstain from violence. The mob burned
the palaces of both brother and sister when rebellion broke out.
The couple took refuge in Caesarea—their last, sad resort.

26

Paul and Agrippa
(Acts 26:1–32)

Agrippa said to Paul, "You are permitted to speak for yourself." Then Paul, stretching forth his hand, began his defense: "King Agrippa, I count myself happy that today I am about to make reply before you against all the charges the Jews have brought against me, especially because you are well informed concerning all the customs and controversies of the Jews. So please hear me patiently. All Jews know the manner of my life from youth, which was spent first among my own people in Jerusalem. And they have known all the time, if they are prepared to tell the truth, that, in accordance with the strictest form of our religion, I lived a Pharisee. And now, I stand on trial for the hope of the promise to our fathers given by God—the promise which our Twelve Tribes, serving earnestly night and day, hope to attain—for which hope, King Agrippa, I am charged by the Jews. What? Is it judged incredible among us that God should raise the dead? In fact, I was myself convinced that I should do much against the name of Jesus of Nazareth. And I did that in Jerusalem and put many of God's people into prison on the authority I received from the chief priests and gave my vote against them when they were being done to death. Through all the synagogues, punishing them again and again, I tried to make them blaspheme. Exceedingly mad against them, I was setting about persecuting them in other cities, too. In the course of which pur-

suit, on the way to Damascus, with power and authority from the
high priests, at midday on the journey, I saw, king, a light from
heaven shine around me and those traveling with me, a light
beyond the brightness of the sun. We all fell to the ground, and
I heard a voice speaking to me and saying in Hebrew, 'Saul,
Saul, why are you persecuting me? It is hard for you to kick
against the goads.' I said, 'Who are you, Lord?' He replied, 'I am
Jesus, whom you are persecuting. But be on your feet, for to this
end I have appeared to you, to appoint you a servant and a
witness both of the things which you have seen and the things in
which I shall be revealed to you, as I deliver you from your
people and the Gentiles. To them I am sending you, to open their
eyes, to turn them from darkness to light, from the power of
Satan to God, to receive forgiveness of sins and an inheritance
with the sanctified, by their faith in me.' Whence, King Agrippa,
I did not prove faithless to the heavenly vision; but, first to those
in Damascus and Jerusalem and through all Judaea, and to the
Gentiles I continued to preach repentance and turning to God,
with deeds to match such repentance. For these reasons the Jews
laid hold of me in the temple and tried to kill me. By God's help,
I stand until this very day, bearing witness to small and great,
saying nothing other than that which Moses and the prophets
said would happen, how that the Messiah must suffer, and how
first, by his resurrection from the dead, he was destined to proclaim light to the people and the Gentiles."

As he was thus making his defense, Festus said with a loud
voice, "You are mad, Paul. Your great learning is turning you to
madness." But Paul said, "I am not mad, most excellent Festus,
but uttering words of truth and a balanced mind, for the king
knows about these things of which I am speaking. I am convinced that not a detail of them escapes him, for this thing has
not been done in a corner. King Agrippa, you believe the
prophets. I know you do."

Agrippa said to Paul, "In short, you are trying to persuade me to become a Christian?" "I would to God," said Paul, "in short or at length, that not only you, but all those who hear me today, could become as I am—except for these chains."

When he said this, the king, the governor, and Bernice stood up, with their whole party. They withdrew and spoke to one another, saying, "This man is doing nothing to deserve death or imprisonment." And Agrippa said to Festus, "This man could have been set free, if he had not appealed to Caesar."

It is difficult to believe that Luke did not in some way secure entrance to this scene. The royal visitor liked display, and the audience chamber would have been crowded to his liking. The small details, those inconsiderable things that mark the report of the eyewitness, are all there: Paul's characteristic opening movement with his hand, like his rueful lifting of his manacled wrists at the end; the slightly pompous tone of the king, a little conscious of his importance; Paul's quite polished and courteous opening words; the rude outburst of Festus, carried right out of his depth by the apologia of the brilliant prisoner or else into realms of spiritual experience explicable to him only as a form of madness. Paul's gentle turning of the situation back to the king's attention and its implied rebuke of Festus is also remarkable. It all leads to the conclusion that here is found firsthand reporting in Luke's most brilliant manner. The slight variations in the account of the incident on the road to Damascus support the same view. Luke wrote as he heard and remembered, and no one account negates the other.

Luke is mainly concerned to show that Agrippa, like Festus, could find no fault in the prisoner. Enlightened Jewish opinion coincided with the verdict of Roman law. Paul lays the stress where the occasion demanded it: the systematic attempt of the Jerusalem hierarchy to eliminate the Christians and the savage and fanatical support that policy had once received from the apostle himself in his unconverted days. How could Paul do other than believe in a risen, living Lord, when his experience had come in the midst of such ferocious opposition?

It is curious how that very testimony seems to form the sticking point with those who, until such moment of challenge, will patiently listen to a more abstract argument. Such had been the situation in Athens. Festus, for all the commendable correctness of his behavior to this point, is driven to an unbecoming interruption, hardly courteous to the visitor to whom, with appropriate grace, he had earlier given precedence.

The small problem of translation occasioned by Agrippa's remark (28) is perhaps reasonably sorted out above. Perhaps Agrippa's Greek was not of the best, and Paul courteously glosses over the fact by a slight play on words. It can be taken for certain that Agrippa was not "almost persuaded," as a once-popular rather mournful hymn takes it. Nor was it bad-tempered. It may have been slightly ironical: "In a word, you want me to be a Christian"—a matter not too remote from Paul's actual intent, if truth be told.

Paul had been vindicated again, and Luke's purpose was to set the fact on record. A charter of Christian liberty was in the process of formation, as history moved into the grim, dark decade of the sixties: the ghastly years after Nero took control; the Jewish War; the "year of the four emperors," A.D. 69. Had it not been for the sequence of events—the Great Fire; Nero's search for scapegoats and Rome's attack, at his evil instance, on the Church—the skies seemed clear for Paul's evangelism and the empire about to recognize that the new faith contained no sedition. To be sure, the emperor worship that was infiltrating the great system might ultimately have precipitated the fatal clash; but, in the meantime, the implacable foes were the Pharisaic synagogues. Luke's whole point was that, from Corinth, to

Philippi, and to Caesarea, authority was declaring *for* the Church, not against it.

Such incidents as the Ephesus riot showed a deep substratum of hostility toward the Church. No doubt, portent lay here, and men of insight might have looked upon that situation with uneasiness. But the Asiarchs had helped Paul in that sinister clash, and Luke had every reason to share Paul's dream of the empire for Christ. Both would have been shocked, could they have read the Apocalypse of a score of years later.

Paul, had he been released at this time, would have been a security problem; but Philip, the evangelist, seems to have dwelt safely in Caesarea. And the refugee could no doubt have been passed from congregation to congregation, up to Tyre and thence out, by ship—to Rome? to Spain? But his appeal was filed, and proceedings could not, apparently, have been reversed.

27

Shipwreck on Malta
(Acts 27:1–44)

And when it was decided that we should go by sea to Italy, they handed over Paul and some other prisoners to a centurion named Julius, of the emperor's special duty corps. Embarking on a ship of Adramyttium bound for ports on the Asian coast, we put to sea. Aristarchus, a Macedonian of Thessalonica, was with us. On the second day we berthed at Sidon, and Julius kindly allowed Paul to go and enjoy the hospitality of his friends there. Sailing from Sidon, we ran under the lee of Cyprus, since the winds were against us; and, cutting across the Cilician and Pamphylian bight, we put in at Myra, a port of Lycia. There the centurion found an Alexandrian vessel bound for Italy, and he put us aboard. For several days we sailed on slowly and with difficulty drew near Cnidus. Here, since the head wind quite frustrated us, we made for the sheltered side of Crete, past Cape Salmone. Coasting along it with difficulty, we arrived at a place called Good Harbors, near the city of Lasea.

All this consumed much time, and navigation was now perilous, for it was well into October. Paul warned them, saying, "Sirs, I see that the voyage is likely to be a matter of much damage and loss, not only to the cargo and the ship, but even to our lives." But the centurion took more notice of the captain and owner of the ship than of Paul's advice, and since the harbor was not convenient to winter in, the majority were for putting to sea, reaching Phenice, if possible, and spending the winter there.

Phenice is a Cretan harbor with its back to the southwest and northwest winds.

When a gentle southerly sprang up, thinking they had just what they required, they weighed anchor and coasted closely along the shore of Crete. But soon there rushed down from the high country a fearsome wind, which they called a nor'easter. The ship was at its mercy, quite unable to make headway against it, so we gave in and were carried before the gale. Running under a small island called Clauda, with difficulty we hauled the ship's boat aboard. When it was lifted in, they braced the hull with tautened cables. Fearing lest they be driven into the African sandbanks, they shortened sail and were driven along. The next day, still hopelessly stormbound, they jettisoned some cargo, and on the third day, with all hands at work, they threw overboard all the fittings of the ship. When for many days there was no sight of sun or stars, all hope of safety vanished.

When no one had eaten anything for a long time, Paul went and spoke to all of them. "Men," he said, "you should have listened to me and not sailed from Crete to suffer this damage and loss. But now I beg you to keep your courage up. There will be no life lost, only the ship. For last night the messenger of God, to whom I belong, and whom I serve, stood by my side and said, 'Do not be afraid, Paul. You must stand before Caesar, and God has granted you of his grace the lives of those who sail with you.' So courage, men, for I believe God and that it shall be as it was told me. We must run the ship ashore on a certain island."

When the fourteenth night was come, and we were being driven along in the Adrian Sea, about midnight, the sailors suspected that there was land ahead. Sounding, they found twenty fathoms. A little later, sounding again, they found fifteen. Fearing lest we should run on some rocky shore, they threw four anchors from the stern and prayed for daylight to come. The crew, with the idea of abandoning ship, had actually lowered the boat, on the pretext of running anchors from the bow. Paul said to the centurion and his men, "Unless these stay by the ship, you cannot be saved." Then the soldiers cut the cables of the boat and let it fall away. And as day was beginning to break, Paul begged them all to take food. "This is the fourteenth day," he said, "that you continue on watch without proper meals, taking nothing. So I beg you to take food, for this makes for your well-being. For not a hair from the head of one of you shall perish." With these words, he took bread, said grace, and, standing before them all, he broke it and began to eat. Thus encouraged, they, too, all took food. All told were two hundred and seventy-six souls on board. When they had eaten all they wanted, they set about lightening the ship, throwing out the corn into the sea.

When day broke, they could not identify the land; but they could see a bay with a beach, on which they purposed, if they could, to run the ship aground. They untied the anchors and left them in the sea, slackened the rudder bands, hoisted the foresail to the wind, and made for the beach. And, running onto a sand-bank with deeper water on both sides, they grounded the vessel. The prow stuck fast, but the stern began to break up under the swell. The soldiers were for killing the prisoners, in case someone should dive overboard and escape, but the centurion, determined to save Paul, vetoed this plan. Those who could swim he told to go overboard first and get ashore, and then the rest, on planks and other flotsam from the ship. And so it came about that all reached land safely.

The Augustan Cohort, under whose commander, Julius, Paul and his fellow prisoners were placed, still awaits full explanation. It is the sort of problem which some chance scrap of epigraphical or papyrological information could, at any time, simply solve. It was, in all likelihood, a special-duty corps of picked troops, probably from the Praetorian Guard, detailed for special duties: the escort of important prisoners or diplomatic security men in delicate areas and so on. Properly, a cohort was one-tenth of a legion, 600 men, and a centurion was normally in command of a single century. Perhaps the cohort was of the traditional strength and was officered by leading praetorian centurions. We have no means of knowing how many men were in the section sailing on this occasion.

It is obvious that again in Julius (one of the two New Testament centurions whose names we know), we encounter a soldier of breeding, humanity, and worth. One characteristic of the Roman imperial system at its best was inherited from that consummate diplomat, Augustus, himself: an ability to pick men. Even under Nero, Seneca and Burrus, in virtual charge for Nero's first five years, maintained this tradition. Hence Lysias, who was firm, swift, careful of the law, and tactful; hence the gentleman of this story, Julius, who was quiet, effective in command, and notably humane.

Luke, in this chapter, writes one of literature's best-told stories of shipwreck. Ovid, Virgil, Achilles Tatius, and one or two other ancient writers venture into this area of narrative, but none approach Luke for quiet command of practical detail. It is useful to follow a map and imagine the talk, the argument, the apprehensions of this strangely assorted party, as the ship's master—under orders, no doubt, from some Roman shipping firm—risked a late voyage with his valuable cargo of Egyptian wheat for the capital.

The Roman centurion shipped his party in a vessel from Adramyttium, the likeliest vessel to put the company into the stream of east-west trade, for Adramyttium lies on the Aegean, opposite Lesbos. The vessel had beaten north along the low Palestinian coast; cut between Cyprus and the mainland, as the seasonal winds demanded; and then worked west, under the coast of Asia Minor, to Myra, at the extreme southern point of the blunt peninsula. Here the party transferred to an Alexandrian corn ship that had perhaps chosen this northern route because of the lateness of the season.

Wall paintings from Herculaneum and Pompeii, the two towns on the Bay of Naples overwhelmed by the eruption of Vesuvius in August A.D. 79, depict ships which are contemporary with the Alexandrian grain ship which brought Paul to Rome; and the general impression is that of a vessel which differed little in fittings and form of hull from the common ship designs of the next eighteen centuries, save that both ends were similarly shaped. The contour of the sides was almost straight along the middle section, but swept upwards to some height at each end.

It is of interest, in view of Luke's story, to look at a similar description, written by the essayist Lucian, in the middle of the second century. An Alexandrian grain ship was driven by stress of storm to take refuge in Piraeus, where Lucian and his friends visited the monster, to marvel at the mast, count the layers of hide in the sails, and admire the dexterity of the sailors in the rigging. He gives a detailed description:

> The shipwright said it was 120 cubits long, and over a quarter as wide, and from deck to bottom, where it is deepest, in the bilge, 29 cubits. Then, what a tall mast, what a yard to carry! What a forestay to hold it up! How gently the poop curves up, with a little golden goose below! And correspondingly at the opposite end, the prow juts right out in front, with figures of the goddess, Isis, after whom the ship is named, on either side. And the other decorations, the paintings and the topsail colored like fire, anchors in front of them and capstans, and windlasses, and the cabins on the poop . . . . You could call the sailors an army. The vessel was said to carry corn enough to feed all Attica for

a year. And all this a little old man had kept from harm by turning the huge rudders with a tiny tiller.

The rule by which tonnage is calculated is to multiply the length of keel by the extreme breadth, and the product by half the breadth or depth, and divide the whole by 94. Someone has thus made the ship of Lucian to measure 1938 tons.

The grain ship on which Paul traveled had 276 people aboard. Josephus, now increasingly regarded as a reliable historian, states that he traveled to Rome on a ship which had 600 people on board. He wrote:

> I reached Rome after being in great jeopardy at sea. For our ship foundered in the midst of the sea of Adria, and our company of some six hundred souls had to swim all that night. About daybreak, through God's good providence, we sighted a ship of Cyrene, and I, along with about 80 others, were taken aboard.
> *Vita* 3

But, to return to Luke's story: The map reveals the dire hazards. The shipmaster made for Cnidus, a port on the southwest extremity of Asia Minor. He was unable to make the harbor, for a wind offshore drove the heavy galley south, and the shipmaster took refuge from the insistent blast under the lee of the 140-mile-long island of Crete. Halfway along lies Fair Havens, the port where Paul, one of the most experienced travelers of his age, besought them to stay for the winter—the common practice of ancient mariners. The shipmaster rashly decided to try for another anchorage, Phenice, perhaps modern Loutro, the only harbor able comfortably to accommodate so large a ship.

The eastern half of Crete is low, the western quite different.

In great, heaped terraces, it rises into a group of lofty, snow-capped mountains. The old enemy, the northeast wind, funneled down through the clefts of the highlands, now found them again and drove them offshore round the island of Clauda. Clauda is the modern Gaudhos, or Gozzo, an island lying some fifty miles off the southern coast of Crete and the same distance east of the longitude of the western end of Crete. Paul's ship was coasting under Crete to escape the southward driving blast of the *meltemi* which had precluded a direct crossing of the Aegean, but had given a following wind for the pilot's attempt to round Crete and make westward progress under its lee. But when the ship reached the western half of the long island, the wind, pressing on the north of the mountainous mass of that region, spilled over in downdraughts that were disastrous. It was only when the ship, struggling to avoid too much southward drift, briefly came under the lee of Clauda, that they were able to haul in the ship's boat, which, as it was towed, waterlogged, behind, disrupted steering, as the story implies. The passengers were called in to aid the crew in managing the lurching ship, for Luke vividly remembered the fierce struggle under the brief protection of the island.

Danger unites men of diverse character. There were the rugged soldiers, picked men of the centurion's special corps. The centurion himself, the chosen officer in a special brigade, was pulling on the same ropes as one of the greatest scholars of his age—the Roman citizen from Tarsus—and Luke, the cultured historian and physician.

The nor'easter now had the lumbering corn ship in charge. Far to the south, off the African coast, lay the Syrtes, the graveyard of many ships, as underwater archaeology has vividly revealed. Hence the battle to hold a westerly course, aided, it appears, by a veering of the wind to the east, as the cyclonic disturbance shifted.

Paul's tremendous gifts of leadership emerged at the crisis. His advice at Fair Havens had been rejected, and he was human enough to mention the fact, but in Luke's vivid account it is clear that the apostle did wonders to stiffen human resources. They had looped tautened cables round the hull, to bind the straining timbers against the stress of the violent seas and the strong leverage of the mast; they had cut loose and jettisoned all dispensable tackle and gear. And it was all under a murky heaven, with the spray and driving cloud blotting out the stars, and the galley lurching west at nearly forty miles a day.

The end came. Hearing the sound of distant surf, the sailors suspected land or shoals ahead. The lead showed a shelving seabed, so the vessel was hove to for the night, with anchors out astern. This arrangement kept the ship heading in the right direction before the pressure of the still-thrusting wind. It was on the fairly transparent pretext of similarly anchoring the bow that the crew proposed to launch the boat and escape, a plot frustrated by the alert Paul and a few quick sword cuts on the ropes, at the centurion's prompt orders.

At this point the centurion Julius, or the captain, seems to have numbered the ship's complement, a sensible measure before the abandonment of the vessel. They spent the night heaving the cargo of Egyptian wheat overboard and with the dawn saw an unknown coast, a beach, and a practicable bay. A bar, due to a crosscurrent, frustrated the attempt to beach the ship, which probably drew eighteen feet of water; and it was at this point that the escort, who were responsible for their charges, proposed to kill the prisoners. The centurion's admiration for Paul is apparent in his refusal. There was a struggle through the breakers, and the whole ship's company reached the beach. It was a triumph for Paul's faith and no small tribute to his dynamic personality, which was of immense support to the Roman officers.

28

The Maltese
(Acts 28:1–6)

Only then did they find out that the island was Malta. And the
islanders showed us extraordinary kindness. They built a fire and
gave us all shelter, for it was raining and cold. And when Paul
had gathered a great bundle of sticks and was putting it on the
fire, a viper, escaping the heat, laid hold of his hand. When the
natives saw the reptile hanging on his hand, they said to one
another, "No doubt this man is a murderer. He has escaped the
sea, but justice has not allowed him to live." But he shook off the
creature into the fire and suffered no harm. They were expecting
him to become feverish or fall down dead. When they had
watched for some time and saw nothing untoward happen to
him, they changed their minds and said that he was a god.

The "barbarous people," as the King James Version so clum-
sily translates the phrase (2), were the native Maltese, who had
watched the galley smashing through the surf. The Greek *bar-
baros* simply means one who speaks another language than
Greek—one whose speech, in short, sounds to Greek ears as
unintelligible as a lamb's bleating (bar-bar). The Greeks called
their Persian foes "barbaroi," while most freely admitting the
material superiority of Persian civilization. "Foreigners" is the
straightest translation.

Malta had been colonized by Phoenicians, ten centuries before Christ. Six centuries before Christ, the island had come

under the control of the great North African Phoenician city of
Carthage, which, over the space of a century, disputed the possession of the western Mediterranean with Rome. Hannibal,
one of the greatest military commanders of history, was born
on Malta. In 218 B.C., Rome took the island and never lost it.
The position, as all history has shown, is strategically vital, a
bridgehead between two continents.

The peasantry of Malta continued to speak their native Phoenician, a Semitic tongue as closely allied, perhaps, to Hebrew
and Aramaic as Arabic is to modern Israeli. It is not impossible
that Paul could make some sense of what they said. Hence the
knowledge of what the bystanders thought when Paul, ready as
ever to lend a hand at humble work, shook the torpid snake
into the fire. And so, on Paul's second contact with "barbar-
ians," he had made a similar impression to that which he had
made, at Lystra, on its Lycaonian community. They thought he
was someone more than mortal.

A Respite
(Acts 28:7–10)

> In the neighborhood were the lands of the chief man of the
> island, whose name was Publius. He made us welcome and gen-
> erously entertained us for three days. It happened that Publius'
> father was lying ill with intermittent fever and dysentery. Paul
> visited him, prayed, laid hands on him, and healed him. After
> this the rest of the island's sick kept arriving and finding relief.
> They showed us all manner of respect; and, when we sailed, put
> on board what we needed.

As usual, Luke is correct with the title. The chief Roman
official was called "the First" or "First Man," a title verified
epigraphically; he was probably an appointee of the praetor of

Syracuse, the senior Roman governor of the area. Luke's medical terms are also precise and in common usage. The actual course of events in Malta, where the large party found three months' accommodation and where they finally embarked, is rapidly passed by. Luke is anxious to get Paul to Rome.

On to Rome
(Acts 28:11–16)

After three months, we set sail in an Alexandrian ship which had wintered in the island and whose sign was Castor and Pollux. We put in to Syracuse and spent three days there. Thence, with a wide tack, we came to Rhegium; and, after one day, a south wind springing up, we made Puteoli on the second day out. We found brethren there, who invited us to stay a week. And so we came to Rome. The brethren from Rome, having had news of us, came as far as Appius' Market and the village of Three Shops to meet us. When Paul saw them, he thanked God and took heart. When we reached Rome, the centurion handed the prisoners over to the prefect of the Praetorian Guard. Paul was allowed to live privately, with a soldier to guard him.

Malta was hardly a good place to winter in, for a large vessel, but the Alexandrian freighter had perhaps been forced in by the weather that had fallen in fuller fury on Paul's vessel. The Great Twin Brethren, Castor and Pollux—the Saint Elmo's fire of the old Mediterranean sailor superstition, whose electrical discharges play round the masts—were patron deities of sailors.

Paul again is the recipient of Julius' kindness. He had preserved Paul when his men were all for killing the prisoners as the galley ran ashore. The detachment, after all, was responsible for the secure delivery of the persons in their charge. In Puteoli, the same centurion allowed Paul to lodge with the

Christians. It is remarkable that the Christians were so promptly to be found or that communication between the Christian groups in the empire was such that the Christians of the busy port were aware of the coming of Paul on such and such a ship. It could have been the group whose well-preserved upper room, overwhelmed by Vesuvius less than twenty years later, at Herculaneum, is still to be seen. There is what appears to be the charred remains of a cross on the wall. The place was in walking distance of Puteoli, the modern Pozzuoli.

Paul must have been supremely trusted. This, for Julius, was a much more chancy situation than that off the small island of Malta. The port was big and cosmopolitan. It was full of hiding places. The Christians were obviously in touch with their brethren in Rome. Rome, with its population of a million people, was a great warren into which any man could disappear, as Onesimus was soon to do. Paul could have been spirited away, up the Via Appia, with the greatest of ease. It shows courage, acute judgment, and even friendly regard on the part of the senior soldier, to allow such freedom.

To be trustworthy as a citizen and a man was, of course, a lesson Paul taught. Writing, soon afterwards, to Philippi, he besought the Church to "live as citizens worthily of the Gospel of Christ" (Philippians 1:27). He was himself a prime example. He had appealed to Rome. He was ready to go there. The centurion duly delivered him to the prefect of the Praetorian Guard. This was the competent Burrus, who had only two more years to live—he who, along with Seneca, was giving the empire its brief years of good government.

But this anticipates. There was a journey, by road, to the city, and it must have been with some excitement that Paul saw the crumbling monuments and tombs thicken beside the flagstoned Appian Way. The smoke and noise of the capital lay ahead, and the traveler had no reason to anticipate anything but justice there. Many more years were to pass before John wrote into the visions of the last book of the Bible a picture of a Rome far different from that which occupied the mind of Paul on the cold February or March morning. The writer of the Apocalypse had seen the empire turn to persecution, and he pictured her as a woman "arrayed in purple and scarlet and decked with gold . . . . drunken with the blood of the martyrs" (Revelation 17:4, 6). But when Paul arrived, in A.D. 59 or 60, Rome had not viciously turned on the innocent, and Paul saw the beckoning of opportunity. True, he came a prisoner when he had hoped to come in freedom; but he may have reflected, ironically, that he also came at Rome's expense. A million strong, Rome awaited him, and Rome's need was great. The world weariness of the age was written into the inscriptions he could read on the tombs by the wayside. "What I ate and drank I have with me," ran one. "The rest is lost." "Come and have a spot with me," said another.

South of Rome, today, there are bits and pieces of the landscape that must be much as they were nineteen centuries ago. The umbrella pines stood then as they do today. So, too, the pointing candles of the dark cypresses, the dry stone walls, the crumbling, pumiceous soil. There are bits of the city rampart which Paul may have seen, grey green olives, hill slopes of hungry soil.

Paul must have found the challenge daunting and a burden on his heart. Hence the lift of spirits when a band of Christians, alerted by their friends at Puteoli, appeared with welcome at Forum Appii, forty miles south; and at the village of Three Shops, thirty-three miles from Rome.

Rome's praetorians provided the guard for Paul in his house confinement and gave him a sphere of evangelism of which we get only one glimpse. It is in the letter to the Philippians, written from Rome. Correctly translated, Philippians 1:13 runs: "It has become clear, through the whole praetorian barracks, that it is because I am a Christian that I am in confinement." The words indicate some wide interest among Rome's household troops.

Augustus had established this special corps in 27 B.C. Half a century later, Tiberius' designing prefect of the Praetorian Guard, Sejanus, concentrated its nine cohorts, till then scattered, into a single camp just outside the city walls. It was from this dangerous action that the political importance of the guard and its commanders dated. They proclaimed Claudius and Nero as emperors and sealed Nero's doom by deserting him. They killed Galba, first of the four emperors to be proclaimed in the fearsome civil strife of A.D. 68 and 69.

Having murdered Galba, the praetorians supported Otho, second of the four emperors whom that year of blood was to see. They supported Vitellius, who defeated and succeeded Otho and were destroyed by a running fight in the streets of Rome and the final storming of their camp by the vanguard of the legions which raised Vespasian to power. Thus was "the beast," wounded almost to death, "healed of his deadly wound, and all the world wondered " (Revelation 13:3), as John was to write in the Apocalypse perhaps seventeen or more years later.

These scenes of violence and manifold disaster took place eight or nine years after the final events of Luke's story. If Paul succeeded in bringing some of the troops to Christ, they could have been among those involved in the street fighting and the battle for the barracks, which were only some of the incidents of blood and carnage that cursed the whole land of Italy in the horrible year before Vespasian seized and held power.

With the changing of the guard at each watch, it could be that, over the space of two years, half of the 4500 troops in the guard had some contact with the notable prisoner. It was their day of opportunity, had they but known it. It is quite certain that Paul used the hours to advantage.

The Synagogue
(Acts 28:17-29)

After three days, Paul called together the leaders of the Jews. When they had gathered, he said to them, "Brethren, I was handed over to the Romans, a prisoner, from Jerusalem, though I had committed no offense against the people. They heard my case and were of a mind to set me free, for there was no reason for a death penalty in me. When there were protests from the Jews, I was forced to appeal to Caesar—not that I had any charge to make against my nation. For this reason, then, I have invited you to see and speak with me, because it is for the hope of Israel that I lie in this bondage." They replied, "For our part, we have not received from Judaea any communication regarding you, nor has any one of our brethren reported or said anything ill of you; but we are glad to hear your ideas, for concerning this movement we know that it is everywhere spoken against."

Arranging a day, many of them came to his lodging. To them he carefully explained and bore witness to the kingdom of God, seeking to convince them about Jesus from the Law of Moses and the prophets, from early morning until the evening. Some were convinced by what he said, and some refused to believe. They broke up in disagreement, after one word from Paul. "The Holy Spirit spoke well to our fathers through the prophets, 'Go to this people and say: "You shall indeed hear but in no wise understand. Seeing, you shall see and shall in no wise perceive. For this nation's heart has grown callous, and with their ears they hardly hear, and they have shut their eyes—lest they should seek with their eyes, and hear with their ears, and understand with their heart, and should turn about and I should heal them."' Let it then be known to you, that the salvation of God has been sent to the Gentiles, and they will listen." When he had said this the Jews departed with much debating among themselves.

These are Paul's last words in Acts—sad and solemn and an echo of the quotation with which Christ began his parabolic teaching. It was another crisis, another step along a tragic road.

Paul's theme in this long discussion with the Roman Jews would undoubtedly follow the argument of the letter to the Roman Christians, which he had written two or three years before. That famous document was to be a treatise for the Church, but its very nature reveals the strength of the Jewish section of the Roman community, and the synagogue would be familiar with it, because it must have been the inevitable subject of debate among Jews—Christian and orthodox.

The Jews, according to Paul's consistent policy, even under his straitened circumstances, had the first chance. They were back in Rome, and obviously Claudius' decree of banishment (18:2) must have been rescinded. Claudius was a learned man, and it could have been his whim to apply what the Athenians called "ostracism," whereby, without criminal charge against him, a person was asked, for the good of the city, to leave for a period of ten years.

In consequence, if some attempt is made to see matters from the point of view of the Roman rabbis, it is fair to concede that they had their difficulties. Nero had succeeded Claudius, and we have had occasion to note that, during the first five years of his principate, that sinister and dissolute youth left affairs largely in the hands of the competent Burrus and the wise Seneca. If one or both of these men were instrumental in allowing the Jews to return, it would have been on condition that they should diligently keep the peace. And, if Suetonius is rightly read, the earlier troubles had origin in the first impact of Christian teaching in Rome.

And now a notoriously controversial figure had arrived, one whose path through the eastern and central lands of the Mediterranean had been strewn with riot and disorder. Or so, at least, the career of Paul could be represented by the timid and the cautious, not to mention the openly hostile. No Jew cared to have his hard-pressed community wantonly disrupted. Reception, in consequence, was mixed (24), and Paul set before them the stern words of Isaiah. We are allowed to be present at the last interview, when, with some severity, the apostle again announces his turning to the Gentiles.

The Church
(Acts 28:30, 31)

> For two years Paul stayed in his rented premises and welcomed all who came to see him. He proclaimed the kingdom of God and taught, with all confidence and no constraint, all about the Lord Jesus Christ.

The origin of the Roman Christian church is unknown. If a major preacher or apostle had been in the capital of the empire, the fact would surely have been mentioned in this chapter. There is no trace of a ministry of Peter in Rome before Paul's visit. Peter could easily have visited the city later, and 1 Peter 5:13 seems to demand a sojourn. The Roman Christians, perhaps a legacy of Pentecost (2:10) or the converts of such international figures as Aquila and Priscilla, seem to have had no outstanding leadership. No one is specifically mentioned. There was abundant Jewish material to afford a field for wide evangelism there. The Jewish ghetto occupied a whole Transtiber ward. The chapter of greetings which closes the letter to the Romans contains Greek and Latin names, as well as Jewish ones, and gives no notion of the nature of the faith they held, whether it was Pauline or not. The letter, in fact, argues for a highly intelligent group, but one standing in great need of theological instruction and of unified guidance.

Little more can be said. The Jewish converts Paul won in Jerusalem and the many of undisclosed background who came to him over his two years of uninterrupted ministry may have added to the difficulties of the congregation, as they might also have promoted its coherence. There are two sources of knowledge—one Christian, one secular—that give a little light on the nature of the Roman congregation.

First consider the epistle to Philippi (which, along with the letters to Ephesus, Colossae, and Philemon, was a rich product of this imprisonment). In the letter that Epaphroditus—recovered from a dire illness—carried back to Macedonia, half of the first chapter contains some vital information about the church in Rome during the two years of Paul's confinement there. First, let it be with some assurance affirmed that the congregation had been established at least ten or twelve years before, if the above-mentioned riots in the ghetto, at the end of the forties, are to be interpreted as arising from hostility toward the Christians.

What was the group that was proclaiming Christ "out of party spirit, insincerely" (Philippians 1:16), thinking to make Paul's imprisonment even more burdensome than it was? He does not seem to disapprove of the general content of their preaching, so there can hardly have been elements of the Galatian Judaistic heresy involved. Magnanimously, though he deplores the spirit of the Roman partisans, he even sees a certain propaganda value in their efforts. Perhaps they were the old leaders of the Roman Christians. Corinth is evidence for embryonic sects, based on diversity of leadership and teaching. Apollos, too, is evidence for some variety of doctrine. So is the first Ephesian church. It is possible that some feared for the future of their teaching, and human nature is tragically prone to treasure a system of thought and to shun the agony of reappraisement. Pride, too, most pervasive of the mind's faults, can

enter in and corrupt even sacred things. Good men took courage from Paul's brightened prospects and preached Christ from
purity of motive. With purpose less pure, others took occasion
to establish their own version of the faith, in the absence of the
dynamic personality who was confined at Caesar's pleasure.
Many a pet doctrine may have been menaced by Paul's authoritative elucidation of the truth, and such doctrines are difficult
to give up. Paul, a man of conspicuous intellect, may not have
gladly suffered pretentious error.

The second reference to the Roman church comes from the
historian Tacticus' account of Nero's hideous persecution in the
late summer of A.D. 64. In search of a scapegoat for the Great
Fire of Rome, Nero blamed "a body of people detested for
their abominations, and popularly known by the name of Christians." He says "a vast number were condemned, not so much
on the charge of incendiarism as for their hatred of the human
race. . . ."

It is not relevant, here, to speak of the horror, the base slan-
der, and the sheer wickedness of the attack on the church of
Rome. But Christians constituted "a multitude," that, because
of its challenge to a close-knit proletariat, as at Ephesus, had
acquired an unpopularity that, in Rome, Nero canalized and
used.

Paul had clearly prospered as an evangelist, and at this point
Luke abruptly leaves us. The book ends, like Coleridge's *Kubla
Khan,* almost with a comma. Luke must have intended to write
a third book, and what a book it would have been! The hearing
before Nero, or some assessor appointed by the ruler, would
have been a highlight. It is a fair assumption that the case
lapsed. Festus' documents may have gone down in the wreck.
Festus was dead and proper statements may have been impossible to come by. The Sanhedrin had silenced their foe for five
vital years; their own personnel was changing; and, anyway,

Jerusalem, as the land darkened to the explosion of A.D. 66, had troubles enough to preoccupy it. There may have been a statute of limitations by which an appeal to Caesar, in default of finalizing accusations, lapsed after a two-year period; but no clear evidence seems to be available for this assumption.

At any rate, Paul expected to visit Philemon and Colossae and probably did, after a presumed release in A.D. 62. Some argue for A.D. 63, but it is certain that he was free before the horrors of A.D. 64 fell. Sensing, like Peter, the darkening skies, he set about writing his pastoral epistles to Timothy and Titus, perhaps in A.D. 65. His subsequent movements are difficult to trace. From Titus 1:5 and 3:12 it could be assumed that he visited Crete and Dalmatia and perhaps fulfilled his wish to visit Spain (Romans 15:24, 28). There could have been characteristically active years of work, up to A.D. 67.

Nero's panic-stricken persecution died down and may have been largely confined to Rome, but it appears to have left the Church in the position of a proscribed body. There also appears to have been widespread persecution in the equally panic-stricken years between the serious and ill-managed plot against Nero in A.D. 65 and the final debacle, at the end of A.D. 68.

Was Paul arrested in Troas in A.D. 66 or 67? He left his cloak and precious notes and books behind him there, perhaps to avoid incriminating his hosts or because he was roughly apprehended and hustled to Rome. He wrote to Timothy, at this time, without hope of release, and according to overwhelming tradition, died a martyr. Did Luke perish in the same tragic sequence of events? At any rate, the world was denied his third book.

But he has left, in the book we have concluded, a magnificent account of the founding of the Church, in one long swath of territory, from Jerusalem to Rome. Other apostles and evangelists were working, perhaps with equal effectiveness, elsewhere.

But the Christians were loose in the world, and although Rome was to miss the day of her visitation and fail to choose the faith of the despised and misrepresented Church as her cement of empire, the world was never to be the same again. Look at those who have moved through the book. The Christians of its thirty-year story would make a typical congregation for any church. They range from the servant girl Rhoda, to the brilliant intellectual Paul. They include the physician Luke, the businesswoman Lydia, the jailer of Philippi, two synagogue heads, a member of Athens' most sophisticated judicial body, an Ethiopian cabinet minister, a country boy from Lystra, two canvas workers from Rome, a lame beggar from Jerusalem, a Cypriot landowner, and a wrongheaded young man who quarreled with an elder Christian.

They came from a dozen cities, Jewish, Greek, Roman in race. They were far from perfect, for on their periphery were sly, deceitful folk like Ananias and Sapphira, scamps like Simon, and charlatans like Sceva and his sons. Their enemies ranged from Herod the king, to the Sadducees and Pharisees of the Sanhedrin, the head of an Asian trade guild, and the rabble of a Greek marketplace. Their message was received with yells of rage and the throwing of stones, with the polite deferment of Stoics, the mirth of Epicureans, the fear and self-seeking of one Roman governor, the impatience of another, and the irony of a well-informed puppet king.

A document of immense historical importance was given to anyone interested in the most remarkable political institution of ancient times: the vast system called the Roman Empire, which gave the world the Roman Peace. The empire is seen at work: the magistrates—men of cool integrity, like Gallio; anxious, like Festus; calculating and taking risks with peace, like Felix. One can sense the atmosphere of Judaea, sliding forward to the Great Rebellion. There were the lesser levels of authority, functioning smoothly: the Asiarchs of Ephesus, the Areopagus of Athens, Lysias and the Jerusalem garrison. It is almost a conducted tour of major cities of the Graeco-Roman world, as a leading modern historian has remarked. We see the crowds, the minorities, the majorities, the sects, the denizens of the streets, the proletariat, the philosophers, the sailors, the soldiers, and an island peasantry. It is the same world, the same men and women, the same Church—fortunately, it is the same Christ, patient and powerful to save.